T0350862

The Impact of IFRS on Industry

Mohan R. Lavi

WILEY

This edition first published 2016
© 2016 Mohan R. Lavi

Registered office
John Wiley & Sons Ltd, The Atrium, Southern Gate, Chichester, West Sussex, PO19 8SQ, United Kingdom

For details of our global editorial offices, for customer services and for information about how to apply for permission to reuse the copyright material in this book please visit our website at www.wiley.com.

The right of the author to be identified as the author of this work has been asserted in accordance with the Copyright, Designs and Patents Act 1988.

All rights reserved. No part of this publication may be reproduced, stored in a retrieval system, or transmitted, in any form or by any means, electronic, mechanical, photocopying, recording or otherwise, except as permitted by the UK Copyright, Designs and Patents Act 1988, without the prior permission of the publisher.

Wiley publishes in a variety of print and electronic formats and by print-on-demand. Some material included with standard print versions of this book may not be included in e-books or in print-on-demand. If this book refers to media such as a CD or DVD that is not included in the version you purchased, you may download this material at http://booksupport.wiley.com. For more information about Wiley products, visit www.wiley.com.

Designations used by companies to distinguish their products are often claimed as trademarks. All brand names and product names used in this book are trade names, service marks, trademarks or registered trademarks of their respective owners. The publisher is not associated with any product or vendor mentioned in this book.

Limit of Liability/Disclaimer of Warranty: While the publisher and author have used their best efforts in preparing this book, they make no representations or warranties with respect to the accuracy or completeness of the contents of this book and specifically disclaim any implied warranties of merchantability or fitness for a particular purpose. It is sold on the understanding that the publisher is not engaged in rendering professional services and neither the publisher nor the author shall be liable for damages arising herefrom. If professional advice or other expert assistance is required, the services of a competent professional should be sought.

Library of Congress Cataloging-in-Publication Data is Available

Names: Lavi, Mohan R., author.
Title: The impact of IFRS on industry / Mohan R. Lavi.
Description: Hoboken : Wiley, 2016. | Series: Wiley regulatory reporting |
  Includes index.
Identifiers: LCCN 2015043944 (print) | LCCN 2015044761 (ebook) |
  ISBN 9781119047582 (paperback) | ISBN 9781119047551 (ePDF) |
  ISBN 9781119047483 (epub)
Subjects: LCSH: Financial statements—Standards—Handbooks, manuals, etc. |
  Accounting—Standards—Handbooks, manuals, etc. | BISAC: BUSINESS &
  ECONOMICS / International / Accounting.
Classification: LCC HF5626 .L384 2016 (print) | LCC HF5626 (ebook) |
  DDC 657/.320218—dc23
LC record available at http://lccn.loc.gov/2015043944

Cover Design & Image: Wiley

Set in 11/12.3pt and TimesLTstd by SPi-Global, Chennai, India

Printed in Great Britain by TJ International Ltd, Padstow, Cornwall, UK

10 9 8 7 6 5 4 3 2 1

CONTENTS

PREFACE

During the course of my lectures across India and abroad on International Financial Reporting Standards (IFRS) and other accounting related topics, I was always fascinated by the questions that the participants put forward. Each session was different and so was each question. There were, of course, questions that were not in any way related to accounting or standards but that is to be expected anywhere. Probably what fascinated me more was that accountants were able to pose questions on how, for instance, a refractor should be accounted considering its use, or whether an internally generated brand qualifies for recognition as an intangible asset when the brand has been hypothecated to a bank and funds obtained. Most of my employment was with companies that were based in the United States and hence I had exposure to the industry-specific provisions of US GAAP. As IFRS grew in importance, my mind was filled with thoughts as to how different industries would be impacted if they transitioned to IFRS. Those thoughts are set out in this book.

Having worked in different industries, I have extrapolated an IFRS-implementation scenario in these industries to ascertain the impact. For other industries, I have researched the annual reports of large companies operating in these industries and asked questions of friends and associates working in these industries. As always, the internet threw up way too much information – I have digested this information and present only the relevant parts of which I am absolutely sure, and which are supported by other tangible evidence.

This book is primarily intended for entities that are yet to transition to IFRS and are considering an impact assessment. Entities that have already moved over to IFRS could find the book useful in the impact of revised IFRS Standards that are to come out in the future or the impact that annual impairment tests or fair valuation would have. Others who are interested in IFRS as academics or students could find the book useful for their areas of work.

The book is divided into six chapters. Chapter 1 discusses the origin of accounting standards and how they appear to be moving to an industry-based era. Chapter 2 summarizes all the disclosure requirements of IFRS. Chapter 3 details the impact that IFRS Standards would have on all industries while Chapter 4 discusses this impact for specific industries. Chapter 5 discusses the collateral impact of IFRS while Chapter 6 concludes with a discussion on how future IFRS Standards could impact specific industries. The book concludes with an appendix that contains a tabular summary of the impact discussed.

Readers are encouraged to read the book in any order they prefer.

I do hope readers enjoy this book.

Bangalore
January 31, 2016

ACKNOWLEDGEMENTS

The easy part of writing this book was to complete the chapters on industries in which I have worked – software, retail and industries where property, plant and equipment constitute a significant component of the balance sheet. The not-so-tough part was writing the chapters on industries whose business model everyone is familiar with – airlines, for instance. The tough parts were the chapters on industries which were highly technical in nature – pharmaceutical and the oil and gas industries are examples.

As in other things, the internet has a lot of information on the impact of IFRS on industry – sometimes there is too much information. Deloitte, KPMG, EY, PWC, GT, BDO and other large accounting firms have a number of publications on how IFRS would impact certain industries. There are quite a few research publications written by researchers at different universities that analyse issues with regard to IFRS. Many regulators across the world have published their impact analysis of IFRS in their area of regulation.

This book would have remained only an idea if not for the support received from the entire team at John Wiley and Sons. It commenced with a person (I am not sure who) @ Wiley responding and forwarding my Twitter message on July 10, 2014 to the right people very fast. Then, Steven Mullaly, Executive Commissioning Editor and Gemma Valler, Commissioning Editor, interacted with me and have been very supportive throughout this project that has taken about a year to finish. They have been extremely patient with me though I delayed sending them this book by quite a bit. In IFRS-speak, their patience was not impaired and they dealt with my delays at fair value. All credit for this book being published should go to them.

A word of immense thanks is also due to John Duggan who patiently proofread the book, identified and corrected the many errors I had made in the book. Thanks, John.

My parents, R R T Lavi and Vasanta Lavi, wife Rekha K R and daughter Brinda have been a source of amazing encouragement to me throughout. They have endured a lot with me and dedicating this book to them is one small though insufficient way of thanking each one of them.

Mohan R Lavi
Bangalore, India

1 INTRODUCTION: THE BACKGROUND AND EVOLUTION OF IFRS, AND A DISCUSSION ON WHY IFRS WOULD HAVE AN IMPACT ON INDUSTRY

At first blush, it would appear that a book on the impact that IFRS would have on industry is needless and unnecessary as all IFRS Standards are principle-based and, irrespective of the nature and peculiarities of a particular industry, the same principles would apply. However, accounting history has shown us that a general principle cannot take into account the accounting nuances of each and every industry. There could be interpretational issues when applying the same principles across all industries. As an illustration, let us take the principle of transfer of risks and rewards required in IAS 18 *Revenue* to recognise revenue on sale of goods. The transfer of risks and rewards could occur at different times for a software product company that sells its goods on the internet and a machinery manufacturer which transports its machinery to the customer's premises at its own risk. In the latter case, the transfer of risks would occur at a different time if the customer bore the risk of transporting the goods to his premises. Since IAS 18 only lays down a principle, determining the timing of transfer of risks and rewards is not very clear from the accounting standard. This gap in IAS 18 would however appear to have been rectified by its successor IFRS 15.

1.1 RULE-BASED VS. PRINCIPLE-BASED STANDARDS

Readers are probably aware that it was an Italian mathematician named Luca Pacioli who invented the double entry system of accounting. Being a mathematician, he was most likely content if the debit mathematically matched the credit. In those days transactions were simple, and cost would have been the basis of most accounting. However, as business flourished, accounting issues did too.

It would appear that actual pressures on the accounting profession to establish uniform accounting standards began to surface after the stock market crash of 1929 in the United States. Some feel that insufficient and misleading financial statement information led to inflated stock prices and that this contributed to the stock market crash and the subsequent depression. The 1933 Securities Act and the 1934 Securities Exchange Act were designed to restore investor confidence. The 1933 act sets forth accounting and disclosure requirements for initial offerings of securities, stocks and bonds. The Financial Accounting Standards Board (FASB) was formed in the United States to develop accounting standards. It was in 1938 that the Committee on Accounting Procedures was formed – this committee issued what would be probably the first set of accounting standards – and issued 51 Accounting Research Bulletins on an eclectic variety of topics including business combinations. Though accountants had something to refer to, with the passage of time, these bulletins attracted a lot of criticism for giving too many options and not dealing with complicated situations and transactions. In June 1973, the International Accounting Standards Committee (IASC) was formed to develop international accounting standards. There seemed to be an unwritten rule that the FASB would formulate accounting standards that would apply only in the United States – a rule that applies even now to a limited extent. Over the years, both the accounting bodies issued numerous accounting standards. In doing so, and maybe unwittingly, they developed standards based on totally different concepts – the FASB developed Standards based on rules while the IASC developed Standards based on principles. As subsequent events would prove, there is a world of difference between these two concepts. Rule-based standards suggest that the quantity of standards is due more to the fact that rules have to be established for different industries, while principle-based standards appear much simpler – just lay down the principle and leave the rest to the user of the standard.

The debate on whether principle-based standards score over rule-based standards has been going on for some time now and will probably continue in the future too. Purely on the basis of historical experience, it can be stated with some authority that both approaches have their pros and cons.

Principles-based standards require more judgment that firms could exploit opportunistically. In 2002, the FASB observed that a principles-based approach could lead to abuse, whereby the principles in accounting standards are not applied in good faith consistent with the intent and spirit of the standards. Ironically, the Enron episode occurred a few months later. Critics were quick to point out that aggressive accounting is likely to be easier to justify (or detect by auditors) under rules-based standards because detailed guidance or thresholds are explicitly stated. It was also felt that principles-based standards might lead to more informative earnings since they allow greater flexibility for firms to choose accounting methods that better reflect their economic realities. Following this reasoning, the SEC and FASB have both indicated a preference for principles-based standards because they allow accounting professionals to operationalise accounting treatments in a manner that best fulfils the objective of each standard and thereby best captures the underlying economic reality. On the other hand, from the perspective of statement preparers and auditors, the principles-based accounting system presents higher uncertainty due to lack of detailed guidance. The risk of being perceived as out of compliance may cause preparers to stray from the desired accounting treatment due to the increased risk of second-guessing.

Prior research that directly tests the effect of principles-based versus rules-based accounting standards on accounting quality has been conducted mostly in experimental settings. Evidence from these experimental studies generally supports the notion that principles-based standards improve accounting quality over rules-based standards. For example, in their experiments Agoglia, Doupnik, and Tsakumis (2011) find that CFOs are less likely to report aggressively under a principles-based standard than a rules-based standard.

The end of Enron signalled the beginning of a period in which the world started looking differently at the entire circle of accounting – accounting standards, accounting regulators and auditors. It was felt that having a single set of accounting standards would be the way to go forward – however idealistic that may sound. Both the International Accounting Standards Board (IASB, which succeeded the IASC) and the FASB decided to do something about it.

1.2 THE NORWALK AGREEMENT

Memorandum of Understanding

THE NORWALK AGREEMENT

At their joint meeting in Norwalk, Connecticut, USA on September 18, 2002, the Financial Accounting Standards Board (FASB) and the International Accounting Standards Board (IASB) each acknowledged their commitment to the development of high-quality, compatible accounting standards that could be used for both domestic and cross-border financial reporting. At that meeting, both the FASB and IASB pledged to use their best efforts to (a) make their existing financial reporting standards fully compatible as soon as practicable, and (b) to coordinate their future work programmes to ensure that once achieved, compatibility was maintained.

To achieve compatibility, the FASB and IASB (together, the "Boards") agree, as a matter of high priority, to:

(a) undertake a short-term project aimed at removing a variety of individual differences between U.S. GAAP and International Financial Reporting Standards (IFRSs, which include International Accounting Standards, IASs);

(b) remove other differences between IFRSs and U.S. GAAP that will remain at January 1, 2005, through coordination of their future work programmes; that is, through the mutual undertaking of discrete, substantial projects which both Boards would address concurrently;

(c) continue progress on the joint projects that they are currently undertaking; and,

(d) encourage their respective interpretative bodies to coordinate their activities.

One of the defining features of rule-based standards is that they prescribe rules depending on the peculiarities of the industry. US GAAP has a bunch of standards that are specific to certain industries. The codification of US GAAP has the following under the heading "Industry."

Topic	Industry
905	Agriculture
908	Airlines
910	Contractors

915	Development Stage Entities
920	Entertainment
930	Extractive Activities
940	Financial Services
952	Franchisors
954	Health Care Entities
958	Not-for-Profit Entities
960	Plan Accounting
970	Real Estate
980	Regulated Operations
985	Software
995	US Steamship entities

Subsequent to the Norwalk Agreement, with all accounting standards issued by both the IASB and the FASB, there has been an attempt to develop them based on common principles. There are, however, still some differences between the standards pronounced by both the regulators. This is to be expected as it would be well nigh impossible to expect one-size-fits-all accounting standards due to the fact that local accounting regulations, practices and cultures differ from country to country. As long as the overall principles between the two sets of standards are not radically different, we can acknowledge that some semblance of uniformity has been achieved.

However, this does not resolve the rule-based vs. principle-based debate since all rule-based standards issued by the FASB are still being used. As in all things where there are two diametrically opposite views, it would appear that the ideal solution would be an equal balance between the two – the mid-path so to speak.

The IASB seems to have found that balance. After IFRS 3, the following standards were issued by the IASB:

IFRS 4 *Insurance Contracts*
IFRS 5 *Non-current assets held for sale*
IFRS 6 *Exploration and Evaluation of Mineral Resources*
IFRS 7 *Financial Instruments – Disclosures*
IFRS 8 *Operating Segments*
IFRS 9 *Financial Instruments*
IFRS 10 *Consolidated Financial Statements*
IFRS 11 *Joint Arrangements*
IFRS 12 *Disclosure of Interests in Other Entities*
IFRS 13 *Fair Value Measurement*
IFRS 14 *Rate Regulated Entities*
IFRS 15 *Revenue from Contracts with Customers*

It would appear that the IASB too is moving towards industry specific standards in cases where it is felt that the existing accounting standards are not elaborate enough to meet the requirements of the Framework to International Accounting Standards. IFRS 4 *Insurance Contracts* and IFRS 6 *Exploration and Evaluation of Mineral Resources* are industry specific. IFRS 14 focuses only on regulatory deferral accounts.

The saying "the only constant is change" is probably as old as change itself. Technology has filtered into everyone's lives and changed the way they live. A decade ago, buying a bestselling book involved going to your nearest bookstore. Often times, the book was not available and the storekeeper was told to inform you when it arrived. These days, you can order a bestseller online even before it is released to the public. You get it at your doorstep immediately after it is released. You can pay cash after ensuring it has been delivered intact (the only thing you probably can't do is to read it and return it!). From vegetables, electronic gadgets to matrimonial alliances, everything is done at the click of a button. With the rapid changes in technology, it was only a matter of time before bricks-and-mortar companies started to provide an online offering, thereby ensuring parity with the competition.

Accounting standards needed to keep pace with these developments. Both the FASB and the IASB have been quick to issue clarifications whenever any issues are raised on their existing accounting standards. In many ways, it is considered that the five-step approach envisaged by IFRS 15 is not only bringing the revenue recognition standard on par with Chapter 606 of US GAAP but also takes into account the changing revenue recognition landscape in different industries. Many of the 64 illustrative examples in IFRS 15 show the principles of revenue recognition in different industries.

Apart from the new generation industries, such as e-commerce, the traditional manufacturing industries also seem to be changing. Entities are hiving off divisions which they cannot manage profitably – bringing into play IFRS 3 *Business Combinations* – or are outsourcing segments of their manufacturing process that are provided more cheaply by third parties. This would bring into play questions of revenue recognition and in some instances, determining who owns and controls the property, plant and equipment to recognise it under IAS 16.

Entities that engage with the government in public private partnerships invariably enter into service concession arrangements with the government. The erstwhile International Accounting Standards provided limited guidance on how to recognise revenue in such arrangements or whether the right to charge an amount for utilising that public service gave rise to any intangible assets. IFRIC 12 *Service Concession Arrangements* fixes this conundrum.

All IFRS Standards go through a very detailed process before being published. Despite this, a Standard may not be able to provide solutions to specific situations experienced in particular industries. A recent discussion in the IASB focused on whether telecommunication towers owned by tower companies should be reflected as investment property under IAS 40 or property, plant and equipment under IAS 16. The IASB brought out International Financial Reporting Standards Interpretations (IFRIC) and Standard Interpretations Committee (SIC) to resolve such specific issues. In a limited way, IFRIC and SIC are looking at industry-specific issues.

The focus of IFRS on industry-specific standards appears to be further confirmed if one looks at the major projects of the IASB for the future. Re-deliberation is planned on IFRS 4 in Q1 of 2015, and the all-new IAS 17 *Leases* is expected to be issued at the latest by the end of 2015. That apart, a further public consultation on rate regulation is expected to be commenced in Q1 2015.

The twin factors of IFRS evolving, and dynamic changes in the way business is conducted and industries are aligned, will ensure that there will more industry-specific standards that will come out in the future from the IASB.

Some experts aver that IFRS is all about fair value and disclosures. They opine that the extensive disclosures mandated by every IFRS Standard provide ready-made information to competitor to know everything that a competitor needs to know about an entity – the fair value of its assets and liabilities, as well as a detailed breakdown of the amounts paid in a business combination. This is a spin-off effect that IFRS has had on industry – the availability of too much information about an entity. While using these vast amounts of disclosure data can do no harm, misuse of this data can create issues between entities and their competitors. However, it should be stated here that all the accounting accidents that happened over the last decade and more – be it an Enron, WorldCom, Parmalat, Lehmann Brothers or Satyam – suffered from a common shortcoming: the lack of detailed disclosures in the areas of accounting where they deviated from the norms. Accounting regulators feel – and rightly so – that it is better to disclose more rather than less, or only what is deemed essential. In the IFRS era, entities operating in different industries should learn the art of disclosing both good and not-so-good information.

We can reasonably conclude from the above discussion that, irrespective of the basis on which accounting standards have been developed, they will have an impact on specific industries. During the course of writing this book, I found to my pleasant surprise that the industry most impacted by IFRS was the airline industry. They have different types of leases, componentisation of PPE, borrowing costs, impairment, intangible assets such as airport landing rights, revenue recognition dilemmas (customer loyalty programmes) and financial instruments. It would probably not be an exaggeration to state that apart from the industry specific Standards such as IFRS 4 *Insurance Contracts* and IFRS 6 *Exploration for and Evaluation of Mineral Resources* most of the other Standards would apply in some way or the other to the airline industry. This conclusion sets the tone for the remaining chapters of the book.

2 SUMMARY OF DISCLOSURES UNDER IFRS STANDARDS

To many, IFRS is all about disclosures. The insertion of the words "financial reporting" in place of "accounting" in the erstwhile International Accounting Standards was intended to send out a message that accounting is *passé*, financial reporting is in. Financial reporting in essence means disclosures. The disclosure requirements in IFRS are, to say the least, intense. Apart from the disclosure requirements mentioned in most Standards, IFRS has Standards exclusively for disclosures: IAS 24 *Related Party Transactions*, IFRS 7 *Financial Instruments: Disclosures*, IFRS 8 *Operating Segments* and IFRS 11 *Disclosure of Interests in Other Entities* are examples. However, it has to be mentioned that the disclosure requirements in other Standards are equally intense: IAS 36 requires extensive disclosures to be made when an asset tests positive for impairment. In stark contrast, the disclosure requirements required by IAS 23 *Borrowing Costs* are mentioned only in about four paragraphs. The mantra for an entity moving over to an IFRS world will be "just disclose it."

A summary of the disclosure requirements in major IFRS Standards is provided here. A disclaimer has to be made here – the list is by no means exhaustive since some paragraphs in IFRS Standards draw references to other IFRS Standards. An entity doing IFRS for the first time would do well do develop a detailed checklist for disclosures. There are quite a few available online but it would be ideal to get one done internally because it just seems like the right thing to do.

2.1 IFRS 3 *BUSINESS COMBINATIONS*

The acquirer shall disclose information that enables users of its financial statements to evaluate the nature and financial effect of a business combination that occurs either:

(a) during the current reporting period; or
(b) after the end of the reporting period but before the financial statements are authorised for issue.

The acquirer shall disclose information that enables users of its financial statements to evaluate the financial effects of adjustments recognised in the current reporting period that relate to business combinations that occurred in the period or previous reporting periods.

2.2 IFRS 4 *INSURANCE CONTRACTS*

An entity need not apply the disclosure requirements in this IFRS to comparative information that relates to annual periods beginning before 1 January 2005, except for the disclosures about accounting policies, and recognised assets, liabilities, income and expense (and cash flows if the direct method is used).

If it is impracticable to apply a particular requirement to comparative information that relates to annual periods beginning before 1 January 2005, an entity shall disclose that fact. Applying the liability adequacy test to such comparative information might sometimes be impracticable, but it is highly unlikely to be impracticable to apply other requirements to such comparative information. IAS 8 explains the term "impracticable."

An entity need not disclose information about claims development that occurred earlier than five years before the end of the first financial year in which it applies this IFRS. Furthermore, if it is impracticable, when an entity first applies this IFRS, to prepare information about claims development that occurred before the beginning of the earliest period for which an entity presents full comparative information that complies with this IFRS, the entity shall disclose that fact.

2.3 IFRS 5 *NON-CURRENT ASSETS HELD FOR SALE*

An entity shall disclose the following information in the notes in the period in which a non-current asset (or disposal group) has been either classified as held for sale or sold:

(a) a description of the non-current asset (or disposal group);
(b) a description of the facts and circumstances of the sale, or leading to the expected disposal, and the expected manner and timing of that disposal;
(c) the gain or loss recognised and, if not separately presented in the statement of comprehensive income, the caption in the statement of comprehensive income that includes that gain or loss;
(d) if applicable, the reportable segment in which the non-current asset (or disposal group) is presented in accordance with IFRS 8 *Operating Segments*.

If applicable, an entity shall disclose, in the period of the decision to change the plan to sell the non-current asset (or disposal group), a description of the facts and circumstances leading to the decision and the effect of the decision on the results of operations for the period and any prior periods presented.

2.4 IFRS 6 *EVALUATION AND EXPLORATION OF MINERAL RESOURCES*

An entity shall disclose information that identifies and explains the amounts recognised in its financial statements arising from the exploration for and evaluation of mineral resources.

An entity shall disclose:

(a) its accounting policies for exploration and evaluation expenditures including the recognition of exploration and evaluation assets;
(b) the amounts of assets, liabilities, income and expense and operating and investing cash flows arising from the exploration for and evaluation of mineral resources.

An entity shall treat exploration and evaluation assets as a separate class of assets and make the disclosures required by either IAS 16 or IAS 38 consistent with how the assets are classified.

2.5 IFRS 7 *FINANCIAL INSTRUMENTS: DISCLOSURES*

The two main categories of disclosures required by IFRS 7 are:

1. information about the significance of financial instruments; and
2. information about the nature and extent of risks arising from financial instruments.

2.5.1 Information about the significance of financial instruments

2.5.1.1 Statement of financial position

Disclose the significance of financial instruments for an entity's financial position and performance. This includes disclosures for each of the following categories:

- financial assets measured at fair value through profit and loss, showing separately those held for trading and those designated at initial recognition;
- held-to-maturity investments;
- loans and receivables;
- available-for-sale assets;
- financial liabilities at fair value through profit and loss, showing separately those held for trading and those designated at initial recognition; and
- financial liabilities measured at amortised cost.

Other balance sheet-related disclosures

- Special disclosures about financial assets and financial liabilities designated to be measured at fair value through profit and loss, including disclosures about credit risk and market risk, changes in fair values attributable to these risks and the methods of measurement.
- Reclassifications of financial instruments from one category to another (e.g. from fair value to amortised cost or vice versa).
- Information about financial assets pledged as collateral and about financial or non-financial assets held as collateral.
- Reconciliation of the allowance account for credit losses (bad debts) by class of financial assets.
- Information about compound financial instruments with multiple embedded derivatives.
- Breaches of terms of loan agreements.

2.5.1.2 Statement of comprehensive income

- Items of income, expense, gains, and losses, with separate disclosure of gains and losses from:
    - financial assets measured at fair value through profit and loss, showing separately those held for trading and those designated at initial recognition,
    - held-to-maturity investments,

- loans and receivables,
- available-for-sale assets,
- financial liabilities measured at fair value through profit and loss, showing separately those held for trading and those designated at initial recognition,
- financial liabilities measured at amortised cost.

Other income statement-related disclosures
- Total interest income and total interest expense for those financial instruments that are not measured at fair value through profit and loss.
- Fee income and expense.
- Amount of impairment losses by class of financial assets.
- Interest income on impaired financial assets.

2.5.1.3 Other disclosures

- Accounting policies for financial instruments.
- Information about hedge accounting, including:
  - description of each hedge, hedging instrument, and fair values of those instruments, and nature of risks being hedged,
  - for cash flow hedges, the periods in which the cash flows are expected to occur, when they are expected to enter into the determination of profit or loss, and a description of any forecast transaction for which hedge accounting had previously been used but which is no longer expected to occur.
- If a gain or loss on a hedging instrument in a cash flow hedge has been recognised in other comprehensive income, an entity should disclose the following:
  - the amount that was so recognised in other comprehensive income during the period,
  - the amount that was removed from equity and included in profit or loss for the period,
  - the amount that was removed from equity during the period and included in the initial measurement of the acquisition cost or other carrying amount of a non-financial asset or non-financial liability in a hedged highly probable forecast transaction.
- For fair value hedges, information about the fair value changes of the hedging instrument and the hedged item.
- Hedge ineffectiveness recognised in profit and loss (separately for cash flow hedges and hedges of a net investment in a foreign operation).
- Information about the fair values of each class of financial asset and financial liability, along with:
  - comparable carrying amounts,
  - description of how fair value was determined,
  - the level of inputs used in determining fair value,
  - reconciliations of movements between levels of fair value measurement hierarchy additional disclosures for financial instruments whose fair value is determined using level 3 inputs including impacts on profit and loss, other comprehensive income and sensitivity analysis,
  - information if fair value cannot be reliably measured.

- The fair value hierarchy introduces three levels of inputs based on the lowest level of input significant to the overall fair value:
  - Level 1 – quoted prices for similar instruments,
  - Level 2 – directly observable market inputs other than Level 1 inputs,
  - Level 3 – inputs not based on observable market data,
- Disclosure of fair values is not required when the carrying amount is a reasonable approximation of fair value, such as short-term trade receivables and payables, or for instruments whose fair value cannot be measured reliably.

2.5.2 Nature and extent of exposure to risks arising from financial instruments

2.5.2.1 Qualitative disclosures

The qualitative disclosures describe:

- risk exposures for each type of financial instrument;
- management's objectives, policies, and processes for managing those risks; and
- changes from the prior period.

2.5.2.2 Quantitative disclosures

The quantitative disclosures provide information about the extent to which the entity is exposed to risk, based on information provided internally to the entity's key management personnel. These disclosures include:

- summary quantitative data about exposure to each risk at the reporting date
- disclosures about credit risk, liquidity risk, and market risk and how these risks are managed as further described below
- concentrations of risk.

2.5.2.3 Credit risk

Credit risk is the risk that one party to a financial instrument will cause a loss for the other party by failing to pay for its obligation.
Disclosures about credit risk include:

- maximum amount of exposure (before deducting the value of collateral), description of collateral, information about credit quality of financial assets that are neither past due nor impaired, and information about credit quality of financial assets whose terms have been renegotiated
- for financial assets that are past due or impaired, analytical disclosures are required
- information about collateral or other credit enhancements obtained or called.

2.5.2.4 Liquidity risk

Liquidity risk is the risk that an entity will have difficulties in paying its financial liabilities.
Disclosures about liquidity risk include:

- a maturity analysis of financial liabilities
- description of approach to risk management.

2.5.2.5 *Market risk*

Market risk is the risk that the fair value or cash flows of a financial instrument will fluctuate due to changes in market prices. Market risk reflects interest rate risk, currency risk and other price risks.

Disclosures about market risk include:

- a sensitivity analysis of each type of market risk to which the entity is exposed;
- additional information if the sensitivity analysis is not representative of the entity's risk exposure (for example because exposures during the year were different to exposures at year-end).

IFRS 7 provides that if an entity prepares a sensitivity analysis such as value-at-risk for management purposes that reflects interdependencies of more than one component of market risk (for instance, interest risk and foreign currency risk combined), it may disclose that analysis instead of a separate sensitivity analysis for each type of market risk

2.5.2.6 *Transfers of financial assets*

An entity shall disclose information that enables users of its financial statements:

- to understand the relationship between transferred financial assets that are not derecognised in their entirety and the associated liabilities;
- to evaluate the nature of, and risks associated with, the entity's continuing involvement in derecognised financial assets;
- transferred financial assets that are not derecognised in their entirety;
- required disclosures include description of the nature of the transferred assets, nature of risk and rewards as well as description of the nature and quantitative disclosure depicting relationship between transferred financial assets and the associated liabilities;
- transferred financial assets that are derecognised in their entirety;
- required disclosures include the carrying amount of the assets and liabilities recognised, fair value of the assets and liabilities that represent continuing involvement, maximum exposure to loss from the continuing involvement as well as maturity analysis of the undiscounted cash flows to repurchase the derecognised financial assets;
- additional disclosures are required for any gain or loss recognised at the date of transfer of the assets, income or expenses recognise from the entity's continuing involvement in the derecognised financial assets as well as details of uneven distribution of proceed from transfer activity throughout the reporting period.

Note: The above disclosure requirements do not take into consideration the additional disclosure requirements of IFRS 9.

2.6 IFRS 8 *SEGMENT REPORTING*

An entity shall disclose information to enable users of its financial statements to evaluate the nature and financial effects of the business activities in which it engages and the economic environments in which it operates.

An entity shall disclose the following for each period for which a statement of comprehensive income is presented:

(a) general information as described,
(b) information about reported segment profit or loss, including specified revenues and expenses included in reported segment profit or loss, segment assets, segment liabilities and the basis of measurement,
(c) reconciliations of the totals of segment revenues, reported segment profit or loss, segment assets, segment liabilities and other material segment items to corresponding entity amounts.

Reconciliations of the amounts in the statement of financial position for reportable segments to the amounts in the entity's statement of financial position are required for each date at which a statement of financial position is presented. Information for prior periods shall be restated.

2.6.1 General information

An entity shall disclose the following general information:

(a) factors used to identify the entity's reportable segments, including the basis of organisation (for example, whether management has chosen to organise the entity around differences in products and services, geographical areas, regulatory environments, or a combination of factors and whether operating segments have been aggregated);
(b) the judgements made by management in applying the aggregation criteria. This includes a brief description of the operating segments that have been aggregated in this way and the economic indicators that have been assessed in determining that the aggregated operating segments share similar economic characteristics; and
(c) types of products and services from which each reportable segment derives its revenues.

2.6.2 Information about profit or loss, assets and liabilities

An entity shall report a measure of profit or loss for each reportable segment. An entity shall report a measure of total assets and liabilities for each reportable segment if such amounts are regularly provided to the chief operating decision maker. An entity shall also disclose the following about each reportable segment if the specified amounts are included in the measure of segment profit or loss reviewed by the chief operating decision maker, or are otherwise regularly provided to the chief operating decision maker, even if not included in that measure of segment profit or loss:

(a) revenues from external customers;
(b) revenues from transactions with other operating segments of the same entity;
(c) interest revenue;
(d) interest expense;
(e) depreciation and amortisation;
(f) material items of income and expense disclosed in accordance with IAS 1 *Presentation of Financial Statements* (as revised in 2007);

(g) the entity's interest in the profit or loss of associates and joint ventures accounted for by the equity method;

(h) income tax expense or income; and

(i) material non-cash items other than depreciation and amortisation.

An entity shall report interest revenue separately from interest expense for each reportable segment unless a majority of the segment's revenues are from interest and the chief operating decision maker relies primarily on net interest revenue to assess the performance of the segment and make decisions about resources to be allocated to the segment. In that situation, an entity may report that segment's interest revenue net of its interest expense and disclose that it has done so.

An entity shall disclose the following about each reportable segment if the specified amounts are included in the measure of segment assets reviewed by the chief operating decision maker or are otherwise regularly provided to the chief operating decision maker, even if not included in the measure of segment assets:

(a) the amount of investment in associates and joint ventures accounted for by the equity method; and

(b) the amounts of additions to non-current assets1 other than financial instruments, deferred tax assets, net defined benefit assets (see IAS 19 *Employee Benefits*) and rights arising under insurance contracts.

2.7 IFRS 10 *CONSOLIDATED FINANCIAL STATEMENTS*

2.7.1 Significant judgements and assumptions

An entity discloses information about significant judgements and assumptions it has made (and changes in those judgements and assumptions) in determining:

- that it controls another entity;
- that it has joint control of an arrangement or significant influence over another entity;
- the type of joint arrangement (i.e. joint operation or joint venture) when the arrangement has been structured through a separate vehicle.

2.7.2 Interests in subsidiaries

An entity shall disclose information that enables users of its consolidated financial statements to:

- understand the composition of the group;
- understand the interest that non-controlling interests have in the group's activities and cash flows;
- evaluate the nature and extent of significant restrictions on its ability to access or use assets, and settle liabilities, of the group;
- evaluate the nature of, and changes in, the risks associated with its interests in consolidated structured entities,

- evaluate the consequences of changes in its ownership interest in a subsidiary that do not result in a loss of control; and
- evaluate the consequences of losing control of a subsidiary during the reporting period.

2.7.3 Interests in unconsolidated subsidiaries

In accordance with IFRS 10 *Consolidated Financial Statements*, an investment entity is required to apply the exception to consolidation and instead account for its investment in a subsidiary at fair value through profit or loss.

Where an entity is an investment entity, IFRS 12 requires additional disclosure, including:

- the fact that the entity is an investment entity;
- information about significant judgements and assumptions it has made in determining that it is an investment entity, and specifically where the entity does not have one or more of the "typical characteristics" of an investment entity;
- details of subsidiaries that have not been consolidated (name, place of business, ownership interests held);
- details of the relationship and certain transactions between the investment entity and the subsidiary (e.g. restrictions on transfer of funds, commitments, support arrangements, contractual arrangements); and
- information where an entity becomes, or ceases to be, an investment entity.

2.7.4 Interests in joint arrangements and associates

An entity shall disclose information that enables users of its financial statements to evaluate:

- the nature, extent and financial effects of its interests in joint arrangements and associates, including the nature and effects of its contractual relationship with the other investors with joint control of, or significant influence over, joint arrangements and associates; and
- the nature of, and changes in, the risks associated with its interests in joint ventures and associates.

2.7.5 Interests in unconsolidated structured entities

An entity shall disclose information that enables users of its financial statements to:

- understand the nature and extent of its interests in unconsolidated structured entities; and
- evaluate the nature of, and changes in, the risks associated with its interests in unconsolidated structured entities.

2.8 IFRS 13 *FAIR VALUE MEASUREMENT*

An entity shall disclose information that helps users of its financial statements assess both of the following:

(a) For assets and liabilities that are measured at fair value on a recurring or non-recurring basis in the statement of financial position after initial recognition, the valuation techniques and inputs used to develop those measurements.

(b) For recurring fair value measurements using significant unobservable inputs (Level 3), the effect of the measurements on profit or loss or other comprehensive income for the period.

An entity shall consider all the following:

(a) the level of detail necessary to satisfy the disclosure requirements;
(b) how much emphasis to place on each of the various requirements;
(c) how much aggregation or disaggregation to undertake; and
(d) whether users of financial statements need additional information to evaluate the quantitative information disclosed.

If the disclosures provided in accordance with this IFRS and other IFRSs are insufficient to meet the objectives, an entity shall disclose additional information necessary to meet those objectives.

An entity shall disclose, at a minimum, the following information for each class of assets and liabilities measured at fair value (including measurements based on fair value within the scope of this IFRS) in the statement of financial position after initial recognition:

(a) For recurring and non-recurring fair value measurements, the fair value measurement at the end of the reporting period, and for non-recurring fair value measurements, the reasons for the measurement. Recurring fair value measurements of assets or liabilities are those that other IFRSs require or permit in the statement of financial position at the end of each reporting period. Non-recurring fair value measurements of assets or liabilities are those that other IFRSs require or permit in the statement of financial position in particular circumstances (e.g. when an entity measures an asset held for sale at fair value less costs to sell in accordance with IFRS 5 *Non-current Assets Held for Sale and Discontinued Operations* because the asset's fair value less costs to sell is lower than its carrying amount).

(b) For recurring and non-recurring fair value measurements, the level of the fair value hierarchy within which the fair value measurements are categorised in their entirety (Level 1, 2 or 3).

(c) For assets and liabilities held at the end of the reporting period that are measured at fair value on a recurring basis, the amounts of any transfers between Level 1 and Level 2 of the fair value hierarchy, the reasons for those transfers and the entity's policy for determining when transfers between levels are deemed to have occurred. Transfers into each level shall be disclosed and discussed separately from transfers out of each level.

(d) For recurring and non-recurring fair value measurements categorised within Level 2 and Level 3 of the fair value hierarchy, a description of the valuation technique(s) and the inputs used in the fair value measurement. If there has been a change in valuation technique (e.g. changing from a market approach to an income approach or the use of an additional valuation technique), the entity shall disclose that change and the reason(s) for making it. For fair value measurements categorised within Level 3 of the fair value hierarchy, an entity shall provide quantitative information about the significant unobservable inputs used in the fair value measurement. An entity is not required to create quantitative information to comply with this disclosure requirement if quantitative unobservable inputs are not developed by the entity when measuring fair value (e.g. when an entity uses prices from prior transactions or third-party pricing information without adjustment). However, when providing this disclosure an entity cannot ignore quantitative unobservable inputs that are significant to the fair value measurement and are reasonably available to the entity.

For recurring fair value measurements categorised within Level 3 of the fair value hierarchy, a reconciliation from the opening balances to the closing balances, disclosing separately changes during the period attributable to the following:

1. Total gains or losses for the period recognised in profit or loss, and the line item(s) in profit or loss in which those gains or losses are recognised.
2. Total gains or losses for the period recognised in other comprehensive income, and the line item(s) in other comprehensive income in which those gains or losses are recognised.
3. Purchases, sales, issues and settlements (each of those types of changes disclosed separately).
4. The amounts of any transfers into or out of Level 3 of the fair value hierarchy, the reasons for those transfers and the entity's policy for determining when transfers between levels are deemed to have occurred. Transfers into Level 3 shall be disclosed and discussed separately from transfers out of Level 3.

A narrative description of the sensitivity of the fair value measurement to changes in unobservable inputs if a change in those inputs to a different amount might result in a significantly higher or lower fair value measurement. If there are interrelationships between those inputs and other unobservable inputs used in the fair value measurement, an entity shall also provide a description of those interrelationships and of how they might magnify or mitigate the effect of changes in the unobservable inputs on the fair value measurement. To comply with that disclosure requirement, the narrative description of the sensitivity to changes in unobservable inputs shall include, at a minimum, the unobservable inputs disclosed when complying with (d).

For financial assets and financial liabilities, if changing one or more of the unobservable inputs to reflect reasonably possible alternative assumptions would change fair value significantly, an entity shall state that fact and disclose the effect of those changes. The entity shall disclose how the effect of a change to reflect a reasonably possible alternative assumption was calculated. For that purpose, significance shall be judged with respect to profit or loss, and total assets or total liabilities, or, when changes in fair value are recognised in other comprehensive income, total equity.

For recurring and non-recurring fair value measurements, if the highest and best use of a non-financial asset differs from its current use, an entity shall disclose that fact and why the non-financial asset is being used in a manner that differs from its highest and best use.

An entity shall determine appropriate classes of assets and liabilities on the basis of the following:

(a) the nature, characteristics and risks of the asset or liability; and
(b) the level of the fair value hierarchy within which the fair value measurement is categorised.

The number of classes may need to be greater for fair value measurements categorised within Level 3 of the fair value hierarchy because those measurements have a greater degree of uncertainty and subjectivity. Determining appropriate classes of assets and liabilities for which disclosures about fair value measurements should be provided requires judgement. A class of assets and liabilities will often require greater disaggregation than the line items presented in the statement of financial position. However, an entity shall provide information sufficient to permit reconciliation to the line items presented in the statement of financial position. If another IFRS specifies the class for an asset or a liability, an entity may use that class in providing the disclosures required in this IFRS if that class meets these requirements.

An entity shall disclose and consistently follow its policy for determining when transfers between levels of the fair value hierarchy are deemed to have occurred. The policy about the timing of recognising transfers shall be the same for transfers into the levels as for transfers out of the levels. Examples of policies for determining the timing of transfers include the following:

(a) the date of the event or change in circumstances that caused the transfer;
(b) the beginning of the reporting period; and
(c) the end of the reporting period.

For each class of assets and liabilities not measured at fair value in the statement of financial position but for which the fair value is disclosed, an entity shall disclose the information required. However, an entity is not required to provide the quantitative disclosures about significant unobservable inputs used in fair value measurements categorised within Level 3 of the fair value hierarchy. For such assets and liabilities, an entity does not need to provide the other disclosures required by this IFRS.

For a liability measured at fair value and issued with an inseparable third-party credit enhancement, an issuer shall disclose the existence of that credit enhancement and whether it is reflected in the fair value measurement of the liability.

An entity shall present the quantitative disclosures required by this IFRS in a tabular format unless another format is more appropriate.

2.9 IFRS 14 *REGULATORY DEFERRAL ACCOUNTS*

IFRS 14 sets out disclosure objectives to allow users to assess:

• the nature of, and risks associated with, the rate regulation that establishes the price(s) the entity can charge customers for the goods or services it provides – including information about the entity's rate-regulated activities and the rate-setting process, the identity of the rate regulator(s), and the impacts of risks and uncertainties on the recovery or reversal of regulatory deferral balance accounts; and

- the effects of rate regulation on the entity's financial statements – including the basis on which regulatory deferral account balances are recognised, how they are assessed for recovery, a reconciliation of the carrying amount at the beginning and end of the reporting period, discount rates applicable, income tax impacts and details of balances that are no longer considered recoverable or reversible.

2.10 IFRS 15 *REVENUE FROM CONTRACTS WITH CUSTOMERS*

The objective of the disclosure requirements is for an entity to disclose sufficient information to enable users of financial statements to understand the nature, amount, timing and uncertainty of revenue and cash flows arising from contracts with customers. To achieve that objective, an entity shall disclose qualitative and quantitative information about all of the following:

(a) its contracts with customers;

(b) the significant judgements, and changes in the judgements, made in applying this Standard to those contracts; and

(c) any assets recognised from the costs to obtain or fulfil a contract with a customer.

An entity shall consider the level of detail necessary to satisfy the disclosure objective and how much emphasis to place on each of the various requirements. An entity shall aggregate or disaggregate disclosures so that useful information is not obscured by either the inclusion of a large amount of insignificant detail or the aggregation of items that have substantially different characteristics.

An entity need not disclose information in accordance with this Standard if it has provided the information in accordance with another Standard.

2.10.1 Contracts with customers

An entity shall disclose all of the following amounts for the reporting period unless those amounts are presented separately in the statement of comprehensive income in accordance with other Standards:

(a) revenue recognised from contracts with customers, which the entity shall disclose separately from its other sources of revenue; and

(b) any impairment losses recognised (in accordance with IFRS 9) on any receivables or contract assets arising from an entity's contracts with customers, which the entity shall disclose separately from impairment losses from other contracts.

2.10.2 Disaggregation of revenue

An entity shall disaggregate revenue recognised from contracts with customers into categories that depict how the nature, amount, timing and uncertainty of revenue and cash flows are affected by economic factors.

In addition, an entity shall disclose sufficient information to enable users of financial statements to understand the relationship between the disclosure of disaggregated revenue (and revenue information that is disclosed for each reportable segment, if the entity applies IFRS 8 *Operating Segments*.

2.10.3 Contract balances

An entity shall disclose all of the following:

(a) the opening and closing balances of receivables, contract assets and contract liabilities from contracts with customers, if not otherwise separately presented or disclosed;

(b) revenue recognised in the reporting period that was included in the contract liability balance at the beginning of the period; and

(c) revenue recognised in the reporting period from performance obligations satisfied (or partially satisfied) in previous periods (for example, changes in transaction price).

An entity shall explain how the timing of satisfaction of its performance obligations relates to the typical timing of payment and the effect that those factors have on the contract asset and the contract liability balances. The explanation provided may use qualitative information.

An entity shall provide an explanation of the significant changes in the contract asset and the contract liability balances during the reporting period. The explanation shall include qualitative and quantitative information. Examples of changes in the entity's balances of contract assets and contract liabilities include any of the following:

(a) changes due to business combinations;

(b) cumulative catch-up adjustments to revenue that affect the corresponding contract asset or contract liability, including adjustments arising from a change in the measure of progress, a change in an estimate of the transaction price (including any changes in the assessment of whether an estimate of variable consideration is constrained) or a contract modification;

(c) impairment of a contract asset;

(d) a change in the time frame for a right to consideration to become unconditional (i.e. for a contract asset to be reclassified to a receivable); and

(e) a change in the time frame for a performance obligation to be satisfied (i.e. for the recognition of revenue arising from a contract liability).

2.10.4 Performance obligations

An entity shall disclose information about its performance obligations in contracts with customers, including a description of all of the following:

(a) when the entity typically satisfies its performance obligations (for example, upon shipment, upon delivery, as services are rendered or upon completion of service), including when performance obligations are satisfied in a bill-and-hold arrangement;

(b) the significant payment terms (for example, when payment is typically due, whether the contract has a significant financing component, whether the consideration amount is variable and whether the estimate of variable consideration is typically constrained);

(c) the nature of the goods or services that the entity has promised to transfer, highlighting any performance obligations to arrange for another party to transfer goods or services (i.e. if the entity is acting as an agent);

(d) obligations for returns, refunds and other similar obligations; and

(e) types of warranties and related obligations.

2.10.5 Transaction price allocated to the remaining performance obligations

An entity shall disclose the following information about its remaining performance obligations:

(a) the aggregate amount of the transaction price allocated to the performance obligations that are unsatisfied (or partially unsatisfied) as of the end of the reporting period; and

(b) an explanation of when the entity expects to recognise as revenue the amount disclosed which the entity shall disclose in either of the following ways:

    (i) on a quantitative basis using the time bands that would be most appropriate for the duration of the remaining performance obligations; or

    (ii) by using qualitative information.

As a practical expedient, an entity need not disclose the information for a performance obligation if either of the following conditions is met:

(a) the performance obligation is part of a contract that has an original expected duration of one year or less; or

(b) the entity recognises revenue from the satisfaction of the performance obligation.

An entity shall explain qualitatively whether it is applying the practical expedient and whether any consideration from contracts with customers is not included in the transaction price and, therefore, not included in the information disclosed. For example, an estimate of the transaction price would not include any estimated amounts of variable consideration that are constrained.

2.10.6 Significant judgements in the application of this Standard

An entity shall disclose the judgements, and changes in the judgements, made in applying this Standard that significantly affect the determination of the amount and timing of revenue from contracts with customers. In particular, an entity shall explain the judgements, and changes in the judgements, used in determining both of the following:

(a) the timing of satisfaction of performance obligations; and

(b) the transaction price and the amounts allocated to performance obligations.

2.10.7 Determining the timing of satisfaction of performance obligations

For performance obligations that an entity satisfies over time, an entity shall disclose both of the following:

- the methods used to recognise revenue (for example, a description of the output methods or input methods used and how those methods are applied); and
- an explanation of why the methods used provide a faithful depiction of the transfer of goods or services.

For performance obligations satisfied at a point in time, an entity shall disclose the significant judgements made in evaluating when a customer obtains control of promised goods or services.

2.10.8 Determining the transaction price and the amounts allocated to performance obligations

An entity shall disclose information about the methods, inputs and assumptions used for all of the following:

(a) determining the transaction price, which includes, but is not limited to, estimating variable consideration, adjusting the consideration for the effects of the time value of money and measuring non-cash consideration;

(b) assessing whether an estimate of variable consideration is constrained;

(c) allocating the transaction price, including estimating stand-alone selling prices of promised goods or services and allocating discounts and variable consideration to a specific part of the contract (if applicable); and

(d) measuring obligations for returns, refunds and other similar obligations.

2.10.9 Assets recognised from the costs to obtain or fulfil a contract with a customer

An entity shall describe both of the following:

(a) the judgements made in determining the amount of the costs incurred to obtain or fulfil a contract with a customer; and

(b) the method it uses to determine the amortisation for each reporting period.

An entity shall disclose all of the following:

(a) the methods used to recognise revenue (for example, a description of the output methods or input methods used and how those methods are applied); and

(b) an explanation of why the methods used provide a faithful depiction of the transfer of goods or services.

2.11 IAS 2 *INVENTORIES*

The financial statements shall disclose:

(a) the accounting policies adopted in measuring inventories, including the cost formula used;

(b) the total carrying amount of inventories and the carrying amount in classifications appropriate to the entity;

(c) the carrying amount of inventories carried at fair value less costs to sell;

(d) the amount of inventories recognised as an expense during the period;

(e) the amount of any write-down of inventories recognised as an expense in the period;

(f) the amount of any reversal of any write-down that is recognised as a reduction in the amount of inventories recognised as expense in the period;

(g) the circumstances or events that led to the reversal of a write-down of inventories;

(h) the carrying amount of inventories pledged as security for liabilities.

2.12 IAS 3 *CASH FLOW STATEMENTS*

An entity shall disclose the components of cash and cash equivalents and shall present a reconciliation of the amounts in its statement of cash flows with the equivalent items reported in the statement of financial position.

An entity shall disclose, together with a commentary by management, the amount of significant cash and cash equivalent balances held by the entity that are not available for use by the group.

2.13 IAS 10 *EVENTS AFTER THE REPORTING DATE*

An entity shall disclose the date when the financial statements were authorised for issue and who gave that authorisation. If the entity's owners or others have the power to amend the financial statements after issue, the entity shall disclose that fact. If an entity receives information after the reporting period about conditions that existed at the end of the reporting period, it shall update disclosures that relate to those conditions, in the light of the new information. If non-adjusting events after the reporting period are material, non-disclosure could influence the economic decisions that users make on the basis of the financial statements. Accordingly, an entity shall disclose the following for each material category of non-adjusting event after the reporting period:

(a) the nature of the event; and

(b) an estimate of its financial effect, or a statement that such an estimate cannot be made.

2.14 IAS 11 *CONSTRUCTION CONTRACTS*

The disclosures mandated by IAS 11 are as below:

(a) The amount of contract revenue recognised as revenue in the period;

(b) the methods used to determine the contract revenue recognised in the period; and

(c) the methods used to determine the stage of completion of contracts in progress.

An entity shall disclose each of the following for contracts in progress at the end of the reporting period:

    (a) the aggregate amount of costs incurred and recognised profits (less recognised losses) to date;

    (b) the amount of advances received; and

    (c) the amount of retentions.

2.15 IAS 12 INCOME TAXES

The major components of tax expense (income) shall be disclosed separately. The following shall also be disclosed separately:

    (a) the aggregate current and deferred tax relating to items that are charged or credited directly to equity;

    (b) the amount of income tax relating to each component of other comprehensive income;

    (c) an explanation of the relationship between tax expense (income) and accounting profit in either or both of the following forms:

        1. a numerical reconciliation between tax expense (income) and the product of accounting profit multiplied by the applicable tax rate(s), disclosing also the basis on which the applicable tax rate(s) is (are) computed; or

        2. a numerical reconciliation between the average effective tax rate and the applicable tax rate, disclosing also the basis on which the applicable tax rate is computed;

    (d) an explanation of changes in the applicable tax rate(s) compared to the previous accounting period;

    (e) the amount (and expiry date, if any) of deductible temporary differences, unused tax losses, and unused tax credits for which no deferred tax asset is recognised in the statement of financial position;

    (f) the aggregate amount of temporary differences associated with investments in subsidiaries, branches and associates and interests in joint arrangements, for which deferred tax liabilities have not been recognised;

    (g) in respect of each type of temporary difference, and in respect of each type of unused tax losses and unused tax credits:

        1. the amount of the deferred tax assets and liabilities recognised in the statement of financial position for each period presented;

        2. the amount of the deferred tax income or expense recognised in profit or loss, if this is not apparent from the changes in the amounts recognised in the statement of financial position;

    (h) in respect of discontinued operations, the tax expense relating to:

        1. the gain or loss on discontinuance; and

        2. the profit or loss from the ordinary activities of the discontinued operation for the period, together with the corresponding amounts for each prior period presented;

    (i)   the amount of income tax consequences of dividends to shareholders of the entity that were proposed or declared before the financial statements were authorised for issue, but are not recognised as a liability in the financial statements;

    (j)   if a business combination in which the entity is the acquirer causes a change in the amount recognised for its pre-acquisition deferred tax asset the amount of that change; and

    (k)   if the deferred tax benefits acquired in a business combination are not recognised at the acquisition date but are recognised after the acquisition date a description of the event or change in circumstances that caused the deferred tax benefits to be recognised.

An entity shall disclose the amount of a deferred tax asset and the nature of the evidence supporting its recognition, when:

    (a)   the utilisation of the deferred tax asset is dependent on future taxable profits in excess of the profits arising from the reversal of existing taxable temporary differences; and

    (b)   the entity has suffered a loss in either the current or preceding period in the tax jurisdiction to which the deferred tax asset relates.

An entity shall disclose the nature of the potential income tax consequences that would result from the payment of dividends to its shareholders. In addition, the entity shall disclose the amounts of the potential income tax consequences practicably determinable and whether there are any potential income tax consequences not practicably determinable.

2.16 IAS 16 *PROPERTY, PLANT AND EQUIPMENT*

The financial statements shall disclose, for each class of property, plant and equipment:

    (a)   the measurement bases used for determining the gross carrying amount;

    (b)   the depreciation methods used;

    (c)   the useful lives or the depreciation rates used;

    (d)   the gross carrying amount and the accumulated depreciation (aggregated with accumulated impairment losses) at the beginning and end of the period; and

    (e)   a reconciliation of the carrying amount at the beginning and end of the period showing:

        1. additions,

        2. assets classified as held for sale or included in a disposal group classified as held for sale in accordance with IFRS 5 and other disposals,

        3. acquisitions through business combinations,

        4. increases or decreases resulting from revaluations and from impairment losses recognised or reversed in other comprehensive income in accordance with IAS 36,

        5. impairment losses recognised in profit or loss in accordance with IAS 36,

        6. impairment losses reversed in profit or loss in accordance with IAS 36,

7. depreciation,
8. the net exchange differences arising on the translation of the financial statements from the functional currency into a different presentation currency, including the translation of a foreign operation into the presentation currency of the reporting entity, and
9. other changes.

The financial statements shall also disclose:

(a) the existence and amounts of restrictions on title, and property, plant and equipment pledged as security for liabilities;
(b) the amount of expenditures recognised in the carrying amount of an item of property, plant and equipment in the course of its construction;
(c) the amount of contractual commitments for the acquisition of property, plant and equipment; and
(d) if it is not disclosed separately in the statement of comprehensive income, the amount of compensation from third parties for items of property, plant and equipment that were impaired, lost or given up that is included in profit or loss.

If items of property, plant and equipment are stated at revalued amounts, the following shall be disclosed in addition to the disclosures required by IFRS 13:

1. the effective date of the revaluation,
2. whether an independent valuer was involved;

(e) for each revalued class of property, plant and equipment, the carrying amount that would have been recognised had the assets been carried under the cost model; and
(f) the revaluation surplus, indicating the change for the period and any restrictions on the distribution of the balance to shareholders.

2.17 IAS 17 *LEASES*

Lessors shall, in addition to meeting the requirements in IFRS 7, disclose the following for finance leases:

- a reconciliation between the gross investment in the lease at the end of the reporting period, and the present value of minimum lease payments receivable at the end of the reporting period. In addition, an entity shall disclose the gross investment in the lease and the present value of minimum lease payments receivable at the end of the reporting period, for each of the following periods:
  - not later than one year,
  - later than one year and not later than five years,
  - later than five years;
- unearned finance income;
- the unguaranteed residual values accruing to the benefit of the lessor;
- the accumulated allowance for uncollectible minimum lease payments receivable;
- contingent rents recognised as income in the period; and
- a general description of the lessor's material leasing arrangements.

Lessors shall, in addition to meeting the requirements of IFRS 7, disclose the following for operating leases:

(a) The future minimum lease payments under non-cancellable operating leases in the aggregate and for each of the following periods:
  1. not later than one year;
  2. later than one year and not later than five years;
  3. later than five years.
(b) Total contingent rents recognised as income in the period.
(c) A general description of the lessor's leasing arrangements.

2.18 IAS 18 *REVENUE*

An entity shall disclose:

(a) the accounting policies adopted for the recognition of revenue, including the methods adopted to determine the stage of completion of transactions involving the rendering of services;
(b) the amount of each significant category of revenue recognised during the period, including revenue arising from:
  1. the sale of goods,
  2. the rendering of services,
  3. interest,
  4. royalties, and
  5. dividends;
(c) the amount of revenue arising from exchanges of goods or services included in each significant category of revenue.

2.19 IAS 19 *EMPLOYEE BENEFITS*

An entity shall disclose information that:

(a) explains the characteristics of its defined benefit plans and risks associated with them;
(b) identifies and explains the amounts in its financial statements arising from its defined benefit plans; and
(c) describes how its defined benefit plans may affect the amount, timing and uncertainty of the entity's future cash flows.

2.20 IAS 20 *GOVERNMENT GRANTS*

The following matters shall be disclosed:

• the accounting policy adopted for government grants, including the methods of presentation adopted in the financial statements;

- the nature and extent of government grants recognised in the financial statements and an indication of other forms of government assistance from which the entity has directly benefited; and
- unfulfilled conditions and other contingencies attaching to government assistance that has been recognised.

2.21 IAS 21 *THE EFFECTS OF FOREIGN CURRENCY*

An entity shall disclose:

- the amount of exchange differences recognised in profit or loss except for those arising on financial instruments measured at fair value through profit or loss in accordance with IFRS 9; and
- net exchange differences recognised in other comprehensive income and accumulated in a separate component of equity, and a reconciliation of the amount of such exchange differences at the beginning and end of the period.

When the presentation currency is different from the functional currency, that fact shall be stated, together with disclosure of the functional currency and the reason for using a different presentation currency.

When there is a change in the functional currency of either the reporting entity or a significant foreign operation, that fact and the reason for the change in functional currency shall be disclosed.

When an entity presents its financial statements in a currency that is different from its functional currency, it shall describe the financial statements as complying with IFRSs only if they comply with all the requirements of IFRSs including the translation method.

2.22 IAS 23 *BORROWING COSTS*

An entity shall disclose:

(a) the amount of borrowing costs capitalised during the period; and
(b) the capitalisation rate used to determine the amount of borrowing costs eligible for capitalisation.

2.23 IAS 24 *RELATED PARTY DISCLOSURES*

Relationships between a parent and its subsidiaries shall be disclosed irrespective of whether there have been transactions between them. An entity shall disclose the name of its parent and, if different, the ultimate controlling party. If neither the entity's parent nor the ultimate controlling party produces consolidated financial statements available for public use, the name of the next most senior parent that does so shall also be disclosed.

An entity shall disclose key management personnel compensation in total and for each of the following categories:

(a) short-term employee benefits;
(b) post-employment benefits;

(c) other long-term benefits;

(d) termination benefits; and

(e) share-based payment.

If an entity has had related party transactions during the periods covered by the financial statements, it shall disclose the nature of the related party relationship as well as information about those transactions and outstanding balances, including commitments, necessary for users to understand the potential effect of the relationship on the financial statements. At a minimum, disclosures shall include:

(a) the amount of the transactions;

(b) the amount of outstanding balances, including commitments, and:

    1. their terms and conditions, including whether they are secured, and the nature of the consideration to be provided in settlement, and

    2. details of any guarantees given or received;

(c) provisions for doubtful debts related to the amount of outstanding balances; and

(d) the expense recognised during the period in respect of bad or doubtful debts due from related parties.

Amounts incurred by the entity for the provision of key management personnel services that are provided by a separate management entity shall be disclosed.

The disclosures required above shall be made separately for each of the following categories:

(a) the parent;

(b) entities with joint control of, or significant influence over, the entity;

(c) subsidiaries;

(d) associates;

(e) joint ventures in which the entity is a joint venturer;

(f) key management personnel of the entity or its parent; and

(g) other related parties.

2.24 IAS 26 *ACCOUNTING AND REPORTING BY RETIREMENT BENEFIT PLANS*

The financial statements of a retirement benefit plan, whether defined benefit or defined contribution, shall also contain the following information:

(a) a statement of changes in net assets available for benefits;

(b) a summary of significant accounting policies; and

(c) a description of the plan and the effect of any changes in the plan during the period.

2.25 IAS 27 *SEPARATE FINANCIAL STATEMENTS*

An entity shall apply all applicable IFRSs when providing disclosures in its separate financial statements.

When a parent elects not to prepare consolidated financial statements and instead prepares separate financial statements, it shall disclose in those separate financial statements:

(a) the fact that the financial statements are separate financial statements; that the exemption from consolidation has been used; the name and principal place of business (and country of incorporation, if different) of the entity whose consolidated financial statements that comply with International Financial Reporting Standards have been produced for public use; and the address where those consolidated financial statements are obtainable.

(b) a list of significant investments in subsidiaries, joint ventures and associates, including:

1. the name of those investees.
2. the principal place of business (and country of incorporation, if different) of those investees.
3. its proportion of the ownership interest (and its proportion of the voting rights, if different) held in those investees.

(c) a description of the method used to account for the investments listed under (b).

When an investment entity that is a parent prepares separate financial statements as its only financial statements, it shall disclose that fact. The investment entity shall also present the disclosures relating to investment entities required by IFRS 12 *Disclosure of Interests in Other Entities*.

When a parent or an investor with joint control of, or significant influence over, an investee prepares separate financial statements, the parent or investor shall identify the financial statements prepared in accordance with IFRS 10, IFRS 11 or IAS 28 (as amended in 2011) to which they relate. The parent or investor shall also disclose in its separate financial statements:

(a) the fact that the statements are separate financial statements and the reasons why those statements are prepared if not required by law;

(b) a list of significant investments in subsidiaries, joint ventures and associates, including:

1. the name of those investees,
2. the principal place of business (and country of incorporation, if different) of those investees, and
3. its proportion of the ownership interest (and its proportion of the voting rights, if different) held in those investees;

(c) a description of the method used to account for the investments listed under (b).

2.26 IAS 29 *ACCOUNTING IN HYPERINFLATIONARY ECONOMIES*

The following disclosures shall be made:

(a) the fact that the financial statements and the corresponding figures for previous periods have been restated for the changes in the general purchasing power of the functional currency and, as a result, are stated in terms of the measuring unit current at the end of the reporting period;

(b) whether the financial statements are based on a historical cost approach or a current cost approach; and

(c) the identity and level of the price index at the end of the reporting period and the movement in the index during the current and the previous reporting period.

2.27 IAS 33 *EARNINGS PER SHARE*

An entity shall disclose the following:

(a) The amounts used as the numerators in calculating basic and diluted earnings per share, and a reconciliation of those amounts to profit or loss attributable to the parent entity for the period. The reconciliation shall include the individual effect of each class of instruments that affects earnings per share.

(b) The weighted average number of ordinary shares used as the denominator in calculating basic and diluted earnings per share, and a reconciliation of these denominators to each other. The reconciliation shall include the individual effect of each class of instruments that affects earnings per share.

(c) Instruments (including contingently issuable shares) that could potentially dilute basic earnings per share in the future, but were not included in the calculation of diluted earnings per share because they are antidilutive for the period(s) presented.

(d) A description of ordinary share transactions or potential ordinary share transactions, that occur after the reporting period and that would have changed significantly the number of ordinary shares or potential ordinary shares outstanding at the end of the period if those transactions had occurred before the end of the reporting period.

2.28 IAS 36 *IMPAIRMENT OF ASSETS*

An entity shall disclose the following for each class of assets:

- the amount of impairment losses recognised in profit or loss during the period and the line item(s) of the statement of comprehensive income in which those impairment losses are included;
- the amount of reversals of impairment losses recognised in profit or loss during the period and the line item(s) of the statement of comprehensive income in which those impairment losses are reversed;
- the amount of impairment losses on revalued assets recognised in other comprehensive income during the period; and
- the amount of reversals of impairment losses on revalued assets recognised in other comprehensive income during the period.

An entity that reports segment information in accordance with IFRS 8 shall disclose the following for each reportable segment:

(a) the amount of impairment losses recognised in profit or loss and in other comprehensive income during the period; and

(b) the amount of reversals of impairment losses recognised in profit or loss and in other comprehensive income during the period.

An entity shall disclose the following for an individual asset (including goodwill) or a cash-generating unit, for which an impairment loss has been recognised or reversed during the period:

(a) the events and circumstances that led to the recognition or reversal of the impairment loss;

(b) the amount of the impairment loss recognised or reversed;

(c) for an individual asset:
    1. the nature of the asset, and
    2. if the entity reports segment information in accordance with IFRS 8, the reportable segment to which the asset belongs;

(d) for a cash-generating unit:
    1. a description of the cash-generating unit (such as whether it is a product line, a plant, a business operation, a geographical area, or a reportable segment as defined in IFRS 8),
    2. the amount of the impairment loss recognised or reversed by class of assets and, if the entity reports segment information in accordance with IFRS 8, by reportable segment, and
    3. if the aggregation of assets for identifying the cash-generating unit has changed since the previous estimate of the cash-generating unit's recoverable amount (if any), a description of the current and former way of aggregating assets and the reasons for changing the way the cash-generating unit is identified;

(e) the recoverable amount of the asset (cash-generating unit) and whether the recoverable amount of the asset (cash-generating unit) is its fair value less costs of disposal or its value in use;

(f) if the recoverable amount is fair value less costs of disposal, the entity shall disclose the following information:
    1. the level of the fair value hierarchy (see IFRS 13) within which the fair value measurement of the asset (cash-generating unit) is categorised in its entirety (without taking into account whether the "costs of disposal" are observable),
    2. for fair value measurements categorised within Level 2 and Level 3 of the fair value hierarchy, a description of the valuation technique(s) used to measure fair value less costs of disposal. If there has been a change in valuation technique, the entity shall disclose that change and the reason(s) for making it, and
    3. for fair value measurements categorised within Level 2 and Level 3 of the fair value hierarchy, each key assumption on which management has based its determination of fair value less costs of disposal. Key assumptions are those to which the asset's (cash-generating unit's) recoverable amount is most sensitive. The entity shall also disclose the discount rate(s) used in the current measurement and previous measurement if fair value less costs of disposal is measured using a present value technique;

(g) if recoverable amount is value in use, the discount rate(s) used in the current estimate and previous estimate (if any) of value in use.

An entity shall disclose the following information for the aggregate impairment losses and the aggregate reversals of impairment losses recognised during the period for which no information is disclosed:

(a) the main classes of assets affected by impairment losses and the main classes of assets affected by reversals of impairment losses; and

(b) the main events and circumstances that led to the recognition of these impairment losses and reversals of impairment losses.

If any portion of the goodwill acquired in a business combination during the period has not been allocated to a cash-generating unit (group of units) at the end of the reporting period, the amount of the unallocated goodwill shall be disclosed together with the reasons why that amount remains unallocated.

An entity shall disclose the information required by (a)–(f) for each cash-generating unit (group of units) for which the carrying amount of goodwill or intangible assets with indefinite useful lives allocated to that unit (group of units) is significant in comparison with the entity's total carrying amount of goodwill or intangible assets with indefinite useful lives:

(a) The carrying amount of goodwill allocated to the unit (group of units).

(b) The carrying amount of intangible assets with indefinite useful lives allocated to the unit (group of units).

(c) The basis on which the unit's (group of units') recoverable amount has been determined (i.e. value in use or fair value less costs of disposal).

(d) If the unit's (group of units') recoverable amount is based on value in use:
1. Each key assumption on which management has based its cash flow projections for the period covered by the most recent budgets/forecasts. Key assumptions are those to which the unit's (group of units") recoverable amount is most sensitive.
2. A description of management's approach to determining the value(s) assigned to each key assumption, whether those value(s) reflect past experience or, if appropriate, are consistent with external sources of information, and, if not, how and why they differ from past experience or external sources of information.
3. The period over which management has projected cash flows based on financial budgets/forecasts approved by management and, when a period greater than five years is used for a cash-generating unit (group of units), an explanation of why that longer period is justified.
4. The growth rate used to extrapolate cash flow projections beyond the period covered by the most recent budgets/forecasts, and the justification for using any growth rate that exceeds the long-term average growth rate for the products, industries, or country or countries in which the entity operates, or for the market to which the unit (group of units) is dedicated.
5. The discount rate(s) applied to the cash flow projections.

(e) If the unit's (group of units') recoverable amount is based on fair value less costs of disposal, the valuation technique(s) used to measure fair value less costs of disposal. An entity is not required to provide the disclosures required by IFRS 13. If fair value less costs of disposal is not measured using a quoted price for an identical unit (group of units), an entity shall disclose the following information:

1. Each key assumption on which management has based its determination of fair value less costs of disposal. Key assumptions are those to which the unit's (group of units") recoverable amount is most sensitive.

2. A description of management's approach to determining the value (or values) assigned to each key assumption, whether those values reflect past experience or, if appropriate, are consistent with external sources of information, and, if not, how and why they differ from past experience or external sources of information.

   (i) The level of the fair value hierarchy (see IFRS 13) within which the fair value measurement is categorised in its entirety (without giving regard to the observability of "costs of disposal").

   (ii) If there has been a change in valuation technique, the change and the reason(s) for making it.

3. If fair value less costs of disposal is measured using discounted cash flow projections, an entity shall disclose the following information:

   (i) the period over which management has projected cash flows.

4. The growth rate used to extrapolate cash flow projections.

5. The discount rate(s) applied to the cash flow projections.

(f) If a reasonably possible change in a key assumption on which management has based its determination of the unit's (group of units') recoverable amount would cause the unit's (group of units') carrying amount to exceed its recoverable amount:

1. The amount by which the unit's (group of units') recoverable amount exceeds its carrying amount.

2. The value assigned to the key assumption.

3. The amount by which the value assigned to the key assumption must change, after incorporating any consequential effects of that change on the other variables used to measure recoverable amount, in order for the unit's (group of units') recoverable amount to be equal to its carrying amount.

If some or all of the carrying amount of goodwill or intangible assets with indefinite useful lives is allocated across multiple cash-generating units (groups of units), and the amount so allocated to each unit (group of units) is not significant in comparison with the entity's total carrying amount of goodwill or intangible assets with indefinite useful lives, that fact shall be disclosed, together with the aggregate carrying amount of goodwill or intangible assets with indefinite useful lives allocated to those units (groups of units). In addition, if the recoverable amounts of any of those units (groups of units) are based on the same key assumption(s) and the aggregate carrying amount of goodwill or intangible assets with indefinite useful lives allocated to them is significant in comparison with the entity's total carrying amount of goodwill or intangible assets with indefinite useful lives, an entity shall disclose that fact, together with:

(a) the aggregate carrying amount of goodwill allocated to those units (groups of units);
(b) the aggregate carrying amount of intangible assets with indefinite useful lives allocated to those units (groups of units);
(c) a description of the key assumption(s);
(d) a description of management's approach to determining the value(s) assigned to the key assumption(s), whether those value(s) reflect past experience or, if appropriate, are consistent with external sources of information, and, if not, how and why they differ from past experience or external sources of information;
(e) if a reasonably possible change in the key assumption(s) would cause the aggregate of the units' (groups of units') carrying amounts to exceed the aggregate of their recoverable amounts:
  1. the amount by which the aggregate of the units' (groups of units') recoverable amounts exceeds the aggregate of their carrying amounts,
  2. the value(s) assigned to the key assumption(s), and
  3. the amount by which the value(s) assigned to the key assumption(s) must change, after incorporating any consequential effects of the change on the other variables used to measure recoverable amount, in order for the aggregate of the units' (groups of units') recoverable amounts to be equal to the aggregate of their carrying amounts.

2.29 IAS 37 *PROVISIONS*

For each class of provision, an entity shall disclose:

(a) the carrying amount at the beginning and end of the period;
(b) additional provisions made in the period, including increases to existing provisions;
(c) amounts used (i.e. incurred and charged against the provision) during the period;
(d) unused amounts reversed during the period; and
(e) the increase during the period in the discounted amount arising from the passage of time and the effect of any change in the discount rate.

An entity shall disclose the following for each class of provision:

(a) a brief description of the nature of the obligation and the expected timing of any resulting outflows of economic benefits;
(b) an indication of the uncertainties about the amount or timing of those outflows. Where necessary to provide adequate information, an entity shall disclose the major assumptions made concerning future events; and
(c) the amount of any expected reimbursement, stating the amount of any asset that has been recognised for that expected reimbursement.

Unless the possibility of any outflow in settlement is remote, an entity shall disclose for each class of contingent liability at the end of the reporting period a brief description of the nature of the contingent liability and, where practicable:

(a) an estimate of its financial effect;
(b) an indication of the uncertainties relating to the amount or timing of any outflow; and
(c) the possibility of any reimbursement.

2.30 IAS 38 *INTANGIBLE ASSETS*

An entity shall disclose the following for each class of intangible assets, distinguishing between internally generated intangible assets and other intangible assets:

(a) whether the useful lives are indefinite or finite and, if finite, the useful lives or the amortisation rates used;
(b) the amortisation methods used for intangible assets with finite useful lives;
(c) the gross carrying amount and any accumulated amortisation (aggregated with accumulated impairment losses) at the beginning and end of the period;
(d) the line item(s) of the statement of comprehensive income in which any amortisation of intangible assets is included;
(e) a reconciliation of the carrying amount at the beginning and end of the period showing:
    1. additions, indicating separately those from internal development, those acquired separately, and those acquired through business combinations,
    2. assets classified as held for sale or included in a disposal group classified as held for sale in accordance with IFRS 5 and other disposals,
    3. increases or decreases during the period resulting from revaluations and from impairment losses recognised or reversed in other comprehensive income in accordance with IAS 36 (if any),
    4. impairment losses recognised in profit or loss during the period in accordance with IAS 36 (if any),
    5. impairment losses reversed in profit or loss during the period in accordance with IAS 36 (if any),
    6. any amortisation recognised during the period,
    7. net exchange differences arising on the translation of the financial statements into the presentation currency, and on the translation of a foreign operation into the presentation currency of the entity, and
    8. other changes in the carrying amount during the period.

An entity shall also disclose:

(a) for an intangible asset assessed as having an indefinite useful life, the carrying amount of that asset and the reasons supporting the assessment of an indefinite useful life. In giving these reasons, the entity shall describe the factor(s) that played a significant role in determining that the asset has an indefinite useful life;
(b) a description, the carrying amount and remaining amortisation period of any individual intangible asset that is material to the entity's financial statements;

(c) for intangible assets acquired by way of a government grant and initially recognised at fair value:
1. the fair value initially recognised for these assets,
2. their carrying amount, and
3. whether they are measured after recognition under the cost model or the revaluation model;

(d) the existence and carrying amounts of intangible assets whose title is restricted and the carrying amounts of intangible assets pledged as security for liabilities.

If intangible assets are accounted for at revalued amounts, an entity shall disclose the following:

(a) by class of intangible assets:
1. the effective date of the revaluation,
2. the carrying amount of revalued intangible assets, and
3. the carrying amount that would have been recognised had the revalued class of intangible assets been measured after recognition using the cost model;

(b) the amount of the revaluation surplus that relates to intangible assets at the beginning and end of the period, indicating the changes during the period and any restrictions on the distribution of the balance to shareholders.

An entity shall disclose the aggregate amount of research and development expenditure recognised as an expense during the period.

2.31 IAS 40 *INVESTMENT PROPERTY*

The disclosures mandated by IAS 40 are as below:

- Whether it applies the fair value model or the cost model.
- If it applies the fair value model, whether, and in what circumstances, property interests held under operating leases are classified and accounted for as investment property.
- When classification is difficult, the criteria it uses to distinguish investment property from owner-occupied property and from property held for sale in the ordinary course of business.
- The extent to which the fair value of investment property (as measured or disclosed in the financial statements) is based on a valuation by an independent valuer who holds a recognised and relevant professional qualification and has recent experience in the location and category of the investment property being valued. If there has been no such valuation, that fact shall be disclosed.
- The amounts recognised in profit or loss for:
  (i) rental income from investment property,
  (ii) direct operating expenses (including repairs and maintenance) arising from investment property that generated rental income during the period,
  (iii) direct operating expenses (including repairs and maintenance) arising from investment property that did not generate rental income during the period, and
  (iv) the cumulative change in fair value recognised in profit or loss on a sale of investment property from a pool of assets in which the cost model is used into a pool in which the fair value model is used.

An entity that applies the fair value model shall disclose a reconciliation between the carrying amounts of investment property at the beginning and end of the period, showing the following:

(a) additions, disclosing separately those additions resulting from acquisitions and those resulting from subsequent expenditure recognised in the carrying amount of an asset;
(b) additions resulting from acquisitions through business combinations;
(c) assets classified as held for sale or included in a disposal group classified as held for sale in accordance with IFRS 5 and other disposals;
(d) net gains or losses from fair value adjustments;
(e) the net exchange differences arising on the translation of the financial statements into a different presentation currency, and on translation of a foreign operation into the presentation currency of the reporting entity;
(f) transfers to and from inventories and owner-occupied property; and
(g) other changes.

When a valuation obtained for investment property is adjusted significantly for the purpose of the financial statements, for example to avoid double-counting of assets or liabilities that are recognised as separate assets and liabilities, the entity shall disclose a reconciliation between the valuation obtained and the adjusted valuation included in the financial statements, showing separately the aggregate amount of any recognised lease obligations that have been added back, and any other significant adjustments.

In the exceptional cases when an entity measures investment property using the cost model in IAS 16, the reconciliation shall disclose amounts relating to that investment property separately from amounts relating to other investment property. In addition, an entity shall disclose:

(a) the existence and amounts of restrictions on the realisability of investment property or the remittance of income and proceeds of disposal;
(b) contractual obligations to purchase, construct or develop investment property or for repairs, maintenance or enhancements;
(c) if possible, the range of estimates within which fair value is highly likely to lie; and
(d) on disposal of investment property not carried at fair value:
   1. the fact that the entity has disposed of investment property not carried at fair value,
   2. the carrying amount of that investment property at the time of sale, and
   3. the amount of gain or loss recognised.

2.31.1 Cost model

An entity that applies the cost model shall disclose:

(a) the depreciation methods used;
(b) the useful lives or the depreciation rates used;
(c) the gross carrying amount and the accumulated depreciation (aggregated with accumulated impairment losses) at the beginning and end of the period;

(d) a reconciliation of the carrying amount of investment property at the beginning and end of the period, showing the following:
1. additions, disclosing separately those additions resulting from acquisitions and those resulting from subsequent expenditure recognised as an asset,
2. additions resulting from acquisitions through business combinations,
3. assets classified as held for sale or included in a disposal group classified as held for sale in accordance with IFRS 5 and other disposals,
4. depreciation,
5. the amount of impairment losses recognised, and the amount of impairment losses reversed, during the period in accordance with IAS 36,
6. the net exchange differences arising on the translation of the financial statements into a different presentation currency, and on translation of a foreign operation into the presentation currency of the reporting entity,
7. transfers to and from inventories and owner-occupied property, and
8. other changes.
(e) the fair value of investment property. In the exceptional cases when an entity cannot measure the fair value of the investment property reliably, it shall disclose:
1. a description of the investment property,
2. an explanation of why fair value cannot be measured reliably, and
3. if possible, the range of estimates within which fair value is highly likely to lie.

2.32 IAS 41 *AGRICULTURE*

An entity shall disclose the aggregate gain or loss arising during the current period on initial recognition of biological assets and agricultural produce and from the change in fair value less costs to sell of biological assets.

An entity shall provide a description of each group of biological assets.

If not disclosed elsewhere in information published with the financial statements, an entity shall describe:

(a) the nature of its activities involving each group of biological assets; and
(b) non-financial measures or estimates of the physical quantities of:
1. each group of the entity's biological assets at the end of the period, and
2. output of agricultural produce during the period.

An entity shall disclose:

(a) the existence and carrying amounts of biological assets whose title is restricted, and the carrying amounts of biological assets pledged as security for liabilities;
(b) the amount of commitments for the development or acquisition of biological assets; and
(c) financial risk management strategies related to agricultural activity.

An entity shall present a reconciliation of changes in the carrying amount of biological assets between the beginning and the end of the current period. The reconciliation shall include:

- the gain or loss arising from changes in fair value less costs to sell;
- increases due to purchases;
- decreases attributable to sales and biological assets classified as held for sale (or included in a disposal group that is classified as held for sale) in accordance with IFRS 5;
- decreases due to harvest;
- increases resulting from business combinations;
- net exchange differences arising on the translation of financial statements into a different presentation currency, and on the translation of a foreign operation into the presentation currency of the reporting entity; and
- other changes.

If an entity measures biological assets at their cost less any accumulated depreciation and any accumulated impairment losses at the end of the period, the entity shall disclose for such biological assets:

(a) a description of the biological assets;
(b) an explanation of why fair value cannot be measured reliably;
(c) if possible, the range of estimates within which fair value is highly likely to lie;
(d) the depreciation method used;
(e) the useful lives or the depreciation rates used; and
(f) the gross carrying amount and the accumulated depreciation (aggregated with accumulated impairment losses) at the beginning and end of the period.

If, during the current period, an entity measures biological assets at their cost less any accumulated depreciation and any accumulated impairment losses, an entity shall disclose any gain or loss recognised on disposal of such biological assets and the reconciliation required shall disclose amounts related to such biological assets separately. In addition, the reconciliation shall include the following amounts included in profit or loss related to those biological assets:

(a) impairment losses;
(b) reversals of impairment losses; and
(c) depreciation.

If the fair value of biological assets previously measured at their cost less any accumulated depreciation and any accumulated impairment losses becomes reliably measurable during the current period, an entity shall disclose for those biological assets:

(a) a description of the biological assets;
(b) an explanation of why fair value has become reliably measurable; and
(c) the effect of the change.

2.32.1 Government grants

An entity shall disclose the following related to agricultural activity covered by this Standard:

(a) the nature and extent of government grants recognised in the financial statements;

(b) unfulfilled conditions and other contingencies attaching to government grants; and

(c) significant decreases expected in the level of government grants.

3 *IFRS STANDARDS THAT COULD IMPACT ALL INDUSTRIES*

As we have seen earlier, being principle-based, no one could disagree that all IFRS Standards would impact every industry in some manner or the other. However, there are certain standards within the present set of IFRS Standards that would impact all industries only because the standards either deal with a new concept or are to be followed when an entity moves over to IFRS for the first time. Based on a combination of gut feel and experience, here is a list of Standards that could impact all industries:

Standard	Covering
IFRS 1	First time conversion to International Financial Reporting Standards
IAS 36	Impairment of Assets
IAS 40	Investment Property
IFRS 3	Business Combinations
IFRS 5	Non-Current Assets held for Sale
IFRS 8	Operating Segments
IFRS 13	Fair Value Measurement
IAS 39/IFRS 9	Financial Instruments
All IFRS Standards	Disclosure Requirements
IFRS 15	Revenue from Contracts with Customers
IFRS 10	Consolidated Financial Statements

A discussion follows:

3.1 IFRS 1 – FIRST-TIME CONVERSION TO INTERNATIONAL FINANCIAL REPORTING STANDARDS

For any entity, transitioning to IFRS is a project by itself. This is due to the fact that they would have to let go of legacy accounting practices and procedures, apply IFRS principles and educate and train their accounting staff to continue applying the new principles in the future – in short, moving over to IFRS involves a change of mindset and culture. Normally, when entities transition to a new system, they calculate the impact of the transition and disclose this information in their financial statements. In most cases, this transition is done prospectively.

Entities that transition to IFRS normally do what is known as an "Impact Assessment" which is an assessment of how moving over to IFRS would impact their profit and Statement of Financial Position. By mandating an IFRS Opening Balance-Sheet, in a limited way, IFRS 1, assists in making that Impact Assessment.

The fact that this standard would impact all industries becomes obvious from the title of the standard – this is a transition standard that would have to be followed by all entities that are going to embrace IFRS for the first time. If this Standard had not been published, entities transitioning to IFRS could have had issues with ascertaining the date of transition and whether they could carry forward balances are per the previous GAAP. IFRS 1 solves all those issues.

3.1.1 Date of transition to IFRS

One of the first steps in adopting IFRS 1 would be to decide on the date of transition. In most geographies, a regulator or the government announces this. Let us take the example of a country that is yet to transition to IFRS-India. It is expected that the government there is set to announce that presenting financial statements in IFRS would be mandatory for certain set of companies which meet specific criteria with effect from 2016–17 mandatorily and 2015–16 voluntarily. As India follows April–March as their accounting year, the date of transition to IFRS would be 31 March 2017. IFRS 1 requires that an entity shall prepare and present an opening IFRS statement of financial position at the date of transition to IFRSs. In the case of the Indian entity illustrated above, the opening IFRS statement of financial position would be prepared on 1st April 2015 – which is as good as the numbers on 31st March 2015.

On the minimum first financial statements that are required, IFRS 1 states that there should at least three statements of financial position, two statements of profit or loss and other comprehensive income, two separate statements of profit or loss (if presented), two statements of cash flows and two statements of changes in equity and related notes, including comparative information for all statements presented.

3.1.2 Mandatory and optional exceptions

A transition to IFRS involves a significant change. Entities would have got used to a particular method and way of accounting/valuation would need to change their mindset. IFRS 1 recognises the impact this difficulty and as a remedial measure provides some mandatory and some optional exceptions. The exceptions are only for the first time transition to IFRS and cannot be used as the rule.

IFRS 1 provides a large relief to entities who are transitioning to IFRS for the first time by permitting them to continue carrying their previous estimates on the books unless they are made in error. The insertion of this relief would mean that entities would need to take a good hard look at all their estimates and true them up when they are transitioning to IFRS for the first time.

3.1.3 Mandatory exceptions

1. Derecognition of financial assets and financial liabilities
2. Hedge accounting
3. Non-controlling interests
4. Classification and measurement of financial assets
5. Embedded derivatives
6. Government loans

The mandatory exceptions would apply to all industries while the most of the optional ones would be industry specific – the decommissioning liabilities could arise only in certain industries, the exception for insurance costs would be of interest to the insurance industry and the exploration costs to the mining industry. First-time adopters would need to pick and choose which of the optional exceptions they would opt for depending on the information availability and the time and cost involved.

3.1.3.1 Derecognition of financial assets and financial liabilities

A first-time adopter shall apply the derecognition requirements in IFRS 9 prospectively for transactions occurring on or after the date of transition to IFRSs. For example, if a first-time adopter derecognised non-derivative financial assets or non-derivative financial liabilities in accordance with its previous GAAP as a result of a transaction that occurred before occurred before the date of transition to IFRSs, it shall not recognise those assets and liabilities in accordance with IFRSs. However an entity may apply the derecognition requirements in IFRS 9 retrospectively from a date of the entity's choosing, provided that the information needed to apply IFRS 9 to financial assets and financial liabilities derecognised as a result of past transactions was obtained at the time of initially accounting for those transactions.

3.1.3.2 Hedge accounting

As required by IFRS 9, at the date of transition to IFRSs an entity shall:

(a) measure all derivatives at fair value; and

(b) eliminate all deferred losses and gains arising on derivatives that were reported in accordance with previous GAAP as if they were assets or liabilities.

An entity shall not reflect in its opening IFRS statement of financial position a hedging relationship of a type that does not qualify for hedge accounting in accordance with IFRS 9 (for example, many hedging relationships where the hedging instrument is a stand-alone written option or a net written option; or where the hedged item is a net position in a cash flow hedge for another risk than foreign currency risk). However, if an entity designated a net position as a hedged item in accordance with previous GAAP, it may designate as a hedged item in accordance with IFRSs an individual item within that net position, or a net position if that meets the requirements in of IFRS 9, provided that it does so no later than the date of transition to IFRSs.

If, before the date of transition to IFRSs, an entity had designated a transaction as a hedge but the hedge does not meet the conditions for hedge accounting in IFRS 9, the entity shall apply IFRS 9 to discontinue hedge accounting. Transactions entered into before the date of transition to IFRSs shall not be retrospectively designated as hedges.

3.1.3.3 Non-controlling interests

A first-time adopter shall apply the following requirements of IFRS 10 prospectively from the date of transition to IFRSs:

(a) total comprehensive income is attributed to the owners of the parent and to the non-controlling interests even if this results in the non-controlling interests having a deficit balance;

(b) accounting for changes in the parent's ownership interest in a subsidiary that do not result in a loss of control; and

(c) accounting for a loss of control over a subsidiary, and the related requirements of IFRS 5 *Non-current Assets Held for Sale and Discontinued Operations*.

However, if a first-time adopter elects to apply IFRS 3 retrospectively to past business combinations, it shall also apply IFRS 10.

3.1.3.4 Classification and measurement of financial assets

An entity shall assess whether a financial asset meets the conditions in IFRS 9 on the basis of the facts and circumstances that exist at the date of transition to IFRSs.

3.1.3.5 Embedded derivatives

A first-time adopter shall assess whether an embedded derivative is required to be separated from the host contract and accounted for as a derivative on the basis of the conditions that existed at the later of the date it first became a party to the contract and the date a reassessment is required.

3.1.3.6 Government loans

A first-time adopter shall classify all government loans received as a financial liability or an equity instrument in accordance with IAS 32 *Financial Instruments: Presentation*. If a first-time adopter did not, under its previous GAAP, recognise and measure a government loan at a below-market rate of interest on a basis consistent with IFRS requirements, it shall use its previous GAAP carrying amount of the loan at the date of transition to IFRSs as the carrying amount of the loan in the opening IFRS statement of financial position. An entity shall apply IFRS 9 to the measurement of such loans after the date of transition to IFRSs.

An entity may apply the requirements in IFRS 9 and IAS 20 retrospectively to any government loan originated before the date of transition to IFRSs, provided that the information needed to do so had been obtained at the time of initially accounting for that loan.

The requirements and guidance above do not preclude an entity from being able to use the exemptions relating to the designation of previously recognised financial instruments at fair value through profit or loss.

3.1.4 Optional exceptions

There are some further optional exemptions to the general restatement and measurement principles set out above. The following exceptions are individually optional. They relate to:

- business combinations,
- share-based payment transactions,
- insurance contracts,
- fair value, previous carrying amount, or revaluation as deemed cost,
- leases,
- cumulative translation differences,
- investments in subsidiaries, jointly controlled entities, associates and joint ventures,
- assets and liabilities of subsidiaries, associated and joint ventures,

- compound financial instruments,
- designation of previously recognised financial instruments,
- fair value measurement of financial assets or financial liabilities at initial recognition,
- decommissioning liabilities included in the cost of property, plant and equipment,
- financial assets or intangible assets accounted for in accordance with IFRIC 12 *Service Concession Arrangements*,
- borrowing costs,
- transfers of assets from customers,
- extinguishing financial liabilities with equity instruments,
- severe hyperinflation,
- joint arrangements, and
- stripping costs in the production phase of a surface mine.

In order to give a flavour of what IFRS 1 intends by giving these exceptions, some of them are detailed below:

3.1.5 Business combinations

An entity may keep the original previous GAAP accounting, that is, not restate:

- previous mergers or goodwill written-off from reserves,
- the carrying amounts of assets and liabilities recognised at the date of acquisition or merger, or
- how goodwill was initially determined (do not adjust the purchase price allocation on acquisition).

However, should it wish to do so, an entity can elect to restate all business combinations starting from a date it selects prior to the opening balance sheet date.

In all cases, the entity must make an initial IAS 36 impairment test of any remaining goodwill in the opening IFRS balance sheet, after reclassifying, as appropriate, previous GAAP intangibles to goodwill.

The exemption for business combinations also applies to acquisitions of investments in associates, interests in joint ventures and interests in a joint operation when the operation constitutes a business.

3.1.5.1 Deemed cost

Assets carried at cost (e.g. property, plant and equipment) may be measured at their fair value at the date of transition to IFRSs. Fair value becomes the "deemed cost" going forward under the IFRS cost model. Deemed cost is an amount used as a surrogate for cost or depreciated cost at a given date.

If, before the date of its first IFRS balance sheet, the entity had revalued any of these assets under its previous GAAP either to fair value or to a price-index-adjusted cost, that previous GAAP revalued amount at the date of the revaluation can become the deemed cost of the asset under IFRS.

If, before the date of its first IFRS balance sheet, the entity had made a one-time revaluation of assets or liabilities to fair value because of a privatisation or initial public offering, and the revalued amount became deemed cost under the previous GAAP, that amount would continue to be deemed cost after the initial adoption of IFRS.

This option applies to intangible assets only if an active market exists.

If the carrying amount of property, plant and equipment or intangible assets that are used in rate-regulated activities includes amounts under previous GAAP that do not qualify for capitalisation in accordance with IFRSs, a first-time adopter may elect to use the previous GAAP carrying amount of such items as deemed cost on the initial adoption of IFRSs.

Eligible entities subject to rate-regulation may also optionally apply IFRS 14 *Regulatory Deferral Accounts* on transition to IFRSs, and in subsequent financial statements.

3.1.6 IAS 21 – Accumulated translation reserves

An entity may elect to recognise all translation adjustments arising on the translation of the financial statements of foreign entities in accumulated profits or losses at the opening IFRS balance sheet date (that is, reset the translation reserve included in equity under previous GAAP to zero). If the entity elects this exemption, the gain or loss on subsequent disposal of the foreign entity will be adjusted only by those accumulated translation adjustments arising after the opening IFRS balance sheet date.

3.1.7 IAS 27 – Investments in separate financial statements

In May 2008, the IASB amended the standard to change the way the cost of an investment in the separate financial statements is measured on first-time adoption of IFRSs. The amendments to IFRS 1:

- allow first-time adopters to use a "deemed cost" of either fair value or the carrying amount under previous accounting practice to measure the initial cost of investments in subsidiaries, jointly controlled entities and associates in the separate financial statements;
- remove the definition of the cost method from IAS 27 and add a requirement to present dividends as income in the separate financial statements of the investor; and
- require that, when a new parent is formed in a reorganisation, the new parent must measure the cost of its investment in the previous parent at the carrying amount of its share of the equity items of the previous parent at the date of the reorganisation.

3.1.8 Assets and liabilities of subsidiaries, associates and joint ventures: different IFRS adoption dates of investor and investee

If a subsidiary becomes a first-time adopter later than its parent, IFRS 1 permits a choice between two measurement bases in the subsidiary's separate financial statements. In this case, a subsidiary should measure its assets and liabilities as either:

- the carrying amount that would be included in the parent's consolidated financial statements, based on the parent's date of transition to IFRSs, if no adjustments were made for consolidation procedures and for the effects of the business combination in which the parent acquired the subsidiary; or
- the carrying amounts required by IFRS 1 based on the subsidiary's date of transition to IFRSs.

A similar election is available to an associate or joint venture that becomes a first-time adopter later than an entity that has significant influence or joint control over it.

If a parent becomes a first-time adopter later than its subsidiary, the parent should in its consolidated financial statements, measure the assets and liabilities of the subsidiary at the same carrying amount as in the separate financial statements of the subsidiary, after adjusting for consolidation adjustments and for the effects of the business combination in which the parent acquired the subsidiary. The same approach applies in the case of associates and joint ventures.

Entities would need to choose whether they intend to go for these optional exemptions. If yes, they would need to disclose this separately.

To get a better perspective on first time transition to IFRS, let us take a look at the exceptions that Vodafone chose when they first moved over to IFRS.

---

1. IFRS 1 exemptions

IFRS 1, "First-time Adoption of International Financial Reporting Standards" sets out the procedures that the Group must follow when it adopts IFRS for the first time as the basis for preparing its consolidated financial statements. The Group is required to establish its IFRS accounting policies as at 31 March 2006 and, in general, apply these retrospectively to determine the IFRS opening balance sheet at its date of transition, 1 April 2004.

This standard provides a number of optional exceptions to this general principle. The most significant of these are set out below, together with a description in each case of the exception adopted by the Group.

a. Business combinations that occurred before the opening IFRS balance sheet date (IFRS 3, "Business Combinations").

The Group has elected not to apply IFRS 3 retrospectively to business combinations that took place before the date of transition. As a result, in the opening balance sheet, goodwill arising from past business combinations (96,931m pounds Sterling) remains as stated under UK GAAP at 31 March 2004.

b. Employee Benefits – actuarial gains and losses (IAS 19, "Employee Benefits")

The Group has elected to recognise all cumulative actuarial gains and losses in relation to employee benefit schemes at the date of transition. The Group has recognised actuarial gains and losses in full in the period in which they occur in a statement of recognised income and expense in accordance with the amendment to IAS 19, issued on 16 December 2004.

c. Share-based Payments (IFRS 2, "Share-based Payment")

The Group has elected to apply IFRS 2 to all relevant share based payment transactions granted but not fully vested at 1 April 2004.

d. Financial Instruments (IAS 39, "Financial Instruments: Recognition and Measurement" and IAS 32, "Financial Instruments: Disclosure and Presentation")

The Group has applied IAS 32 and IAS 39 for all periods presented and has therefore not taken advantage of the exemption in IFRS 1 that would enable the Group to only apply these standards from 1 April 2005.

Source: Vodafone Annual Report 2004

3.1.9 Retained earnings

The accounting policies that an entity uses in its opening IFRS statement of financial position may differ from those that it used for the same date using its previous GAAP. The resulting adjustments arise from events and transactions before the date of transition to IFRSs. An entity shall recognise those adjustments directly in retained earnings (or, if appropriate, another category of equity) at the date of transition to IFRSs. In case there is a substantial change in Retained Earnings, management may want to give a detailed Explanation to shareholders on the reasons for the change. Though IFRS 1 mandates detailed Reconciliation and Disclosures, management may still want to disclose this information in their analysis.

3.2 IAS 36 *IMPAIRMENT OF ASSETS*

Commencing a business is tough. Continuing a business is tougher. A variety of factors can impact a business adversely – a worsening of the economic environment, change of government policies, recession, high inflation, inability to obtain credit facilities etc. The reason for indicating that IAS 36 *Impairment of Assets* could impact all industries is that any industry is capable of being impacted adversely by, inter-alia, the above-mentioned factors.

There has been a lot of criticism on the concept of Fair Value as a valuation measure. It is often said that fair value is judgemental, not scientific, can be managed, is too aggressive and the like. According to my personal opinion, Accounting Standards on Impairment of Assets are nothing but an extension of the concept of Fair Value.

IAS 36 attempts to ensure that assets are carried at no more than their recoverable amount, and to define how recoverable amount is determined. An **Impairment loss has been defined as** the amount by which the carrying amount of an asset or cash-generating unit exceeds its recoverable amount. **Recoverable amount has been defined to be** the higher of an asset's fair value less costs of disposal and its value in use and **Value in use:** the present value of the future cash flows expected to be derived from an asset or cash-generating unit. IAS 36 provides indicative factors of internal and external input sources that could act as triggers to test the Asset for Impairment.

Impairment Loss = Carrying Amount - Recoverable Amount
Recoverable Amount = Fair Value or Value-in-Use (VIU) whichever is higher.

The terms carrying amount, recoverable amount and Fair Value should be familiar to accountants. However, the VIU could be a new concept. VIU is the present value of the future cash flows expected to be derived from an asset or cash-generating unit. The need to calculate VIU accurately cannot be overemphasised since a wrong estimation of both the cash flows as well as the discount rate can yield very different results.

Worked Example

At the end of 20X0 an entity tests a machine for impairment. The machine was bought five years earlier for CU300,000, when its useful life was estimated to be 15 years and the estimated residual value was nil. At 31 December 20X0, after recognising the depreciation charge for 20X0, the machine's carrying amount was CU200,000 and its remaining useful life was estimated at 10 years.

The machine's value in use is calculated using a pre-tax discount rate of14 per cent per year. Budgets approved by management reflect expected cash inflows net of the estimated costs necessary to maintain the level of economic benefit expected to arise from the machine in its current condition.

Assume, for simplicity, that the expected future cash flows occur at the end of each reporting period. Assume that the Fair Value less costs to sell are CU 175,000.

An estimation of the value in use of the machine at the end of 20X0 is shown below:

Year	Probability Weighted Future Cash Flow CU	PV Factor %	Discounted Cash Flow CU
20x1	22742	0.8772	19,949
20X2	25090	0.7647	19,186
20X3	26794	0.6750	18,085
20X4	35497	0.5921	21,017
20X5	39985	0.5194	20,767
20X6	41959	0.4556	19,116
20X7	43462	0.3996	17,369
20X8	47344	0.3506	16,597
20X9	47287	0.3075	14,541
20Y0	46574	0.2697	12,563

1,79,190

Recoverable Amount is the higher of Fair Value less Costs to Sell or VIU. Since VIU is higher in this case, the Recoverable Amount is CU 179,190. Since Carrying Amount is CU 200,000, there is an Impairment Loss of 200,000–179,190.

For the above example, let us assume a Discount rate of 10%. VIU is as below:

Year	Probability Weighted Future Cash Flow CU	PV Factor %	Discounted Cash Flow CU
20X1	22742	0.92	20,864
20X2	25090	0.84	21,118
20X3	26794	0.77	20,690
20X4	35497	0.71	25,146
20X5	39985	0.65	25,986
20X6	41959	0.60	25,020
20X7	43462	0.55	23,774
20X8	47344	0.50	23,762
20X9	47287	0.46	21,771
20Y0	46574	0.42	19,654
			2,27,785

The Recoverable Amount is greater than the Carrying Amount hence there will be no Impairment Loss recognised.

It is thus extremely critical to estimate the VIU by estimating the correct cash flows and using the appropriate Discount Rate.

3.2.2 Indicators of impairment

As indicated earlier, there could be various indicators of impairment. Some indicators provided in IAS 36 are given below.

3.2.2.1 External sources

- market value declines
- negative changes in technology, markets, economy, or laws
- increases in market interest rates
- net assets of the company higher than market capitalisation

3.2.2.2 Internal sources

- obsolescence or physical damage
- asset is idle, part of a restructuring or held for disposal
- worse economic performance than expected

- for investments in subsidiaries, joint ventures or associates, the carrying amount is higher than the carrying amount of the investee's assets, or a dividend exceeds the total comprehensive income of the investee

Risk factors that could trigger an Impairment Test would differ from industry to industry. In addition to the generic sources indicated above, an attempt has been made in the Table given below to identify specific triggers for Impairment in different industry sectors:

Industry	Indicative Triggers for Impairment test
Goodwill (applicable to all industries)	Failed acquisitions, steep fall in revenue & market share post-acquisition,
Software	Financial Instruments, Investment in Associates
Telecom	Sharp fall in Average Revenue per User (ARPU)
Oil and Gas	Long delay in drilling of wells, new technology
Airlines	Cut-throat competition, sharp fall in revenue per seat, loss of aircraft
Banks and financial institutions	Steep increase in bad loans, steep decrease in market value of financial instruments
Insurance Claims	Huge increase in claims
Automotive	Stiff competition, inability to keep up with change in technology, regular recall of manufactured vehicles
Pharma	Denial of Food and Drug Administration (FDA) approval for drugs and medications, inappropriate acquisitions
Power	Irregularity in timing and amount of receivables
Real Estate & Infrastructure	Extremely high debt,
Shipping	Lack of demand due to a slump, deterioration in quality of fleet, other modes of transport becoming more economical
Retail	Economic Slump resulting in slack demand, Impairment of Financial Instruments

There could be other issues in testing for Impairment. One factor could be the timing of the test. An Annual Review is mandated for Goodwill. However, there could be an asset that satisfies the Impairment Test during an interim financial reporting period. The entity could either report the Impairment in that period or if the frequency of Impairment appears regular, it could accelerate the timing of its Impairment tests – to say twice a year.

In determining Value-in-Use, it is critical to use the appropriate discount rate to arrive at the present value of future cash flows from the Asset. While the accepted practice is to use the cost of capital as the general discount rate, it is a fact that the cost of capital could differ between industries. Using the appropriate discount rate involves judgement and an impartial estimate of the cost of capital.

In 2014, the Japanese giant, Sumitomu, provided an amount of more than 150 billion yen for Impairment Losses. Their note on this Impairment is presented below.

Divestment of certain fixed assets and the recognition of impairment loss

At the meeting of the Board of Directors held on September 29, 2014, Sumitomo resolved to divest part of the fixed assets held by its oil and gas development subsidiary (SDRIII, as defined below) in the Tight Oil Development Project in the U.S., and as a result, the impairment loss will be recognized.

(1) COMPANY PROFILE

1) Summit Shale International Corporation

Name	Summit Shale International Corporation
Location	820 Gessner Rd, Suite 600 Houston, Texas, USA
Representative	Kazuyuki Onose (President & Director)
Business	Investment in oil and gas company
Capital	USD 1,128 million

2) Summit Discovery Resources III LLC

Name	Summit Discovery Resources III LLC
Location	820 Gessner Rd, Suite 600 Houston, Texas, USA
Representative	Kazuyuki Onose (President & CEO)
Business	Exploration, development and investment of oil and gas
Capital	USD 1,100 million

(2) REASONS FOR THE DIVESTMENT

Sumitomo, through Summit Shale International Corporation (hereinafter "**SSIC**"), a wholly owned subsidiary of Sumitomo, and Summit Discovery Resources III LLC (hereinafter "**SDRIII**"), a wholly owned oil and gas development subsidiary of SSIC, have participated in a Tight Oil Development Project (hereinafter the "**Project**") jointly with Devon Energy Corporation (hereinafter "**Devon**"), an independent Oil & Gas E&P company based in Oklahoma, in the Permian Basin, Texas since September, 2012 (Sumitomo's interest in the Project: 30 percent).

Sumitomo resolved to divest the lease properties, wells and related facilities in the northern part of the Project jointly with Devon, where SDRIII holds about 172,000 net acres. Analysing the development results until now in the northern part of the Project, Sumitomo determined that it is difficult to extract the oil and gas efficiently and it cannot expect as much production to recover the investment. Sumitomo will begin the divestment process after discussing the details with Devon.

At present, Sumitomo plans to continue holding its interest in the southern part of the Project (47,000 net acres). The future development of the southern part will be determined considering carefully the development plans and project economics.

(3) DETAILS OF THE ASSETS TO BE DIVESTED

1) Assets: Lease properties, wells and related facilities
2) Location: 9 counties (Kent, Stonewall, Haskell, Scurry, Fisher, Mitchell, Nolan, Sterling, Coke)

Other details such as the sales value, the sales gain or loss, the transferee and the schedule are not determined at present. Sumitomo will disclose the details as soon as they are decided.

(4) CONTENTS OF IMPAIRMENT LOSS

The impairment loss will be recognized in the 2nd quarter of FY 2014 (July, 1, 2014 to September 30, 2014), as a result of revaluating the recoverability of the carrying amount of the assets held by SDRIII, as follows:

(1) Consolidated Financial Statement SDRIII will recognize the loss of approximately 170 billion yen as "Impairment losses on long-lived assets"
(2) Non-consolidated Financial Statement of Sumitomo

Sumitomo will recognize the loss of approximately 93 billion yen as "Valuation loss on investment securities" in relation to the investment in SSIC and the loss of approximately 56 billion yen as "Provision for bad debts reserve of affiliates and others" under "Non-operating expense."

Supplementary note

(1) Description of the Tight Oil Development Project The Tight Oil Development Project involves the extraction of crude oil from shale, limestone and sandstone formations with low-permeability that are classified as source rock (sedimentary rock with petroleum hydrocarbon production capacity) using the same horizontal drilling and hydraulic fracturing technologies used in shale gas development. The by-products, natural gas liquid and natural gas, are produced through the development.
(2) Description of Permian Basin The Permian Basin is an area in the southwestern United States that extends over the states of Texas and New Mexico. This is an area of approximately 200,000 square kilometers and it spreads over 52 counties.

Source: http://www.sumitomocorp.co.jp/files/topics/28039_ext_31_en_0.pdf

3.3 IAS 40 *INVESTMENT PROPERTY*

IFRS was introduced in the European Union in 2004. Till IFRS was introduced, entities were typically following country-specific accounting policies. There were entities who were giants in their respective geographies – be it a Vodafone or a Mercedes Benz who had generated sizeable assets on their balance sheets due to the sheer number of years they were in existence. Some of these giants invested extra cash they had in property.

By definition, investment property is property held for investment – which is typified either by capital appreciation or earnings. IAS 40 permits fair valuation of investment property in subsequent measurements. This option would provide a lot of leeway to entities to increase their balance-sheet size.

Since previous GAAP may not have had an option to reflect Investment Property separately in the balance sheet, IAS 40 would impact entities that have invested in properties. Previous GAAP may or may not have permitted an option to reflect these investment properties at fair value (the word revalued amount is used in some geographies which need not necessarily equal the fair value). Entities who convert to IAS 40 and have followed the cost model could use the fair value approach in subsequent measurements.

We present below how F & C UK Investments Limited accounts for Investment Properties.

Investment properties

Investment properties consist of land and buildings (principally offices, commercial warehouses and retail property) which are not occupied for use by, or in the operations of, the Group, nor for sale in the ordinary course of business, but are held to earn rental income together with the potential for capital and income growth.

Investment properties are initially recognised at cost, being the fair value of consideration given, including transaction costs associated with the investment property. Any subsequent capital expenditure incurred in improving investment properties is capitalised in the period incurred and included within the book cost of the property.

After initial recognition, investment properties are measured at fair value, with unrealised gains and losses recognised in the Consolidated Statement of Comprehensive Income. Fair value is based on the open market valuation provided by DTZ Debenham Tie Leung Limited, chartered surveyors, at the balance sheet date using recognised valuation techniques suitably adjusted for unamortised lease incentives and lease surrender premiums. These techniques comprise both the Yield Method and the Discounted Cash Flow Method. In some cases, the fair values are determined based on recent real estate transactions with similar characteristics and location to those of the Group's assets.

The determination of the fair value of investment properties requires the use of estimates such as future cash flows from assets (such as lettings, tenants' profiles, future revenue streams, capital values of fixtures and fittings, plant and machinery, any environmental matters and the overall repair and condition of the property) and discount rates applicable to those assets. In addition, development risks (such as construction and letting risks) are also taken into consideration when determining the fair value of investment properties under construction. These estimates are based on local market conditions existing at the balance sheet date.

TECHNIQUES USED FOR VALUING INVESTMENT PROPERTY

The traditional method converts anticipated future cash flow benefits in the form of rental income into present value. This approach requires careful estimation of future benefits and application of investor yield or return requirements. One approach to value the property on this basis is to capitalise net rental income on the basis of an Initial Yield, generally referred to as the "All Risks Yield" approach or "Net Initial Yield" approach.

The Discounted Cash Flow Method involves the projection of a series of periodic cash flows either to an operating property or a development property. To this projected cash flow series, an appropriate, market-derived discount rate is applied to establish an indication of the present value of the income stream associated with the property. The calculated periodic cash flow is typically estimated as gross income less vacancy and collection losses and less operating expenses/outgoings. A series of periodic net operating incomes, along with an estimate of the reversion/terminal/exit value (which uses the traditional valuation approach) anticipated at the end of the projection period, are discounted to present value. The aggregate of the net present values equals the market value of the property.

Investment properties held under finance leases and leased out under operating leases are classified as investment property and stated at fair value.

On derecognition, realised gains and losses on disposals of investment properties are recognised in the Consolidated Statement of Comprehensive Income and transferred to the Capital Reserve.

Recognition and derecognition generally occurs on the exchange of signed contracts between a willing buyer and a willing seller.

3.4 IFRS 3 *BUSINESS COMBINATIONS*

In current times, mergers and acquisitions can no longer be called exceptions – they form the rule. Instead of using the term that investment bankers prefer – M & A – IFRS uses a more generic name – Business Combinations. Put simply, they are combinations of businesses.

The credit crisis brought into sharp focus the need for entities to focus on their core competencies and to hive off business divisions that were not yielding adequate returns. Entities started combining businesses in an attempt to achieve economies of scale. There is no industry in which entities would hesitate to combine together to achieve growth. A small textile exporter from a small town called Tirupur in India acquired a Swiss T shirt manufacturer named Swatch. During the course of approvals for the acquisition, he had to restate his financials which were in Indian GAAP to IFRS. IFRS 3 on Business Combinations would apply to any entity in any industry who are the participants in a Business Combination.

One of the critical areas that would be impacted by applying IFRS 3 would be measurement of Goodwill. Since IFRS 3 mandates a Purchase Approach and permits recognition of previously unrecognised Intangible Assets as Assets after the Business Combination has been completed, Goodwill for all practical purposes becomes a residuary item. The previous GAAP may not have permitted recognition of previously unrecognised Intangible Assets and consequentially a lower value of Goodwill.

Apart from its insistence on the Purchase Method, IFRS 3 mandates measuring the assets at acquisition date fair values. This would require that both the acquisition date and the fair values of assets/liabilities as on that date need to be ascertained. The acquisition date is to be determined taking into account all facts and circumstances and Para 45 of IFRS 3 permits the use of approximate Fair Values during the Measurement Period (which has been defined to be one year from the acquisition date). Changes in Fair Value are adjusted in the carrying amount of Goodwill.

Vodafone Essar Limited (formerly Hutchison Essar Limited)

On 8 May 2007, the Group completed the acquisition of 100% of CGP Investments (Holdings) Limited ("CGP"), a company with indirect interests in Vodafone Essar Limited ("Vodafone Essar"), from Hutchison Telecommunications International Limited for cash consideration of US$10.9 billion (£5.5 billion). Following this transaction, the Group has a controlling financial interest in Vodafone Essar.

	Book Value	Fair Value Adjustments	Fair Value
Identified Intangible Assets	xx	xx	xx
Property, Plant and Equipment	xx	xx	xx
Other Investments	xx	xx	xx
Inventory	xx	xx	xx
Taxation Recoverable	xx	xx	xx
Trade and Other Receivables	xx	xx	xx
Cash and Cash Equivalents	xx	xx	xx
Deferred Tax Asset/Liability	xx	xx	xx
Short and long term borrowings	xx	xx	xx
Trade and Other Payables	xx	xx	xx
Provisions	xx	xx	xx
Minority Interests	xx	xx	xx
Written put options over Minority Interests	xx	xx	xx
Goodwill	xx	xx	xx
TOTAL CONSIDERATION PAID	xx	xx	xx

(1) Identifiable intangible assets of £3,189 million consist of licences and spectrum fees of £3,045 million and other intangible assets of £144 million. The weighted average lives of licences and spectrum fees, other intangible assets and total intangibles assets are 11 years, two years and 11 years, respectively.
(2) Included within short term and long-term borrowings are liabilities of £217 million related to written put options over minority interests.
(3) After deducting cash and cash equivalents acquired of £51 million, the net cash outflow related to the acquisition was £5,438 million, of which £5,429 million was paid during the 2008 financial year.

The goodwill is attributable to the expected profitability of the acquired business and the synergies expected to arise after the Group's acquisition of CGP. The results of the acquired entity have been consolidated in the income statement from the date of acquisition. From the date of acquisition, the acquired entity contributed a £219 million loss to the profit attributable to equity shareholders of the Group. As a result of the acquisition of Vodafone Essar, the Group disposed of its 5.60% direct shareholding in Bharti Airtel Limited.

Source: Vodafone Annual Report 2007

3.5 IFRS 5 NON-CURRENT ASSETS HELD FOR SALE

There are some IFRS standards that reign supreme and from which all other IFRS Standards would seek the support of. IAS 39 and IFRS 9 come instantly to mind. IFRS 5 which is much smaller than the Standards on Financial Instruments (at least in length) is another Standard which would fall in the above category. All other IFRS Standards state that if an entity has a non-current asset held for sale (which meets the active plan to sell criteria of IFRS 5), the entity should look to IFRS 5 for guidance on recognition, measurement and disclosure.

Once an asset meets the requirements of Held-for-sale as per IFRS 5, it has to be valued at its Fair Value less Costs to sell and Depreciation on the Asset stops.

IFRS 5 would impact all entities across industries who have non-current Assets that are held for sale.

Bharti Airtel

In this quarter, the Company's subsidiary, Bharti Airtel International (Netherlands) B.V. (BAIN)/its subsidiaries and Eaton Towers Limited (Eaton)/its subsidiaries have entered into agreements for the divestment of over 3,500 telecom towers in six African countries The Company's subsidiaries will have access to a dedicated portion of the towers from Eaton under long-term lease contracts. As the criteria stated in IFRS 5 *Non-current Asset Held for Sale and Discontinued Operations* are met, these assets and relevant liabilities that are part of this sale and will not be leased back, amounting to Rs 15,274 Mn and Rs 1,960 Mn have been re-classified as "assets held for sale" and "liabilities held for sale" respectively in the Statement of Financial Position. As at 30 September, 2014 total "assets held for sale" and "liabilities held for sale" reflected in the statement of financial position is Rs 30,875 Mn and Rs 3,349 Mn respectively.

3.6 IFRS 8 OPERATING SEGMENTS

With its focus on the Chief Operating Decision Maker(CODM), IFRS 8 could alter how entities report their segments. As per IFRS 8, an operating segment is a component of an entity that engages in business activities from which it may earn revenues and incur expenses and whose operating results are reviewed regularly by the entity's chief operating decision maker to make decisions about resources to be allocated to the segment and assess its performance and for which discrete financial information is available

3.6.1 Reportable segments

IFRS 8 requires an entity to report financial and descriptive information about its reportable segments. Reportable segments are operating segments or aggregations of operating segments that meet specified criteria:

- its reported revenue, from both external customers and intersegment sales or transfers, is 10 per cent or more of the combined revenue, internal and external, of all operating segments, or

- the absolute measure of its reported profit or loss is 10 per cent or more of the greater, in absolute amount, of (i) the combined reported profit of all operating segments that did not report a loss and (ii) the combined reported loss of all operating segments that reported a loss, or
- its assets are 10 per cent or more of the combined assets of all operating segments.

Two or more operating segments may be aggregated into a single operating segment if aggregation is consistent with the core principles of the the standard, the segments have similar economic characteristics and are similar in various prescribed respects.

If the total external revenue reported by operating segments constitutes less than 75 per cent of the entity's revenue, additional operating segments must be identified as reportable segments (even if they do not meet the quantitative thresholds set out above) until at least 75 per cent of the entity's revenue is included in reportable segments.

Presented below is how Volkswagen AG reports Operating Segments.

Segments are identified on the basis of the Volkswagen Group's internal management and reporting. In line with the Group's multibrand strategy, each of its brands is managed by its own board of management. The Group targets and requirements laid down by the Board of Management of Volkswagen AG or the Group Board of Management must be complied with to the extent permitted by law. Segment reporting comprises four reportable segments: Passenger Cars, Commercial Vehicles, Power Engineering and Financial Services. Due to a change to the internal management system as of January 1, 2013, light commercial vehicles are no longer allocated to the Passenger Cars and Light Commercial Vehicles segment, but are reported together with trucks and buses in the new Commercial Vehicles segment. The segment designations and prior-year figures were adjusted accordingly. The prior-year figures were also adjusted to reflect the application of IAS 19R.

The activities of the Passenger Cars segment cover the development of vehicles and engines, the production and sale of passenger cars, and the corresponding genuine parts business. As a rule, the Volkswagen Group's individual passenger car brands are combined on a consolidated basis into a single reportable segment.

The Commercial Vehicles segment primarily comprises the development, production and sale of light commercial vehicles, trucks and buses, the corresponding genuine parts business and related services.

The activities of the Power Engineering segment consist of the development and production of large-bore diesel engines, turbo compressors, industrial turbines and chemical reactor systems, as well as the production of gear units, propulsion components and testing systems.

The activities of the Financial Services segment comprise dealer and customer financing, leasing, banking and insurance activities, fleet management and mobility services.

Purchase price allocation for companies acquired is allocated directly to the corresponding segments.

The business of Porsche AG acquired in fiscal year 2012 is allocated to the Passenger Cars segment, with the exception of Porsche's financial services activities, which are presented in the Financial Services segment. The Ducati Group, which was also acquired in fiscal year 2012, is allocated to the Audi operating segment and is thus presented in the Passenger Cars reporting segment.

At Volkswagen, segment profit or loss is measured on the basis of operating profit or loss.

In the segment reporting, the share of the profits or losses of joint ventures is contained in the share of profits and losses of equity-accounted investments in the corresponding segments.

The reconciliation contains activities and other operations that by definition do not constitute segments. It also includes the unallocated Group financing activities. Consolidation adjustments between the segments are also contained in the reconciliation.

Investments in intangible assets, property, plant and equipment, and investment property are reported net of investments under finance leases.

As a matter of principle, business relationships between the companies within the segments of the Volkswagen Group are transacted at arm's length prices.

Source: Volkswagen AG Annual Report 2013, page 233

3.7 IFRS 13 FAIR VALUE MEASUREMENT

If you ask any accountant who has had a limited exposure to IFRS, it should come as no surprise if he states that the F in IFRS stands for Fair Value. IFRS uses Fair Value across all its standards very liberally. To many, Fair Value is the default measurement standard under IFRS unless other measurement basis are specified. The so-called heavy duty IFRS standards – IAS 16 (Property, Plant and Equipment) and IFRS 9 (Financial Instruments: Measurement) provide an option to measure Assets at Fair Value. Even relatively smaller standards such as IAS 40 on Investment Property and IAS 41 on Agriculture bat for Fair Value as a measurement principle. As a concept, Fair Value is judgemental. What is FV to one need not be so for another. Instances abound of differences in Fair Valuation between the auditors and the management. In case the difference of opinion remains unresolved, an independent arbitrator is brought in to arrive at a decisive value. IFRS 13 attempts to provide some benchmarks for Fair Value Measurement and would impact all entities that have to measure their Assets/Liabilities at Fair Value.

What could be the ideal FV is a question that many entities would like an instant answer to. Unfortunately, there is no instant answer. IFRS 13 provides some sort of a ready-reckoner to ascertain the most appropriate FV.

3.7.1 Fair Value Ready Reckoner

Transactional Stages	*Basis*
Asset or Liability	Unit of Account
at	
The Price	Exit Price
In the	
Principal or most advantageous market	Market where market participant would orderly transact the asset or liability
between	

Market Participants	Independent, knowledgeable, able and willing
At the	
Highest and best use for non-financial assets	Current use or alternative use? As a group or on a standalone basis?
Based on	
Valuation Techniques	Market, income or cost approach
Using	
Fair Value Hierarchy	Level 1, 2 and 3 inputs

3.7.2 Explaining the Ready Reckoner

3.7.2.1 Definition

Fair value is defined as "the price that would be received to sell an asset or paid to transfer a liability in an orderly transaction between market participants at the measurement date." The exit price notion embodies expectations about the future cash flows associated with the asset or liability from the perspective of market participants at the measurement date, under current market conditions.

In the context of an actual exchange transaction, the assumption will often be that the price at transaction date represents the fair value at initial recognition of the asset or liability. However, an assessment of the specific transaction should be made to determine whether this is appropriate. Situations in which the transaction price may not represent fair value include:

- the transaction is between related parties;
- the transaction takes place under duress or under circumstances where the seller is forced to accept a price;
- the unit of account of the transaction differs from the unit of account for the asset or liability being measured; or
- the market where the transaction takes place is different from the principal market (or most advantageous market).

3.7.3 The Asset or Liability

A fair value measurement is for a particular asset or liability. Therefore, characteristics such as the condition and location of the asset, as well as restrictions on the sale or use of that asset should be considered, if a market participant would take these characteristics into account.

In accordance with the standard, the asset or liability measured at fair value might be either of the following:

(a) a stand-alone asset or liability; or
(b) a group of assets, a group of liabilities, or a group of assets and liabilities.

For measurement purposes, whether the asset or liability is viewed as stand-alone or as a group depends on its *unit of account*. The unit of account is determined in accordance with the IFRS that requires or permits the fair value measurement in the first place. For example, when valuing the equity interest in a publicly-traded company, the unit of account may be the individual share (e.g. under IAS 39 *Financial Instruments: Recognition and Measurement*) or the entire equity interest (e.g. under IFRS 3 *Business Combinations*).

3.7.4 The Price

In determining the price of an asset or liability in the principal market, *transaction costs* are not included as a component of the price. Transaction costs are considered to be entity specific and will therefore differ depending on how a transaction is structured.

However, *transport costs* are not considered to be entity specific. If the principal (or most advantageous) market requires the asset to be transported from its current location, then the associated transport costs should be considered as component of the price.

3.7.5 The Reference Market

The transaction is assumed to take place in the *principal* market, being the market with the greatest volume and level of activity for the asset or liability, or (if no principal market exists) in the *most advantageous* market where the amount received to sell the asset is maximised or the amount paid to transfer the liability is minimised. In determining which market has the greatest volume and level of activity, it is irrelevant that the entity never transacted in a certain market, provided it has access to such market at the measurement date.

If there is no evidence to the contrary, it is assumed that the principal (or most advantageous) market is the same as the market in which the entity normally transacts. An exhaustive search of all possible markets is not required, but consideration should be given to all reasonably available information.

3.7.6 Market Participants

IFRS 13 formalizes the definition of market participants, which was lacking in other previously issued standards. Market participants are buyers and sellers in the principal (or most advantageous) market who are;

   (i) independent of each other;
  (ii) knowledgeable about the asset or liability; and
 (iii) able and willing to enter into a transaction for the asset or liability.

Fair value is determined using market participant assumptions, not entity-specific assumptions. An entity's own intentions (for example, to hold an asset, or to settle a liability) are not relevant when estimating fair value.

IFRS 13 emphasizes that when measuring fair value it should be assumed that market participants act in their economic best interest (i.e. a value maximising concept).

3.7.7 Fair Value of Assets

The measurement of a non-financial asset should consider a market participant's ability to generate an economic benefit by using the asset in its *highest and best use*, or by selling it to another market participant who will then use the asset in its highest and best use. The highest and best use is determined from the perspective of market participants, who are assumed to maximise the value of the asset or the group of assets (and potentially liabilities) within which the asset would be used. When determining the highest and best use of a non-financial asset, the entity must take into account the use of an asset that is:

Physically possible: any physical attributes that a market participant would consider should be taken into account (for example size and location).

Legally permissible: if market participants would consider any legal restrictions preventing the use of the asset, then these restrictions should also be taken into account by the entity.

Financially feasible: when assessing if a use is financially feasible, the entity must consider that market participants should earn a reasonable return on investment from the use of the asset, after taking into account any costs of converting the asset to that use.

The *highest and best* use of a non-financial asset establishes its *valuation premise*. In other words, it determines whether the asset should be valued on a stand-alone basis or as a group in combination with other assets (or with other assets and liabilities). If the asset's highest and best use is determined to be in combination with of other assets (and potentially liabilities), it is assumed that the complementary assets (and potentially associated liabilities) would be available to market participants.

IFRS 13 clarifies that the concepts of highest and best use and valuation premise do not apply when measuring the fair value of financial assets or of liabilities. An exception is afforded in IFRS 13 by allowing a group of financial assets and financial liabilities to be measured as a group, provided that certain market risk or counterparty credit risk exposures are managed by the entity on a net basis (subject to specific requirements).

3.7.8 Fair Value of Liabilities

The definition of the fair value of a liability is based on a *transfer*, rather than a *settlement*, concept. In other words, the standard requires the assumption that the liability will be transferred to a market participant and that such liability will not be cancelled, or otherwise settled, at the measurement date.

The fair value of a liability reflects non- performance risk, the risk that an entity will not fulfil an obligation, including (but not limited to) the entity's own credit risk. A key notion when measuring the fair value of a liability is the assumption that non-performance risk is the same before and after the transfer. In other words, an implicit assumption is made that a market participant transferee has the same credit standing as the reporting entity.

As with the valuation of assets, the use of observable inputs should be maximised when measuring the fair value of liabilities. However, it is often the case that observable markets do not exist where liabilities are transferred. Nonetheless, if there is a quoted price for an identical item which is traded as an asset in an active market, then the fair value of the liability shall be measured from the perspective of the market participants who hold the identical item as an asset. In this case, if there are factors specific to the asset (e.g. third-party credit enhancements) that are not applicable to the liability being measured, then the quoted price should be adjusted.

If quoted prices in an active market for the identical asset are not available, then the liability is valued using other observable inputs (e.g. prices in an inactive market for the asset), or through a valuation technique.

Where there are restrictions relating to the transfer of a liability, the effects of these restrictions should not be included as a separate input or adjustment.

The standard indicates that when entering into a transaction, market participants already included, either implicitly or explicitly, the effects of the restriction on the transaction price.

3.7.9 Fair Value Hierarchy

The standard introduces the concept of a fair value hierarchy based on the observability of the inputs used to measure fair value. Inputs to fair value measurements should be used in the following order of priority:

3.7.9.1 Level 1

Level 1 inputs are quoted prices (unadjusted) in active markets for identical assets or liabilities. When a Level 1 input is being used in the fair value measurement, the fair value of the asset or liability is the product of the quoted price and the quantity held. This remains the case even where a significant quantity of the asset or liability is held and normal trading activity is not sufficient to absorb the block held.

3.7.9.2 Level 2

Level 2 inputs are inputs (other than quoted prices included in Level 1) that are observable either directly (prices) or indirectly (derived from prices). Level 2 inputs include:
(i) quoted prices for identical assets or liabilities in *inactive* markets;
(ii) quoted prices for similar assets or liabilities in active or inactive markets;
(iii) observable inputs other than quoted prices (interest rates and yield curves, for example); or
(iv) inputs that are corroborated by market data.

3.7.9.3 Level 3

Level 3 inputs are unobservable inputs for the asset or liability. Unobservable inputs should be developed using market participant assumptions, although these assumptions may originally be based on the entity's own data.

When inputs categorised in more than one level are used, the entire fair value measurement is classified in the same hierarchy level as the lowest level input that is significant to the entire measurement. This concept is intended to help increase consistency and comparability in fair value measurements and related disclosures.

3.7.10 How fair is Fair Value?

Though the IASB has attempted to provide detailed guidance on Fair Value, it is a fact that there is a great deal that is still debatable about the concept. Critics of the concept blame the concept for adding fuel to the credit crisis by mandating valuing assets at FV when there was no active market for those assets. Defenders of the concept use a simple mantra "You cannot manage what you cannot measure." They are of the opinion that the cost formula is not a measurement mechanism but only an accounting technique. FV can cause gyrations in the net worth of an enterprise but it certainly assists in sending out a red flag for potential accounting minefields.

Though FV may not be the perfect solution, it is at least a better solution than the cost-depreciation-amortisation model. For instance, IFRS 13 states that the Quoted Market Price in an active market is the best indicator of FV. Everyone knows that markets are not perfect – extending this a bit further and it would be hard not to conclude that the prices quoted therein are also not perfect. Yet, there is at least something to benchmark upon.

If the concept is used judiciously by everyone, it will be hard to dispute its effectiveness.

3.8 IAS 39/IFRS 9 FINANCIAL INSTRUMENTS

It is a very rare company that does not deal in financial instruments these days. The sheer variety of financial instruments available and the fact that many of them can be tailor-made for companies make them extremely attractive as a risk mitigation measure. The definition of Financial Instruments as per IAS 39 is comprehensive enough to include most instruments that companies would normally trade or deal in. The need to fair value/mark-to-market financial instruments can have a significant impact on the financial statements of an enterprise.

Under the International Accounting Standard 39 (IAS 39), all financial assets and financial liabilities have to be recognised on the balance sheet, including all derivatives. Furthermore, the standard requires that the embedded derivative of a hybrid instrument be separated from the host contract, provided certain criteria are met. If it has to be separated, such as a call or put option on debt that is issued at a significant discount, the embedded derivative will have to be fair valued and accounted for individually.

This new accounting standard establishes uniform hedge accounting criteria for all derivatives. Hedge accounting recognises symmetrically the offsetting effects on net income of changes in fair value of the hedging instrument and the hedged item in order to reduce volatility in the income statement. IAS 39 requires that an enterprise must formally designate a hedging instrument to a related item or to a group of similar items being hedged, and to assess and document the effectiveness of transactions that receive hedge accounting.

By increasing the use of fair values in accounting for financial instruments and implementing provisions for certain embedded derivatives, as well as consistent accounting standards for the use of hedge accounting, IAS 39 will affect many companies. Compliance will have major, widespread impacts on users of financial instruments.

Major potential impacts of IAS 39 include volatility in the income statement and in equity, require significant changes in financial risk management strategies and to business processes and systems, as well as modified and additional information to stakeholders. Therefore, companies preparing their financial statements under IAS will have to consider the impact on the functional areas involved in managing, processing, controlling and accounting for financial instruments.

3.8.1 Volatility in Equity and the Income Statement

According to IAS 39, at inception all financial instruments are measured at their fair value. The subsequent remeasurement depends on the initial classification of the financial instrument. Financial assets and liabilities held for trading – including all derivatives – are re-measured to fair value with unrealised gains or losses to be included in the income statement.

Financial assets classified as "available-for-sale" are also re-measured to fair value, but the company has the option to include unrealised gains or losses in equity. Other categorises of financial assets are those classified as "Assets held-to-maturity" which are re-measured at amortised cost and "Originated loans and receivables" which are subsequently measured at cost (without fixed maturity) or amortised cost (with fixed maturity). Financial liabilities – except those held for trading and derivatives – are re-measured at amortised cost (see Figure 3.1 below).

	Initial measurement	*Subsequent measurement*	*Changes in fair value booked to*
Derivatives	Cost	Fair value	Income statement
Loans and receivables	Cost	Cost or Amortised cost	Income statement
Financial assets held for trading	Cost	Fair value	Income statement
Financial assets available for sale	Cost	Fair value	Equity or Income statement
Financial assets held-to-maturity	Cost	Amortised cost	–
Financial liabilities held for trading	Cost	Fair value	Income statement
Other financial liabilities	Cost	Amortised cost	–

Note: The above table would not apply once IFRS 9 is implemented.
Figure 3.1   Measurement of Financial Instruments According to IAS 39

Hedge accounting may be adopted in order to decrease the volatility of the income statement. The standard distinguishes between fair value hedges, cash flow hedges and the hedges of a net investment in a foreign entity.

Whereas the fair value hedge is utilised to hedge the variability of changes in fair value of a recognised asset or liability, a cash flow hedge is used to hedge the exposure to the variability in cash flows associated with a recognised asset or liability, a firm commitment or a forecasted transaction. A hedge on a net investment in foreign entity is applied to hedge the company's share in the net assets of that entity which is not a subsidiary, an associate, or a joint venture.

3.8.2 Significant Changes in Financial Risk Management Strategies

To properly anticipate and manage volatility in equity and the income statement, companies will need to look at current hedging strategies and accounting policies. Financial risk management objectives and strategies have to be re-assessed in order to achieve overall objectives.

Procedures to designate hedging instruments to hedged items and to measure the hedge effectiveness have to be put in place. Since all derivatives have to be fair valued, sources of fair value information have to be identified. Documentation of hedge relations, the measurement of the hedge effectiveness and the valuations of financial instruments has to be ensured.

3.8.3 Changes to Business Processes and a Need for Systems Solutions Upgrade

By applying hedge accounting, IAS 39 prescribes a forward-looking approach to measure expected hedge effectiveness at inception and a backward-looking approach to measure realised hedge effectiveness throughout the life of the hedge. The method an enterprise adopts for assessing hedge effectiveness will depend on its risk management strategy and can vary between different types of hedges, and therefore, has to be carefully selected.

Beyond keeping tabs on fair values, companies will have to track premiums and discounts on items hedged in fair value hedges and amounts deferred in equity for cash flow hedges. Information to meet disclosure requirements has to be compiled and automated journal entries have to be evaluated to determine the magnitude of potential system adoptions and enhancements.

3.8.4 Information to Stakeholders

The new standard requires additional disclosures in the financial statements relating to accounting policies, hedging and financial instruments. The methods and assumptions in estimating fair values, information on the risk management objectives and policies, a description of designated hedges and significant items of gains and losses on financial instruments are only a few of the additional disclosure requirements as set out by IAS 39.

For accounting purposes the chart of accounts and internal reporting packages have to be revised, standard accounting journal entries have to be determined and accounting transition adjustment entries have to be carefully assessed. Management reports should enclose the likely impact on the income statement and equity of the mark-to-fair-value, since this can be of considerable interest. Not least, it is advisable that a clear communication strategy to rating agencies, investors, analysts and other external parties is developed.

3.8.5 Conclusion

With the increased use of fair value accounting for financial instruments, the treatment of embedded derivatives and the hedge accounting principles the IASC created a challenging new accounting principle. Since IAS 39 affects not only accounting, but also other functional areas, the implementation should be planned thoroughly.

A successful implementation requires a multi-disciplinary effort which demands treasury, operations, risk management and accounting expertise.

Presented below the impact of IAS 39 on the financial statements of a bank – the State Bank of Pakistan.

STATE BANK OF PAKISTAN

STATEMENT OF IMPACT OF IAS 39 ON CONSOLIDATED FINANCIAL POSITION

AS AT JUNE 30, 2012

	Note	Impact of application of IAS-39			
		Under existing framework	**Reclassifications**	**Remeasurements**	**After application of IAS-39**
		--------------------(Rs. in '000) ---------------			
ASSETS					
Gold reserves held by the Bank		313,077,419	–	–	313,077,419
Loeal currency - coins		1,814,196	–	–	1,814,196
Foreign currency reserves		1,038,341,770	527,207	–	1,038,868,977
Earmarked foreign currency balances		4,994,808	–	–	4,994,808
Special Drawing Rights of the International Monetary Fund (IMF)		91,334,177	–	–	91,334,177
Reserve tranche with the IMF under quota arrangements		17,104	–	–	17,104
Securities purchased under agreements to resale		112,898,648	–	–	112,898,648
Current accounts of Governments		12,744,407	350,073	–	13,094,480
Investments	3	1,827,251,187	41,100	125,361,020	1,952,653,307
Loans, advances, bills of exchange and commercial papers	4	340,046,025	2,525,730	(75,793,585)	266,778,170
Assets held with the Reserve Bank of India	5	6,311,529	(6,311,529)	–	–
Balances due from Governments of India and Bangladesh (Former East Pakistan)	6	6,797,433	(6,797,433)	–	–
Property and equipment		23,450,893	–	–	23,450,893
Intangible assets		30,882	–	–	30,882
Other assets	3 & 4	6,024,442	(4,170,337)	–	1,854,105
Total assets		**3,785,134,920**	**(13,835,189)**	**49,567,435**	**3,820,867,166**

LIABILITIES

Bank notes in circulation		1,776,962,388	–	–	1,776,962,388
Bills payable		587,542	–	–	587,542
Current accounts of the Governments		148,815,907	–	–	148,815,907
Securities sold under agreement to repurchase		12,240,388	–	–	12,240,388
Deposits of banks and financial institutions		396,172,467	–	–	396,172,467
Other deposits and accounts		153,534,625	270,679	–	153,805,304
Payable to the International Monetary Fund		656,185,305	1,394,116	–	657,579,421
Other liabilities	7	107,523,858	(15,499,984)	–	92,023,874
Deferred liability – staff retirement benefits		21,457,079	–	–	21,457,079
Endowment fund		67,281	–	–	67,281
Total liabilities		**3,273,546,840**	**(13,835,189)**	**–**	**3,259,711,651**
NET ASSETS		**511,588,080**	**–**	**49,567,435**	**561,155,515**

STATE BANK OF PAKISTAN

Notes to the Statements of Impact of IAS 39 on consolidated financial position and consolidated financial performance for the year ended June 30, 2012.

BASIS OF PREPARATION

Statements of Impact of IAS 39:

Financial Instruments: Recognition and Measurement (IAS 39) on the consolidated financial position and the consolidated financial performance (the Statements) of State Bank of Pakistan (the Bank) and its wholly owned subsidiaries SBP Banking Services Corporation (the Corporation) and National Institute of Banking and Finance (Guarantee) Limited (the Institute) have been prepared to analyse the impact of the application of IAS 39 on carrying values of asset, liabilities, equity and reserves of the Group as at 30 June 2012 and profit and loss of the Group for the year then ended as reported in consolidated financial statements. The figures in consolidated financial statements are reported in accordance with accounting framework adopted by the Central Board of the Bank i.e. IAS 1 to IAS 38 and policies for bank notes and coins, investments, gold reserves and transactions and balances with International Monetary Fund (IMF) as stated in notes 4.2, 4.3, 4.6 and 4.17 respectively to the consolidated financial statements. Separate audit opinion is issued on consolidated financial statements of the Group for the year ended 30 June 2012. These Statements are not complete financial statements and incorporate only the adjustments to analyse the impact of the application of IAS 39 on the financial position and performance of the Group and should be read in conjunction with the audited consolidated financial statements of the Group for the year ended June 30, 2012.

USE OF ESTIMATES AND JUDGEMENTS

The preparation of these statements to appropriately reflect the impact of the application of IAS 39 requires the use of certain critical accounting estimates. It also requires the management to exercise its judgment in the process of the application of IAS 39. Estimates and judgments are continually evaluated and are based on historical events. This represents the remeasurement to fair value of the Group's strategic investments in listed shares at their quoted prices as at June 30, 2012. The remeasurement is the difference between the historical cost at which these investments are carried in the audited consolidated financial statements and fair values, as determined from the rates quoted at the Karachi Stock Exchange (KSE), of these shares amounting to Rs. 125,361 million (2011: Rs. 120,459 million). The resulting unrealised gain on remeasurement is taken to equity.

LOANS, ADVANCES, BILLS OF EXCHANGE AND COMMERCIAL PAPERS

4.1 Reclassification

This includes reclassification of accrued interest amounting to Rs. 3,027 million on loans to Governments, Government owned/controlled financial institutions, private sector financial institutions and employees from "Other Assets – accrued interest/mark-up, discount and return" to bring these loan at amortised cost. The reclassification also includes provision for impairment of loans and advances to financial institutions in Bangladesh (former East Pakistan). Provision for these loans amounting to Rs. 501.749 million (2011: Rs. 565.218 million) is included in Other Liabilities – Provision for other doubtful assets in the audited consolidated financial statements.

4.2 Remeasurement

This represents provision for impairment on loans given by the Bank to the agriculture, industrial, export and housing sectors amounting to Rs. 75,794 million (2011: Rs. 74,240 million). Consequent effect of these provisions include charge in profit and loss account amounting to Rs. 75,794 million (2011: Rs. 74,240 million) until 30 June 2012 and reversal of appropriation from unappropriated profit to reserve fund amounting to Rs. 13,000 million (2011: Rs. 13,000 million).

ASSETS HELD WITH THE RESERVE BANK OF INDIA

This reclassification represents netting of Assets Held with Reserve Bank of India (RBI) amounting to Rs. 6,311 million (2011: Rs. 1,308 million) with related provision for impairment which is included in Other Liabilities – Provision for doubtful assets in the consolidated financial statements. The realisability of these assets is subject to final settlement between the Governments of Pakistan and India.

BALANCES DUE FROM THE GOVERNMENTS OF INDIA AND BANGLADESH (FORMER EAST PAKISTAN)

This reclassification represents netting of Balances due from Governments of India and Bangladesh amounting to Rs. 6,797 million (2011: Rs. 6,313 million) with related provision for impairment which is included in Provision for doubtful assets, Overdue markup and return and Others reported under Other liabilities in the consolidated financial statements. The realisability of these assets is subject to final settlement between the Governments of Pakistan, India and Bangladesh.

OTHER LIABILITIES

The reclassification mainly represents the provision for impairment and suspended markup against the assets held with Reserve Bank of India, balances due from the Governments of India and Bangladesh and loans and advances to financial institutions in Bangladesh amounting to Rs. 13,835 million (2011: Rs. 8,518 million) which have been reclassified to their respective accounts.

Source: http://www.sbp.org.pk/reports/annual/arFY12/Vol-2/eng/Chapter-16.pdf

3.9 IFRS 10 CONSOLIDATED FINANCIAL STATEMENTS

When can an entity said to control another entity? The erstwhile IAS 27 had a combination of both mathematical and non-mathematical tests to ascertain if an entity controlled another – control over a majority of the voting power was a mathematical test while the ability to control the operating and financial policies were non-mathematical. The replacement to IAS 27- IFRS 10 – changed the definition of control to mean "power to control the variable returns from an investee." Since it used the word investee, it immediately excluded investment entities from the Standard, which meant that private equity, and other such investors need not consolidate the companies they have invested in. Though entities would fall back on the voting rights and other mathematical measures to ascertain power to control, it is possible that an entity can have a majority holding in another and yet not control it. Similarly, it is possible that an entity may have a minor shareholding in another and yet control it. With business combinations increasing across the world, applying the tests of control in IFRS 10 would pose a challenge to all most entities.

Vodafone provides an example of having a majority shareholding but not consolidating that entity:

> The Group considered the existence of substantive participating rights held by the minority shareholder provide that shareholder with a veto right over the significant financial and operating policies of Vodafone Omnitel N.V., and determined that, as a result of these rights, the Group does not have control over the financial and operating policies of Vodafone Omnitel N.V., despite the Group's 76.9% ownership interest.

Source: Vodafone Annual Report 2008 Page 111.

In their financial statements, Vodafone presented Vodafone Omnitel N.V as a joint venture.

3.10 IFRS 15 REVENUE FROM CONTRACTS WITH CUSTOMERS

IFRS 15 has already generated enough discussion worldwide. This was to be expected because the Standard can be called a game-changer for recognition of revenue. Apart from the core of the Standard which is the five-step mantra for revenue recognition, two other features of the Standard stood out – its length and the level of detail it went into. On hindsight, its predecessor – IAS 18 – is simplistic. The worldwide discussions have forced both the FASB and the IASB to postpone implementation of the Standard by one year.

Being a comprehensive standard, IFRS 15 impacts all industries. Since IAS 11 on Construction Contracts, IAS 18 on Revenue, IFRIC 13 on Customer Loyalty Programmes, IFRIC 15 on Agreements for Construction of Real Estate, IFRIC 18 on Transfer of Assets to Customers and SIC 31– Barter Transactions involving Advertising Services which have morphed into IFRS 15, IFRS 15 would impact the construction industry, advertising industry and all industries that have customer loyalty programmes. Even though it cannot be said that the basic concepts of transfer of risks and rewards and percentage of completion method are redundant, every company would need to test the five-step approach prior to recognising revenue. The five steps are:

1. Identify the contract(s) with a customer
2. Identify the performance obligations in the contract
3. Determine the transaction price
4. Allocate the transaction price to the performance obligations in the contract
5. Recognise revenue when (or as) the entity satisfies a performance obligation.

Every entity applying IFRS 15 would have to take a relook at their contracts, the performance obligations embedded therein and would have to allocate the transaction price to their performance obligations either at a single point in time or over a period of time. Needless to say, this would have an impact on many industries.

Key Takeaways

IFRS 1

- Ascertain date of transition
- Do an impact assessment
- Choose the exceptions the entity opts for
- Document the entire first time adoption process in detail

IAS 40

- Does the property meet the definition of Investment Property?
- Get the subsequent fair valuation right

IFRS 3

- Is it a Business Combination?
- Ascertaining Acquisition Date Fair Values.

- Recognising and measuring Intangible Assets.
- Goodwill Measurement

IFRS 5

- Is the Asset Held for Sale or Abandoned?
- What is the active plan to sell the Asset?
- Determining the Fair Value

IFRS 13

- Getting the Fair Value right or the Right Fair Value (both of which are different but can be difficult to ascertain with accuracy)

Detailed Disclosures could involve entities spending a lot of time and resources on these disclosures.

4 *THE IMPACT OF IFRS STANDARDS ON SPECIFIC INDUSTRIES*

4.1 AIRLINES

4.1.1 Overview

Starting an airline and operating it needs deep pockets. Initial investments are very high, and aircrafts are normally acquired by long-term lease arrangements. The revenue does not come with the same velocity due to differential pricing adopted by airlines to manage competition.

4.1.2 IFRS Standards that could impact the industry

4.1.2.1 IAS 16 Property, Plant and Equipment

IAS 16 *Property, Plant and Equipment* seems to have a liking for airline entities. It illustrates airline entity examples in four different instances:

- Aircraft interiors such as seats and galleys may require replacement several times during the life of the airframe.
- A condition of continuing to operate an item of property, plant and equipment (for example, an aircraft) may be performing regular major inspections for faults regardless of whether parts of the item are replaced.
- A class of property, plant and equipment is a grouping of assets of a similar nature and use in an entity's operations. "Aircraft" is one in a list of eight examples of separate classes.
- It may be appropriate to depreciate separately the airframe and engines of an aircraft, whether owned or subject to a finance lease.

Aircraft acquisition costs

Aircraft are initially recorded at cost. Aircraft acquisition costs normally include purchase costs, duties and taxes, foreign exchange gains and losses and borrowing costs. The costs associated with major inspection activities or overhauls that result in future economic benefits should be recognised as a separate "component" and depreciated through the next major maintenance. Similarly, major spare part inventories may be capitalised as Property, Plant and Equipment.

The component approach

An aircraft is a complicated and costly asset with numerous components. Under IFRS, each significant component must be depreciated separately. As indicated above,

IAS 16 itself indicates that the airframe and engine of an aircraft may be depreciated separately. Choosing components is a management decision, which will have to be done with some technical expertise and judgement.

Measurement

Under IFRS, companies have a choice on how to measure PP&E. They can choose to use either the historical cost method and carry the assets at cost less accumulated depreciation and impairment charges or the revaluation method and revalue the assets regularly to fair value.

For assets carried under the historical cost method or revaluation method, it is important for companies to review the assets' useful life, residual value, and depreciation method.

Residual Values

In normal industries, the residual value of assets is normally determined to be a percentage of the total asset value. However, due to the nature of the assets owned by an airline and the fact that their costs are significant, the residual value could be much higher than in normal industries. Airframes, engines and other assets owned by airlines usually have significant residual values. The residual value and the useful life of an asset under IFRS should be reviewed at least at each financial year-end with the following criteria in mind:

- technological obsolescence,
- operating cycles, and
- repair and maintenance policy.

The financial statements of Lufthansa provide an example of a change in the useful life as well as a change in the residual value.

Lufthansa

Tangible assets used in business operations for longer than one year are valued at cost less regular straight-line depreciation. The cost of production includes all costs directly attributable to the manufacturing process as well as appropriate portions of the indirect costs relating to this process. Borrowing costs in close connection with the financing of the purchase or production of a qualifying asset are also capitalised. In the reporting year borrowing costs of EUR 19m (previous year: EUR 14m) were capitalised. The financing rate used was 3.6 per cent (previous year: 4.5 per cent). The useful lives applied to tangible assets correspond to their estimated/expected useful lives in the Group.

Until the end of the financial year 2012, new commercial aircraft and reserve engines were depreciated over a period of twelve years to a residual value of 15 per cent. Technological developments and the higher demands made of their cost-effectiveness due to increasing competition have resulted in significant changes to the forecast useful economic life of the commercial aircraft and reserve engines used in the Lufthansa Group. In line with the fleet strategy, which takes these aspects into account, as well as with external considerations, commercial aircraft and reserve engines have been depreciated over a period of 20 years to a residual value of five per cent since 1 January 2013. The adjustment to their useful lives was made prospectively as a change in an accounting estimate in accordance with IAS 8.32. The change was therefore not made retrospectively for past reporting periods. As a result of the change in the accounting estimate of the useful economic life of these assets, depreciation and amortisation was EUR 68m lower in the financial year 2013 and impairment losses were EUR 76m lower. In future reporting periods, the adjustment to useful lives will reduce depreciation and amortisation by around EUR 340m for the financial year 2014, by EUR 350m for the financial year 2015 and by around EUR 250m p. a. for the five subsequent financial years.

A useful life of between 20 and 45 years is assumed for buildings, whereby buildings, fixtures and fittings on rented premises are depreciated according to the terms of the lease or over a shorter useful life. Depreciation rates are mainly between 10 and 20 per cent per annum. A useful life of up to ten years is fixed for plant and machinery. Operating and office equipment is depreciated over three to ten years in normal circumstances.

Assets acquired second-hand are depreciated over their expected remaining useful life

Source: Lufthansa Annual Report 2013 page 147

Lufthansa have stated that repairable spare parts for aircraft are held at continually adjusted prices based on average acquisition costs. For measurement purposes, spare parts are assigned to individual aircraft models and depreciated on a straight-line basis depending on the lifetime of the fleet models for which they can be used.

4.1.2.2 IAS 36 **Impairment of Assets**

It may come as a surprise to some that the number of airlines that have shut down operations or have been liquidated exceeds 100. Wikipedia lists them by continent and then by individual country. It should come as no surprise then that Impairment of Assets would be an extremely critical standard for the airline industry.

The airline industry requires significant capital investment and is exposed to economic cycles and market volatility, which affect the fair values of flight equipment. Indicators for impairment are therefore likely to exist over time and under IFRS may result in earlier impairment charges. Impairment is measured under IFRS on individual assets, unless an individual asset does not generate cash inflows that are largely independent from other assets or groups of assets. In these cases, impairment is measured at the cash generating unit (CGU) level. A CGU is the smallest identifiable group of assets that generates cash inflows, largely independent of cash inflows from other assets or groups of assets.

CGU determination within the airline industry should be considered carefully, since the determination of the number of CGUs will depend on the ability to generate cash inflows, largely independent from other assets or groups of assets.

4.1.2.3 *Lease contracts*

Classification of leases

Airlines enter into leases for a variety of assets including aircraft, spare engines, ground support equipment, machinery and facilities, and other equipment and tools. Leases, including those within the scope of IFRIC 4 *Determining Whether an*

Arrangement Contains a Lease, are classified as either operating or finance leases based on the facts and circumstances at their inception.

IAS 17, *Leases,* defines a finance lease as one that transfers substantially all the risks and rewards incidental to ownership to the lessee. The asset's title may or may not eventually be transferred to the lessee. Operating leases have a negative definition – they are defined as all leases that are not finance leases.

Under IFRS, classification depends on substance rather than legal form, IAS 17 lists the following indicators that individually or in combination would lead to a finance lease:

- The lease transfers ownership of the asset to the lessee.
- The lessee has the option to purchase the asset at below market value so that it is reasonably certain that the lessee will exercise the option.
- The lease term is for the major part of the asset's economic life.
  - The present value of the minimum lease payments is close to the fair value of the leased asset when the lease contract is signed.
  - The leased assets are of a specialised nature so that only the lessee can use them without major modifications.
  - The lessor's losses associated with the cancellation of a lease are borne by the lessee.
- Gains or losses from the fluctuation in the fair value of the residual accrue to the lessee – for example, in the form of a rent rebate equalling most of the sales proceeds at the end of the lease.
- The lessee extends the lease term at substantially below-market rent.

Determining whether an aircraft lease is an operating or a finance lease involves significant judgement and will have to done very carefully. For instance, use of a wrong discount rate to calculate the present value of the minimum lease payments could change the nature of classification of the Lease.

Sale and leaseback transactions

Sale and leaseback transactions are frequently used to raise capital in the airline industry. The transaction involves the sale of an aircraft or other assets and the leaseback of the same assets, usually under a finance lease. The future lease payments and the sale price are often interdependent because they are negotiated as a package.

The accounting treatment of such a transaction, under IFRS, depends on classification of the leaseback as either a finance lease or an operating lease. If the leaseback results in a lease classified as a finance lease, any gain is deferred and amortised to income over the lease term. If the sales proceeds are less than the carrying amount, the loss is also deferred unless there has been an impairment of the asset's value. If the leaseback results in a lease classified as an operating lease, the accounting treatment is more complex because the sale price must be compared with the asset's fair value. If the sale price is at fair value or below fair value, the resulting profit or loss is recognised in the profit or loss account immediately. If the sale price is above fair value, the excess over fair value should be deferred and amortised to adjust the future rent over the period for which the asset is expected to be used.

The proposed revision to IAS 17 *Leases* would significantly impact the airline industry – this has been discussed in the chapter on future IFRS standards that could impact industries. As the new Standard has radically altered the method of recognising Lease Assets, it is expected that the value of these Assets on the Balance Sheets of airlines would increase. This may improve their financial condition and borrowing capacity – however this could take time since lenders would need to get used to the concept of recognising a Leased Asset as an Asset in the books of the Lessee.

4.1.2.4 IAS 18/IFRS 15 Revenue recognition

Once airline companies implement IFRS 15, there will be an impact on the revenue they have recognised. As per IFRS 15, an entity would identify the contract with the customer, identify the separate performance obligations in the contract, determine the transaction price, allocate the transaction price to the separate performance obligations, and recognise revenue when the entity satisfies each performance obligation. It is a practice in the airline industry for customers to cancel their tickets, change their tickets, defer their travel or change their route. Airlines normally charge for such additional services. Airlines would need to determine whether such changes form a single contract or are separate contracts. This determination would alter their revenue recognition.

Liabilities from unused flight documents

Until they are used, sold flight documents are recognised as an obligation from unused flight documents. Once a passenger coupon or an airfreight document has been used, the amount carried as a liability is recognised as traffic revenue in the income statement. Coupons that are unlikely to be used are also recognised at the end of the year as traffic revenue in the income statement at their estimated value. The estimate is based on past statistical data.

Source: Lufthansa Annual Report 2013, page 151

Frequent flier accounting

Airlines grant award credits as part of sales transactions, including awards that can be redeemed for goods and services not supplied by the entities, through their customer loyalty programmes. The most common customer loyalty programme in the airline industry is the frequent flier programmes.

IFRS requires that awards, loyalty, or similar programmes, whereby a customer earns credits based on the purchase of goods or services, be accounted for as multi-element arrangements. As such, IFRS requires that the fair value of the award credits (otherwise attributed in accordance with the multiple-element guidance) be deferred and recognised separately upon achieving all applicable criteria for revenue recognition.

The above-outlined guidance applies whether the credits can be redeemed for goods or services supplied by the entity or whether the credits can be redeemed for goods or services supplied by a different entity. In situations where the credits can be redeemed through a different entity, a company should also consider the timing of recognition and appropriate presentation of each portion of the consideration received given the entity's potential role as an agent versus as a principal in each aspect of the transaction.

Obligations under bonus mile programmes

Calculation of the obligations arising from bonus miles programmes is based on several estimates and assumptions. In accordance with IFRIC 13 Customer Loyalty Programmes, accumulated but as yet unused bonus miles are deferred using the deferred revenue method to the extent that they are likely to be used on flights by airlines in the Lufthansa Group. Bonus entitlements are measured at fair value. The fair value of the air miles is determined as the value for which the miles could be sold separately, i.e. the average revenue, taking booking class and traffic region into account. Miles that are likely to be used on flights with partner airlines are valued at the price per mile to be paid to the partners in question.

No provisions are recognised for miles that are expected to lapse. The quota of miles that have been allowed to lapse in the past is used to estimate the number of miles that will probably lapse according to current expiry rules.

The fair value of miles accumulated on the Group's own flights is recognised under deferred revenue and the points collected from third parties are shown under other non-financial liabilities.

A total of 209 billion miles (previous year: 205 billion miles) were to be measured as of 31 December 2013. The resulting obligations were recognised in other non-financial liabilities (EUR 648m; previous year: EUR 638m) and in deferred revenue (EUR 1,063m; previous year: EUR 1,022m).

Lufthansa Annual Report 2013 Page 151

Joint ventures

Joint ventures are common in the airline industry because they allow entities to share the risks and capital costs of new aircraft, routes and facilities. The key principle in IFRS 11 Joint Ventures is that parties to a joint arrangement recognise their contractual rights and obligations arising from the arrangement. It focuses on the recognition of assets and liabilities by the parties to the joint arrangement. The proportionate consolidation for a jointly controlled entity has been eliminated – only the equity method can be used. A single joint arrangement may contain more than one type – for example, joint assets and a joint venture. Parties to such a joint arrangement account first for the assets and liabilities of the joint assets arrangements and then use a residual approach to equity accounting for the joint venture part of the joint arrangement.

Provisions

Airlines are exposed to the potential for various claims and litigations related to aircraft damage, personal injury, other property damage, environmental liability and other matters.

The amount recognised as a provision for IFRS is the best estimate of expenditure required to settle the present obligation as of the balance sheet date. The anticipated cash flows are discounted to their present value if the effect of discounting is material.

Onerous contracts

The industry commonly uses long-term contractual arrangements – for example, codeshare or outsourcing agreements including those with regional airlines. These contracts can become onerous over time if they cannot be cancelled without payment of a significant penalty or other compensation to the counterparty. Management should analyse specific facts and circumstances and, if appropriate, recognise a provision for the expected loss in accordance with IAS 37 *Provisions, Contingent Liabilities and Contingent Assets*. IAS 37 requires a provision for the minimum unavoidable costs of meeting the obligations under a contract where the costs exceed the economic benefits expected to be received under the contract.

The standard also prohibits making a provision for future operating losses.

4.1.3 First-time Conversion to IFRS

Given below are extracts from the financial statements of Ryanair.

Transition to IFRS

This summary sets out the most significant changes required to Ryanair's consolidated financial statements as a result of the transition to IFRS from Irish GAAP during the fiscal year ended March 31, 2006.

(A) IAS 19: PENSION AND OTHER POST RETIREMENT BENEFITS

In accordance with IAS 19 ("Employee Benefits"), the assets and liabilities of the defined benefit pension plans operated by Ryanair have been recognised, gross of deferred tax, in the balance sheet at the date of transition to IFRS in accordance with the valuation and measurement requirements of the standard.

Deferred tax has been computed in respect of the group's pension liabilities arising as a result of the application of IAS 19 and the related deferred tax assets have been included in the restatements at the various balance sheet dates.

In accordance with the option afforded under the amendment to IFRS 1, the group has elected to recognise all cumulative actuarial gains and losses attributable to its defined benefit pension schemes as at the transition date.

Also in line with the amendment to IAS 19, actuarial gains and losses arising after the transition date are dealt with in retained income via the Statement of Recognised Income and Expense, and all other pension scheme movements have been accounted for in the group's income statement.

(B) IFRS 3: BUSINESS COMBINATIONS

The group has elected to restate the acquisition of Buzz on April 10, 2003 (the group's only business combination to date) in accordance with the provisions of IFRS 3 ("Business Combinations"). As the principal assets and liabilities acquired at that time related to takeoff and landing slots at Stansted airport, and onerous leases for aircraft, the restatement of the business combination under IFRS 3 has given rise to the following cumulative adjustments in the periods to March 31, 2005:

(i)   Reversal of goodwill amortisation since the date of the acquisition amounting to €4.5 million.

(ii) Reallocation of all of the fair value of assets acquired at the time (being €46.8 million) from goodwill to intangible assets, represented by takeoff and landing rights ("slots") at Stansted airport. This adjustment was required to recognise the fair value of assets required to be recognised under the provisions of IFRS 3 and IAS 38 "Intangible Assets." This asset is considered to be indefinite lived because the slots do not expire as long as they continue to be utilised and it is Ryanair's intention to utilise these slots for the foreseeable future. Accordingly, the slots acquired have not been amortised. The slots acquired have also been subsequently reviewed for impairment in accordance with the provisions of IAS 36 "Impairment of Assets" and no impairment of this asset is considered to have occurred since the date of acquisition.

(iii) A provision for onerous leases was recognised in the balance sheet at the date the business combination was effected. On transition to IFRS, no change was recorded to the provisional fair value of onerous leases taken over on acquisition as the impact of discounting such amounts was not considered to be material in the context of the group's results. Subsequent to the acquisition, however, Ryanair renegotiated the terms and conditions of these leases and agreed to return the aircraft to the lessors in late 2005, thereby releasing Ryanair from any remaining lease obligations at that time. Irish GAAP permitted that such an adjustment could be made to the provisional value of the assets and liabilities acquired as part of the original business combination, provided that the adjustment was made either in the reporting period that the combination took place or in the first full financial period following the transaction. IFRS 3, however, only allows such an adjustment to be made in the 12 month period following the acquisition, and accordingly, as the event occurred more than 12 months after the acquisition date, under IFRS this adjustment was made to the group's income statement instead. This gives rise to a credit of €11.9m to the income statement in the period to March 31, 2005.

(C) IFRS 2: SHARE BASED PAYMENTS

IFRS 2 ("Share Based Payment") requires the group to recognise any share-based payments made to employees during a reporting period as a charge to the income statement over the vesting period of the options, together with a corresponding increase in equity. The charge of €0.5 million for the year ended March 31, 2005 for share option grants has been computed using the Binomial Lattice methodology.

Ryanair has availed of the transition provisions in IFRS 1 for share based payments by only applying the fair value calculation to share option grants that were made after November 7, 2002 but which had not vested by January 1, 2005. There was no share based payment charge in the periods prior to March 31, 2005 accordingly. Had Ryanair recognised all vested grants of shares between November 7, 2002 and January 1, 2005, the group's equity at March 31, 2005 would have increased by €9.4m with a corresponding reduction in retained earnings.

(D) IAS 16: PLANT, PROPERTY AND EQUIPMENT

IAS 16 requires that all spare parts held by an entity are classified as Property, Plant and Equipment if they are expected to be used for more than one period and not held for resale. This has resulted in a reclassification of the stock of spare aircraft parts from inventories to Property, Plant and Equipment. The related depreciation expense relating to the stock of spare aircraft parts has also been reclassified from "maintenance, materials & repairs" to "depreciation and amortisation." This reclassification was made following the release of our published explanation of the financial impact following the adoption of IFRS.

(E) IAS 39: FINANCIAL INSTRUMENTS

IAS 39 ("Financial Instruments: Recognition and Measurement") requires that all financial instruments are recorded at fair value or amortised cost dependent on the nature of the financial asset or financial liability. Derivatives are measured at fair value with changes in value arising from fluctuations in interest rates, foreign exchange rates or commodity prices. Under Irish GAAP, where the derivatives formed part of a hedging agreement, these were not initially measured on the balance sheet and any related gains or losses arising are deferred until the underlying hedged item impacted on the financial statements.

Ryanair has taken advantage of the exemption from the requirement to restate comparative information for IAS 39 contained in IFRS 1. As a result of this exemption the information presented for all periods up to March 31, 2005 has been accounted for in accordance with Irish/UK GAAP.

At April 1, 2005 Ryanair has accounted for all of its derivatives in accordance with IAS 39, with the result that an opening unrealised loss of €146.4 million together with a related deferred tax benefit of €18.3 million has been recorded directly in the opening cash flow hedging reserve, principally relating to the company's interest rate swaps, which were entered into at a time when underlying interest rates were higher than present market rates. The company also recorded the following entries in respect of fair value hedges for firm commitments; an increase of €2.7 million in derivative financial assets held and a corresponding increase in other creditors, with no amount of ineffectiveness recorded in the income statement. The unrealised losses on these interest rate swaps continue to be significant and amounted to €81.7m as at March 31, 2006. These will have a consequent impact on future operating profits until they expire for up to 12 years the from balance sheet date.

Source: Ryanair Annual Report 2006

TRANSITION EFFECTS

IFRS 1 permits those companies adopting IFRS for the first time to avail of certain exemptions from the full requirements of IFRS on transition. Ryanair intends to avail of the following key exemptions:

Pensions and post-retirement benefits: At the transition date Ryanair has re-evaluated its defined benefit pension plans in accordance with IAS 19, and all cumulative actuarial gains and losses have been recognised in the opening balance sheet within pension assets or pension liabilities, and adjusted against retained income.

Financial instruments: Financial instruments in the comparative periods are recorded using the existing Irish/UK GAAP basis, rather than being restated in accordance with IAS 32, Financial Instruments: Disclosure and Presentation, and IAS 39, Financial Instruments: Recognition and Measurement. The requirements of IAS 32 and 39 will instead be applied from 1 April 2005, as permitted by IFRS

Share-based payments: IFRS 2 has been adopted from the transition date and is only being applied to equity settled share options granted on or after 7 November 2002 which had not vested by 1 January 2005. Ryanair has elected to avail of the option not to apply full retrospective application of the standard.

Business combinations: Ryanair has elected to restate its only business combination (the acquisition of Buzz on 10 April 2003) to comply with IFRS 3 "Business Combinations," and has also applied the provisions of IAS 36 *Impairment of Assets* and IAS 38 *Intangible Assets* from the same date.

Source: Ryanair Annual Report and Financial Statements 2006, pages 69 and 70.

Key Takeaways

- Revenue Recognition on tickets sold as well as Customer Loyalty Programmes
- Determining Useful lives of Property, Plant and Equipment and their residual value
- Impairment of Assets

4.2 AGRICULTURE

4.2.1 Overview

Is Agriculture an Industry? Or is it a mere profession? The general feeling about Agriculture is probably that it is a profession. Like all trades and professions, Agriculture too has evolved over the years and is no longer restricted to growing crops. Recognising this, the IASB has issued a separate Standard on Agriculture IAS 41. IAS 41 is of the opinion that a biological transformation of living animals or plants would constitute an agricultural activity to come within the scope of the Standard.

4.2.2 IFRS Standards that could impact the industry

4.2.2.1 *IAS 41* Agriculture

It is obvious that IAS 41 would be the go-to Standard for the Agricultural industry. Since the concept of an Accounting Standard for agricultural activities is relatively new in a few geographies, there could be issues in interpreting and applying the Standard.

1. *Is it an Agricultural Activity?*

The Standard defines Agricultural Activity to mean management by an entity of the biological transformation and harvest of biological assets for sale or for conversion into agricultural produce or into additional biological assets. It also provides a representative list of biological assets, agricultural produce and the post-harvest product that would invariably be accounted for as Inventory.

Biological Assets	*Agricultural Produce*	*Products that are the result of processing after harvest*
Sheep	Wool	Yarn/Carpet
Trees in a plantation forest	Felled Trees	Logs, Lumber
Plants	Cotton	Thread, Clothing
Dairy Cattle	Milk	Cheese
Pigs	Carcasses	Sausages
Bushes	Leaf	Tea
Vines	Grape	Wine
Fruit Trees	Picked Fruit	Processed Fruit

Entities would need to exercise judgement while ascertaining if the activity falls under IAS 41. For instance, normal activities in a zoo or a gaming sanctuary would not fall under IAS 41, as there is no biological transformation. Similarly, whether stem-cell culture would fall under the ambit of IAS 41 would depend on whether there is a biological transformation.

Some time ago, there was a discussion as to whether bearer plants should be within the scope of IAS 41 or IAS 16. IAS 41 *Agriculture* currently requires all biological assets related to agricultural activity to be measured at fair value less costs to sell. This is based on the principle that the biological transformation that these assets undergo during their lifespan is best reflected by fair value measurement. However, there is a subset of biological assets, known as bearer plants, which are used solely to grow produce over several periods. At the end of their productive lives they are usually scrapped. Once a bearer plant is mature, apart from bearing produce, its biological transformation is no longer significant in generating future economic benefits. The only significant future economic benefits it generates come from the agricultural produce that it creates.

The IASB decided that bearer plants should be accounted for in the same way as property, plant and equipment in IAS 16 *Property, Plant and Equipment*, because their operation is similar to that of manufacturing.

Holmen

BIOLOGICAL ASSETS

The Group divides all its forest assets for accounting purposes into growing forests, which are recognised as biological assets at fair value, and land, which is stated at cost. Any changes in the fair value of the growing forests are recognised in the income statement. Holmen's assessment is that there are no relevant market prices available that can be used to value forest holdings as extensive as Holmen's. Valuation is therefore carried out by estimating the present value of expected future cash flows (after deduction of selling costs) from the growing forests. See Note 11. In the parent company, biological assets are valued in accordance with RFR 2. This means that biological assets classified as non-current assets are recognised at cost adjusted for revaluations taking into account the need, if any, for impairment in value. Felling rights are stated as inventories. They are acquired with a view to securing Holmen's raw material requirements through harvesting. No measurable biological change occurs between the acquisition date and harvesting.

Source: Holmen Annual Report 2013 Page 70

---

2. Measurement and Disclosures

IAS 41 requires biological assets to be measured on initial recognition and at each balance sheet date at their fair value less costs to sell, except in limited circumstances. There are two occasions where the standard permits departure from current fair value:

- at the early stage of an asset's life; and
- when fair value cannot be measured reliably on initial recognition.

Arriving at an appropriate Fair Value for biological assets as per the requirements of IFRS 13 could pose some challenges. Quoted prices in an active market may not be available and observable inputs could be minimal. In such instances, reliance on unobservable inputs would be high. Another factor, which would impact the appropriate fair valuation of biological assets, would be the fact that some biological assets are seasonal. What discount factor would an entity give to a biological asset that is classified as Inventory in the month of June but is sold in the month of December?

An entity that is new to IFRS and has to follow IAS 41 could find the disclosure requirements pretty intense as compared to their erstwhile disclosures.

Holmen

NOTE 11. BIOLOGICAL ASSETS

Forest assets are recognised in the consolidated accounts as growing forest, which is stated as a biological asset at fair value, and land, which is stated at cost. Holmen's assessment is that no relevant market prices are available that can be used to value forest holdings as extensive as Holmen's. The valuation is therefore made by calculating the present value of future expected cash flows from the growing forests. Fair value measurement is based on measurement level 3. This calculation of cash flows is made for the coming 100 years, which is regarded as the harvesting cycle of the forests. The cash flows are calculated on the basis of harvesting volumes according to Holmen's current harvesting plan and assessments of future price and cost changes. The cost of re-planting has been taken into account, because re-planting after harvesting is a statutory obligation. The cash flows are discounted using an interest rate of 5.5 per cent. In total, Holmen owns 1,034,000 hectares of productive forest land, with a volume of standing forest totalling 120 million m3 growing stock, solid over bark, According to the harvesting plan, valid from 2011, harvesting will amount to 3.2 million m3 sub per year, of which 0.2 million m3 sub will be biofuel in the form of branches and treetops. It is believed that this level will remain largely unchanged until 2030. Thereafter, harvesting is expected to increase gradually to over 4 million m3 sub per year by 2110. Around 40 per cent of the wood harvested consists of pulpwood that is sold to the pulp and paper industry, 50 per cent is timber sold to sawmills and the remainder mainly consists of branches and treetops, which are used primarily as forest fuel. The valuation is based on a long-term trend price that is on a par with the average price over the past 10 years but slightly higher than current market prices. The trend price is adjusted upwards annually by an inflation rate of 2 per cent. The cost forecast is based on present-day levels and is adjusted upwardly by just over 2 per cent per year. Holmen's forest holdings are reported at SEK 16 517 million before tax. A deferred tax liability of SEK 3 654 million is stated in relation to that figure. This represents the tax that is expected to be charged against the earnings from harvesting in the future. On that basis, the growing forest, net after tax, is stated at SEK 12 863 million.

Source: Holmen Annual Report 2013 Page 81

3. Impairment of Assets

IAS 36 *Impairment of Assets* is another Standard that would impact Agriculture. Most Agricultural activities depend on the weather, rains, temperature and other such natural resources for their growth and development. If there is too little rain, crops don't grow and if there is too much rain, crops get destroyed. There would be very clear internal as well as external indicators of impairment. Most Biological Assets are meant to be consumed within a particular time frame failing which their value could be eroded. It would appear that tests of Impairment would need to be much quicker for biological assets in the IFRS regime.

4.2.3 First time conversion

Presented below is an extract from the financial statements of Holmen when they first converted to IFRS.

Holmen

BIOLOGICAL ASSETS

The Group divides all its forest assets for accounting purposes into growing forests, which are recognised as biological assets at fair value, and land, which is stated at cost. Any changes in the fair value of the growing forests are recognised in the income statement. Holmen's assessment is that there are no relevant market prices available that can be used to value forest holdings as extensive as Holmen's. Valuation is therefore carried out by estimating the present value of expected future cash flows (after deduction of selling costs) from the growing forests.

In the parent company, biological assets are valued in accordance with RFR 2. This means that biological assets classified as non-current assets are recognised at cost adjusted for revaluations taking into account the need, if any, for impairment in value.

Felling rights are stated as inventories. They are acquired with a view to securing Holmen's raw material requirements through harvesting. No measurable biological change occurs between the acquisition date and harvesting.

ADOPTION OF IFRS

As of 1 January 2005, Holmen applies the International Financial Reporting Standards (IFRS) to its consolidated financial statements. This is a consequence of an EU directive that applies to all listed companies in the EU. Adoption of IFRS means that the comparative figures for 2004 have been adjusted, except for IAS 39, IFRS 4 and IFRS 5 in accordance with voluntary exception in IFRS 1. The rules for the adoption of IFRS and recomputation of figures can be found in IFRS 1 First-time Adoption of IFRS. The Swedish Financial Accounting Standards Council's recommendations have been harmonised with the IFRS rules in many areas. As far as Holmen is concerned, the adoption of IFRS has mainly involved the changes and adjustments commented on below.

IAS 19 *EMPLOYEE BENEFITS*

Holmen has been applying IAS 19 since 2003. The adoption of IFRS involves the zeroing as of 1 January 2004 of unrecognised actuarial gains and losses in respect of defined benefit pension plans. This has resulted in a reduction of MSEK 65 in the pension deficit (difference between pension assets and commitments under defined benefit pension plans), which reduced net financial liabilities by the same amount. After deduction of deferred tax, equity has increased by MSEK 47.

IAS 1 *PRESENTATION OF FINANCIAL STATEMENTS*

According to IAS 1, minority interests in the balance sheet are to be stated as a separate item within equity. However, Holmen has opted not to reclassify these, as the outstanding minority interests were acquired in March 2005.

IAS 39 *FINANCIAL INSTRUMENTS*

Recognition and Measurement

According to IAS 39, all financial assets and liabilities, including derivatives, shall be stated at either fair value or acquisition cost, depending on how they are classified. In the case of assets and liabilities that are stated at fair value, the revaluation result arising shall be stated in the income statement or taken against equity in the balance sheet, depending on whether or not hedge accounting is used. In Holmen's case, the primary change is that the fair value of financial assets and liabilities that are hedge accounted are stated in the balance sheet. Holmen uses hedge accounting in accordance with IAS 39 in respect of currency hedging of transaction and translation exposures, hedging of interest rate risk, and hedging of electricity price risk. Holmen applies the right to value liabilities at fair value according to the fair value option in the case of a loan that satisfies the applicable criteria. The loan has a fair value of MSEK 438 on 31 December and an acquisition cost of MSEK 452.

The introduction of IAS 39 means that working capital as at 1 January 2005 increased by MSEK 107, net financial debt by MSEK 60, deferred tax by MSEK 13 and equity by MSEK 34. The result stated in Holmen's accounts is largely unchanged in relation to past practice. The introduction of IAS 39 has therefore had an insignificant effect on the consolidated result for 2005.

IAS 41 *AGRICULTURE*

Holmen's forest holdings have earlier been stated at acquisition cost after adjustment for write-ups. According to IFRS, forest assets are to be divided into growing forests, which are stated in accordance with IAS 41, and land, which is stated in accordance with IAS 16. According to IAS 41, growing forest shall be valued and stated at fair value at the end of each accounting period. Changes in fair value are stated in the income statement. In the absence of market prices or other comparable valuation, biological assets shall be valued at the discounted value of the future cash flow from the assets. The land on which the forest is growing is valued at acquisition cost in accordance with IAS 16. The adoption of IFRS meant that the book value of Holmen's forest assets on 1 January 2004 increased from MSEK 6,301 to MSEK 8,661, of which growing forest represents MSEK 8,561. The deferred tax liability on forest assets at the same time rose from MSEK 1,715 to MSEK 2,397. Equity increased by MSEK 1,678. At the end of 2004, the value of growing forest was MSEK 8,622. Change in the value of the growing forest is taken into the income statement, which meant that for 2004 the operating profit increased by MSEK 60, in relation to the previous accounting principles. The tax charge has at the same time increased by MSEK 17, which corresponds to the change in deferred tax on the growing forest.

IFRS 3 *BUSINESS COMBINATIONS*

IFRS 3 means that goodwill is not subject to systematic depreciation. In Holmen's case, this means that the goodwill arising on the acquisition of Holmen Paper Madrid in 2000 is no longer depreciated according to plan. Instead, this goodwill will be reviewed annually to determine the need, if any, for a write-down in value. Goodwill on Holmen's balance sheet at 1 January 2004 amounted to MSEK 528. The operating profit for 2004 has improved by MSEK 32, in relation to previous accounting principles. Holmen has not recalculated acquisitions made before 1 January 2004. There were no acquisitions in 2004.

Key Impact Areas

- Identifying whether an Asset qualifies as a Biological Asset for IAS 41 to apply.
- Obtaining proper indicators for Fair Value on the basis of observable or non-observable inputs since these Assets may have previously been recorded at Cost.
- Ascertaining the future cash flows when there is an Impairment Test is triggered due to external factors such as weather.

4.3 AUTOMOTIVE

4.3.1 Overview

The automotive industry is capital intensive. They have a long supply chain. They have complicated agreements with suppliers. They keep incurring Research and Development costs and have to keep bringing out new models of vehicles. In case of defects in vehicles, they recall them and incur costs to rectify the defect.

4.3.2 IFRS Standards that could impact the industry

The following IFRS Standards could impact the automotive industry:

Standard	Description
IAS 16	*Property, Plant and Equipment*
IAS 36	*Intangible Assets*
IAS 18	*Revenue*
IAS 2	*Inventories*
IAS 37	*Provisions, Contingent Liabilities and Contingent Assets*

4.3.2.1 IAS 16 Property, Plant and Equipment

Constructing a plant to manufacture automobiles is a costly and time-consuming process. Car factories are huge, sprawling complexes that occupy acres of land which are dotted with different buildings. Property, plant and equipment is accounted for in accordance with IAS 16. All costs such as material costs, labour and related benefits, installation costs and site preparatory costs that are directly attributable to bringing an asset to the present condition and location necessary for its intended use are capitalised. However, costs that are not directly attributable, such as allocations of general overhead, including training costs, are not capitalised under IFRS. Accordingly, automotive entities, on conversion to IFRS may need to carefully review their asset capitalisation policies. In addition, entities reporting under IFRS are required to allocate the initial amount relating to an item of property, plant and equipment into its significant parts or "components" and depreciate each part separately. This may involve significant judgement on the part of the automotive entity.

Master Supply Agreements

However, car factories of the future are not expected to be located in huge, sprawling complexes. This is because car companies have discovered the art of outsourcing manufacture of various components of a car to different suppliers. Only a small portion of the actual car manufacturing process, if any at all, takes place in the factory. The car manufacturer and the supplier enter into Master Supply Agreements (MSA).

MSAs can bring in some complications in accounting for Property, Plant and Equipment. For instance, the car manufacturer could supply some tools to the component supplier which were capitalised in the books. The tools may never come back from the supplier as they are being used to manufacture a car component. The car manufacturer would have to go back to the Framework to test whether the tool meets the definition of an Asset.

Daimler

PROPERTY, PLANT AND EQUIPMENT

Property, plant and equipment are measured at acquisition or manufacturing costs less accumulated depreciation. If necessary, accumulated impairment losses are recognised.

The costs of internally produced equipment and facilities include all direct costs and allocable overheads. Acquisition or manufacturing costs include the estimated costs, if any, of dismantling and removing the item and restoring the site. Plant and equipment under finance leases are stated at the lower of present value of minimum lease payments or fair value less the respective accumulated depreciation and any accumulated impairment losses. Depreciation expense is recognised using the straight-line method. The residual value of the asset is considered.

Source: Daimler 2013 Annual Report, page 199

Intangible Assets

Due to the very nature of the car industry, there is a need to invest in Research and Development to bring out new models of cars or to alter known defects in existing models. IAS 38 provides guidance on capitalising Research and Development costs and reflecting them as Intangible Assets. Research costs (original investigation undertaken to gain new knowledge) are expensed as incurred. Development costs (application of research to new or substantially improved products) are capitalised provided that they meet specific criteria. Car factories would need to be extremely careful in applying this judgement.

Daimler

OTHER INTANGIBLE ASSETS

Intangible assets acquired are measured at cost less accumulated amortisation. If necessary, accumulated impairment losses are recognised.

Intangible assets with indefinite lives are reviewed annually to determine whether indefinite-life assessment continues to be appropriate. If not, the change in the useful-life assessment from indefinite to finite is made on a prospective basis.

Intangible assets other than development costs with finite useful lives are generally amortised on a straight-line basis over their useful lives (three to ten years) and are tested for impairment whenever there is an indication that the intangible asset may be impaired. The amortisation period for intangible assets with finite useful lives is reviewed at least at each year end. Changes in expected useful lives are treated as changes in accounting estimates. The amortisation expense on intangible assets with finite useful lives is recorded in functional costs.

Development costs for vehicles and components are recognised if the conditions for capitalisation according to IAS 38 are met. Subsequent to initial recognition, the asset is carried at cost less accumulated amortisation and accumulated impairment losses. Capitalised development costs include all direct costs and allocable overheads and are amortised on a straight-line basis over the expected product life cycle (a maximum of ten years). Amortisation of capitalised development costs is an element of manufacturing costs and is allocated to those vehicles and components by which they were generated and is included in cost of sales when the inventory (vehicles) is sold.

Source: Daimler Annual Report 2013, page 194

Revenue Recognition

As per the mandate of IAS 18, revenue from the sale of products is recognised when substantially all risks and rewards from ownership of the goods are transferred to the customer. In the normal course, revenue would be recognised when the vehicle is handed over to the customer since it is generally felt that physical delivery is the best example of transfer of risks and rewards. However, the concept of risks and rewards could change if the vehicle is sold to/by a manufacturer, wholesaler or retailer. The terms of the contract would need to be looked in detail to determine recognition of revenue. This could prove to be a bit complicated due to aggressive selling tactics by dealers and sales dumping by manufacturers.

Multiple-component arrangements

It is normal for car companies to provide a certain number of free services and warranties. IAS 18 states that when the selling price of a product includes an identifiable amount for subsequent servicing, that amount is deferred and recognised as revenue over the period during which the service is performed. Conversely, the recognition criteria are applied to two or more transactions together when they are linked in such a way that the commercial effect cannot be understood without reference to the series of transactions as a whole. For example, an entity may sell goods and, at the same time, enter into a separate agreement to repurchase the goods at a later date, thus negating the substantive effect of the transaction; in such a case, the two transactions are dealt with together.

Car manufacturers would need to closely look at both their contracts with suppliers and customers as well as the provisions of IFRS 15 to ascertain when and how much revenue they would need to recognise on the sale of a car to a customer with services bundled in.

Discount arrangements and incentives

An automotive entity may provide incentives to a customer as part of an arrangement. Examples of sales incentives offered by a seller include cash incentives, discounts and volume rebates, free/discounted goods or services and vouchers. In many cases the arrangement or incentive may need to be identified as a separate component of the transaction, with revenue being attributed and accounted for separately; in other cases it may be appropriate to deduct the amount of the incentive from revenue.

Revenue Recognition at Daimler Benz

ACCOUNTING POLICIES REVENUE RECOGNITION

Revenue from sales of vehicles, service parts and other related products is recognised when the risks and rewards of ownership of the goods are transferred to the customer, the amount of revenue can be estimated reliably and collectability is reasonably assured. Revenue is recognised net of sales reductions such as cash discounts and sales incentives granted. Daimler uses sales incentives in response to a number of market and product factors, including pricing actions and incentives offered by competitors, the amount of excess industry production capacity, the intensity of market competition, and consumer demand for the product. The Group may offer a variety of sales incentive programmes at a point in time, including cash offers to dealers and consumers, lease subsidies which reduce the consumers' monthly lease payment, or reduced financing rate programmes offered to costumers. Revenue from receivables from financial services is recognised using the effective interest method. When loans are issued below market rates, related receivables are recognised at present value and revenue is reduced for the interest incentive granted. If subsidised leasing fees are agreed upon in connection with finance leases, revenue from the sale of a vehicle is reduced by the amount of the interest incentive granted. The Group offers an extended, separately priced warranty for certain products. Revenue from these contracts is deferred and recognised into income over the contract period in proportion to the costs expected to be incurred based on historical information. In circumstances in which there is insufficient historical information, income from extended warranty contracts is recognised on a straight-line basis. A loss on these contracts is recognised in the current period if the sum of the expected costs for services under the contract exceeds unearned revenue. For transactions with multiple deliverables, such as when vehicles are sold with free or reduced-in-price service programmes, the Group allocates revenue to the various elements based on their estimated fair values. Sales in which the Group guarantees the minimum resale value of the product are accounted for as an operating lease. The guarantee of the resale value may take the form of an obligation by Daimler to pay any deficiency between the proceeds the customer receives upon resale and the guaranteed amount, or an obligation to reacquire the vehicle after a certain period of time at a set price. Gains or losses from the resale of these vehicles are included in gross profit in the consolidated statement of income. Revenue from operating leases is recognised on a straight-line basis over the lease term. Among the assets subject to operating leases are Group products which are purchased by Daimler Financial Services from independent third-party dealers and leased to customers. After revenue recognition from the sale of the vehicles to independent third-party dealers, these vehicles create further revenue from leasing and remarketing as a result of lease contracts entered into. The Group estimates that the revenue recognised following the sale of vehicles to dealers equals approximately the additions to leased assets at Daimler Financial Services. Additions to leased assets at Daimler Financial Services were approximately €8 billion in 2013 (2012: approximately €8 billion).

Source: Daimler Benz Annual Report 2013, page 197

Leased Assets

It is normal for car manufacturing companies to have separate finance arms to provide finance to customers to purchase the cars they sell. Normally, the agreements with the customers are operating leases for the car manufacturer who would also have to look into the provisions of IAS 18 to recognise interest income and any fees that it receives for the financing transaction. The accounting for these would become relevant to the car manufacturer since the financing company would invariably be a subsidiary and hence would need to be consolidated as per the requirements of IFRS 10.

Financing being a risk-based business, there will be an impact of customers not paying up for which a provision would need to be made.

Daimler

EQUIPMENT ON OPERATING LEASES

Daimler regularly reviews the factors determining the values of its leased vehicles. In particular, it is necessary to estimate the residual values of vehicles at the end of their leases, which constitute a substantial part of the expected future cash flows from leased assets. In this context, assumptions have to be made regarding the future supply of and demand for vehicles, as well as the development of vehicle prices. Those assumptions are determined either by qualified estimates or by expertise provided by third parties; qualified estimates are based, as far as they are publicly available, on external data with consideration of internally available additional information such as historical experience of price developments and recent sale prices. The residual values thus determined serve as a basis for systematic depreciation; changes in residual values lead either to prospective adjustments to the systematic depreciation or, in the case of a significant drop in expected residual values, to impairment.

If systematic depreciation is prospectively adjusted, changes in estimates of residual values do not have a direct effect but are equally distributed over the remaining periods of the lease contracts.

COLLECTABILITY OF RECEIVABLES FROM FINANCIAL SERVICES

The Group regularly estimates the risk of default on receivables from financial services. Many factors are taken into consideration in this context, including historical loss experience, the size and composition of certain portfolios, current economic events and conditions and the estimated fair values and adequacy of collateral. Changes in economic conditions can lead to changes in our customers' creditworthiness and to changes in used vehicle prices, which would have a direct effect on the market values of the vehicles assigned as collateral. Changes to the estimation and assessment of these factors influence the allowance for credit losses with a resulting impact on the Group's net profit.

Source: Daimler Annual Report 2013, page 204

Decommissioning and restoration liabilities under IFRS – contractual and constructive

Car factories are normally set up on land acquired from the Government. In many instances, the Government may insist that the car manufacturer return the lands to the Government at the end of a specified period in "broom-clean" condition. This would entail the car manufacturer incurring significant costs to decommission the Plant and restore the land to "broom-clean" condition. The car manufacturer would need to account for both a liability as well as an Asset for the amount of Decommissioning and Restoration Costs. They would also need to take into account the provisions of IFRIC 1 *Changes in Existing Decommissioning, Restoration and Similar Liabilities*.

As per IAS 37 *Provisions, Contingent Liabilities and Contingent Assets*, entities recognise obligations, both contractual and constructive, as part of the carrying amount of an asset. Liabilities for automotive entities often include a significant environmental component from storage tanks and chemicals used in the manufacturing process. An accurate estimate of the liability needs to be done.

Recall of Vehicles

It is the norm these days for automotive manufacturers to recall vehicles to rectify some defect in the vehicles. This would involve some costs. Automotive companies need to estimate if they would need to make a provision for these costs are per IAS 37. They key would be to determine the timing of when the current obligation from past events occurs and create a provision for possible expenses accordingly. Automotive companies should be aware of the fact that creating a general provision for possible expenses on recall of vehicles would impact their credibility and thereby possible future sales.

Daimler

A provision is recognised when a liability to third parties has been incurred, an outflow of resources is probable and the amount of the obligation can be reasonably estimated. The amount recognised as a provision represents the best estimate of the obligation at the balance sheet date. Provisions with an original maturity of more than one year are discounted to the present value of the expenditures expected to settle the obligation at the end of the reporting period. Provisions are regularly reviewed and adjusted as further information becomes available or circumstances change.

A provision for expected warranty costs is recognised when a product is sold, upon lease inception, or when a new warranty programme is initiated. Estimates for accrued warranty costs are primarily based on historical experience.

Daimler records the fair value of an asset retirement obligation from the period in which the obligation is incurred.

Restructuring provisions are set up in connection with programmes that materially change the scope of business performed by a segment or business unit or the manner in which business is conducted. In most cases, restructuring expenses include termination benefits and compensation payments due to the termination of agreements with suppliers and dealers. Restructuring provisions are recognised when the Group has a detailed formal plan that has either commenced implementation or been announced.

Source: Daimler Annual Report 2013, page 203

4.3.2.2 IAS 2 Inventories

As car manufacturing is a capital-intensive industry, players in this industry would carry a lot of inventory on their books. The Inventory could be of different types and values. The list of individual items could also run into thousands. Inventory Management is a very critical task for a car manufacturer. IAS 2 defines Inventory and mandates valuing it at cost or Net Realisable Value whichever is lower.

Net realisable value is the estimated selling price less the estimated costs of completion and sale. When net realisable value is less than cost, inventory is written down to net realisable value. Conversely, when the value of an item of inventory that has been written down subsequently increases, the write-down is reversed. Inventory write-downs are common in the industry due to the risks implicit in long-term master supply agreements prevalent in the industry and the need to hold tens of thousands of different spare parts for possible sale to consumers for extended periods.

Daimler

Inventories are measured at the lower of cost and net realisable value. The net realisable value is the estimated selling price less any remaining costs to sell. The cost of inventories is generally based on the specific identification method and includes costs incurred in acquiring the inventories and bringing them to their existing location and condition. Costs for large numbers of inventories that are interchange-able are allocated under the average cost formula. In the case of manufactured inventories and work in progress, cost also includes production overheads based on normal capacity.

Source: Daimler Annual Report 2013, page 200

Key Takeaways

- Accounting for Property, Plant and Equipment
- Accounting for the impact of Master Supply Agreements
- Accounting for Intangible Assets
- Provision for possible expenses on recall of vehicles

4.4 BANKING

4.4.1 Overview

Banking is a highly regulated sector with a regulator in each country overseeing the functioning of banks. Accounting in a banking industry should not only look at complying with accounting standards but also with the diktats of the regulator.

Banks thrive (or deprive themselves) on Financial Instruments. For all practical purposes, their financial statements reflect the impact of transactions in Financial Instruments. The IFRS Standards on Financial Instruments would have a significant impact on the banking industry.

4.4.2 IFRS Standards that could impact the industry

IAS 32, 39, IFRS 7 & IFRS 9	*Financial Instruments:* Recognition, Measurement, Derecognition and Disclosures & Hedge Accounting
IAS 36	Impairment of Assets
IFRS 10	*Consolidated Financial Statements*
IAS 17	*Leases*

4.4.2.1 IAS 32, 39, IFRS 7 and IFRS 9

Financial Instruments

To the treasury function of a bank or a financial institution, financial instruments are almost like inventories.

Financial instruments are initially measured at fair value, which most often, but not always, is the transaction price. After initial recognition they are measured at fair value, amortised cost, or cost. "Amortised cost" is a concept similar to cost, but involves adjusting the balance sheet amount for the effect of calculating the yield on certain financial instruments by spreading fees, transaction costs and discounts or premiums over the lives of those instruments.

The types of financial assets that can be accounted for under amortised cost are mostly limited to debt instruments held to maturity and those not quoted in an active market. Financial assets that do not meet the amortised cost criteria are accounted for at fair value with gains and losses recognised either in profit or loss or in other comprehensive income.

Derivatives are generally accounted for at fair value with gains and losses generally recognised in profit or loss. If derivatives are "embedded" in other contracts (those contracts may or may not be financial instruments) they may have to be separated and accounted for separately from the host contract, at fair value, with gains and losses recognised in profit or loss.

Equity investments are generally accounted for at fair value. There is a limited exemption for unlisted equity investments when fair value cannot be reliably measured, which are accounted for at cost less impairment.

Impact of IFRS 9

The standard removes the "cost" accounting category for investments in equity instruments and introduces new classification criteria. Under its requirements, financial assets are eligible for accounting at amortised cost only if they are held within a business model whose objective is to collect contractual cash flows and their contractual terms give rise to cash flows that are solely payments of principal and interest.

Financial assets that do not meet the criteria for amortised cost accounting are measured at fair value with gains and losses recognised in profit or loss. For equity investments, an election can be made to recognise gains and losses in other comprehensive income. Accounting for financial liabilities remains similar to that in IAS 39 except that the effect of changes in credit risk on financial liabilities designated as at fair value is generally recognised in other comprehensive income. Requirements relating to derecognition of financial instruments are complex, requiring a comprehensive analysis of the transaction. The requirements are a mixture of "risk and rewards" and "control" models.

Impairment of Assets

The impairment of financial assets is currently measured on an "incurred loss" basis. This means that no impairment allowance can be established at initial recognition of a financial asset. Impairment is recognised if objective evidence indicates that an asset is impaired due to events occurring after initial recognition. An impairment loss is measured differently for financial assets accounted for at amortised cost than those accounted for at fair value with gains and losses recognised in other comprehensive income (the latter measurement category is called Available for Sale, or AFS). For financial assets measured at amortised cost, the impairment loss is measured as the difference between an asset's carrying amount and the present value of the estimated future cash flows, discounted at the asset's original rate of return. For AFS assets impairment is measured as the difference between acquisition cost and fair value.

Expected Losses model

As a part of the amendments to IFRS 9, the IASB has replaced the incurred loss approach with an approach based on expected losses (i.e. expected cash flow approach). Under this model the initial estimate of credit losses would be spread over the expected lives of the financial assets as part of the recognition of return from those assets. Any subsequent changes to the initial estimate would be recognised immediately in profit or loss. Extensive additional disclosures are also proposed. The proposals are likely to be very challenging for banks to implement. Unlike IAS 39, the new IFRS 9 will only require an impairment assessment on assets measured at amortised cost; therefore, the expected cash flow model would become the single impairment model for financial assets.

Banks normally have their own robust internal mechanisms to estimate credit losses. A very basic example of the differences between the expected losses approach and the incurred loss approach is given below.

Assume that a finance company has a portfolio of $500,000 of Receivables. The ageing schedule of the receivables is provided in the example. Out of these, the company has subsequently come to know that one debtor A who is in the >365 days bracket has filed for bankruptcy. Another debtor B who is in the >300 days bracket is due $50,000 but has agreed to pay $25,000 in full and final settlement to which the finance company has agreed.

The company has made its own estimates of the expected losses from receivables. The differences between IAS 39 and IFRS 9 is captured below:

Portfolio breakdown	Amount	Incurred Loss	Expected Loss	Loss
	$	$		$
>365 days	200,000	40,000	5%	48,000
>300 days	100,000	25,000	4%	28,000
>180 days	50,000		3%	1,500
>120 days	50,000		2%	1,000
>90 days	45,000		1%	450
>60 days	25,000		1%	250
>30 days	30,000		1%	300
	500,000	65,000		79500
		IAS 39		IFRS 9

Disclosures

IFRS 7 *Financial Instruments: Disclosures* requires extensive qualitative and quantitative information explaining the significance of financial instruments to an entity's financial statements, its exposure to risk and how this exposure is managed. The financial crisis has had a significant impact on the banking sector, and there is considerable demand from financial statement users to improve the quality of the disclosures, including explanation of significant management judgement and sensitivity analysis, a move away from so-called "Boiler Plate" compliance with the standard. Some of the information required by IFRS 7 may not be readily available and new systems, processes and internal controls may need to be put in place to collect it.

Hedge Accounting

Hedge accounting is often used to minimise profit or loss fluctuation arising due to volatility in foreign exchange, interest rates, and other changes in fair values of certain financial instruments and other non-financial items. As under IFRS generally all derivatives have to be accounted for at fair value, with gains and losses recognised in profit or loss, hedge accounting aims to mitigate profit or loss impact in respect of the portion of the hedge that is effective.

There are three types of hedging relationships under IAS 39: fair value hedges, cash flow hedges and hedges of a net investment in a foreign operation. Accounting implications of each are as follows:

For fair value hedges, the gains and losses relating to both the hedged item and the hedging instrument are recognised in profit or loss.

For cash flows hedges and hedges of a net investment in foreign operation, the gains and losses on the hedging item are recognised in other comprehensive income.

In addition, IFRS specifically allows some types of portfolio hedges in which many derivatives can be used to hedge many assets/liabilities in a single relationship. This so-called "macro-hedging" can be very useful in minimising documentation requirements.

A hedging relationship only qualifies for hedge accounting if certain criteria are met, including formal designation and documentation of the hedging relationship at inception of the hedge. It should also be demonstrated, both at the outset and throughout the existence that the hedge is expected to be and has been highly effective, that is, remaining within the 80–125 per cent range. The initial documentation and subsequent effectiveness testing can be time consuming and systems-based solutions may be helpful in monitoring the effectiveness of the hedging relationships.

Hedge accounting requirements are detailed and prescriptive. They define the items that can be hedged (including components and risks) and the allowed hedging instruments. Care needs to be taken to ensure that hedge relationships are identified in a manner that meets the requirements of the standard and, in particular, that the effectiveness tests are designed in a way that minimises the risk of future hedge relationships failure.

4.4.2.2 IFRS 10

Consolidated Financial Statements

Consolidated financial statements should include all subsidiaries of the parent company. The definition of a subsidiary focuses on the concept of control, which is defined in IFRS 10 as the power to govern the financial and operating policies of an entity so as to obtain benefits from its activities.

IFRS contains specific guidance on the application of the control concept to SPEs, as many SPEs have pre-determined objectives and so it is more difficult to determine who controls them. An SPE is defined as an entity created to accomplish a narrow and well-defined objective (e.g. securitisation of receivables). In practice, judgement is often needed to conclude whether an entity should be regarded as an SPE.

Presentation: Debt vs. Equity

IAS 32 *Financial Instruments: Presentation* addresses the liability or equity classification of financial instruments. The classification is dependent on the substance of the contractual arrangements rather than legal form.

In general, an instrument is classified as a financial liability if it contains a contractual obligation to transfer cash or another financial asset, or if it may be settled in a variable number of the entity's own equity instruments. An obligation to transfer cash may arise from a requirement to repay principal or to pay interest or dividends. An equity instrument is any contract that evidences a residual interest in the assets of an entity after deducting all of its liabilities.

An exception to the rules are puttable instruments, which give the holder the right to put the instruments back to the issuer for cash or another financial asset or instruments imposing an obligation on an entity only in liquidation. If certain criteria are met, then such instruments are classified as equity.

Some contracts may contain both equity and liability components, which may have to be accounted for separately. An example is a convertible bond that comprises a debt instrument and an equity conversion option. The equity conversion option would require analysis to determine whether it meets the definition of equity.

This is an example of another area that requires contract-by-contract analysis during the IFRS conversion process.

In general, an instrument is classified as a financial liability if it contains a contractual obligation to transfer cash or another financial asset, or if it may be settled in a variable number of the entity's own equity instruments. An obligation to transfer cash may arise from a requirement to repay principal to pay interest or dividends. An equity instrument is any contract that evidences a residual interest in the assets of an entity after deducting all of its liabilities.

An exception to the rule is puttable instruments, which gives the holder the right to put the instruments back to the issuer for cash or another financial asset.

4.4.2.3 IAS 17 Leases

Accounting for leases under IFRS currently depends on whether a lease is a finance or an operating lease. Finance leases are accounted for by the lessor as financing transactions. Operating leases require the lessor to continue to recognise the leased assets on its balance sheet. Classification of a lease does not depend on which party has legal ownership of the leased asset, but rather on which party has substantially all of the risks and rewards of ownership. Lease accounting under IFRS may affect those banks that under local GAAP keep assets off-balance sheet as operating leases, when the substance of the arrangement is that the bank obtains substantially all of the risks and rewards incidental to ownership of the asset. As a result, many more leases could be recognised on the balance sheet upon conversion to IFRS. Determining whether an arrangement constitutes an operating or a finance lease may require judgement.

In addition, an entity may enter into an arrangement comprising a transaction or a series of transactions that do not take the legal form of a lease but convey the right to use an asset. Such arrangements would have to be reviewed on conversion to IFRS to determine whether they contain a lease and therefore whether lease accounting is appropriate.

4.4.2.4 IFRS 4 Insurance Contracts

IFRS has minimal guidance on accounting for insurance contracts. IFRS 4 *Insurance Contracts* only provides minimum accounting criteria, which in most cases allow companies to continue using existing GAAP and require some specific disclosures. However, IFRS 4 does define an insurance contract and some contracts entered into by an insurance business may not meet the definition of an insurance contract and instead may have to be accounted for as a financial instrument under IAS 39. An insurance contract is defined as one "under which one party accepts significant insurance risk from another party (policyholder) by agreeing to compensate the policyholder if a specified uncertain future event adversely affects the policyholder." For example, insurers often offer what are substantially investment products in which mortality or other insurance risk is minimal or non-existent. Such instruments are required to be accounted for as financial instruments.

4.4.3 First time conversion

We present here the differences between IFRS and UK GAAP that Barclays Bank identified when they first converted to IFRS in 2005.

UK GAAP	IFRS
(a) Consolidation and presentation The Group financial statements consolidate the assets, liabilities and the profits and losses of subsidiaries using the acquisition method. Entities which do not qualify as subsidiaries but which in substance give rise to benefits that are in essence no different from those that would arise were the entity a subsidiary, are included in the consolidated financial statements. In accordance with FRS 5, securitisation transactions which qualified are accounted for on the basis of linked presentation.	The Group financial statements consolidate the assets, liabilities and the profits and losses of subsidiaries using the acquisition method. A subsidiary is an entity which the Group controls, including special purpose entities which are in substance controlled by the Group. Linked presentation is not available under IFRS. Therefore, the gross assets and the related funding are presented separately.
(b) Life assurance In order to reflect the different nature of the shareholders' and policyholders' interests in the retail long-term assurance business, the value of the long-term assurance business attributable to other shareholders is included in Other assets and the assets and liabilities attributable to policyholders are classified under separate headings in the consolidated balance sheet. The value of the shareholders' interest in the retail long-term assurance fund represents an estimate of the net present value of the profits inherent in the in-force policies, (embedded value accounting). All life assurance products are accounted for in the same way; there is no distinction between investment contracts and insurance contracts.	The retail long-term assurance business is consolidated on a line-by-line basis with assets, liabilities and income and expenditure, whether attributable to shareholders or attributable to policyholders, being included in the lines that reflect their nature. In accordance with IFRS from 2005, life assurance products are divided into investment contracts, which are accounted for under IAS 39 and insurance contracts, which under IFRS 4 continue to be accounted for under UK GAAP. The life fund is closed to new business and the volume of contracts which fall to be accounted for as insurance contracts under IFRS is not significant. Therefore, it was considered more appropriate to change the accounting policy for insurance contracts to a Modified Statutory Solvency Basis. This change will allow the insurance contracts to be accounted for on a similar basis to investment contracts from 2005. This change in policy applies from 1st January 2004 and the Modified Statutory Solvency Basis has been applied to all contracts, whether they will be classified as insurance contracts or as investment contracts in 2005.
(c) Investments in associated companies and joint ventures Investments in associated companies and joint ventures are accounted for using the equity method where the Group has the ability to exert significant influence and actually does so. Where incurred, losses are recognised in full.	Investments in associates and joint ventures are accounted for using the equity method where the Group has the ability to exert significant influence or control jointly. Losses are recognised up to the point where the investment in the entity or joint venture has been eliminated, and subsequent profits only to the extent that unrecognised cumulative losses have been made good.

Before using the equity accounting method, adjustments are made to ensure that the results of associates and joint ventures have been prepared based on Group accounting policies. The difference between accounts prepared using UK GAAP policies and IFRS policies has resulted in a restatement of the investments in associates and joint ventures as at 1st January 2004.

(d) Goodwill

Goodwill arising on acquisitions of subsidiaries and associated companies and joint ventures is capitalised and amortised through the profit and loss account on a straight-line basis over its expected economic life. Capitalised goodwill is written off when judged to be impaired. Prior to 1998, goodwill arising on the acquisition of subsidiaries was eliminated directly against reserves.

Goodwill arising on acquisitions of subsidiaries and associates and joint ventures is capitalised and tested annually for impairment.

Amounts recognised in the UK GAAP balance sheet at 1st January 2004 have been carried forward without adjustment into the balance sheet prepared in accordance with IFRS as deemed cost after being tested for impairment. Goodwill previously written off to reserves in accordance with UK GAAP has not been reinstated on the balance sheet. Goodwill amortised under UK GAAP in 2004 has been written back in the 2004 IFRS financial statements.

(e) Share-based payment

Where shares are purchased, the difference between the purchase price and any contribution made by the employee is charged to the profit and loss account in the period to which it relates. Where shares are issued or options granted, the charge made to the profit and loss account is the difference between the fair value at the time the award is made and any contribution made by the employee. For these purposes, fair value is equal to intrinsic value.

An annual charge is made in the income statement for share options and other share-based payments based on the fair value of options granted or shares awarded on the date of the grant or award. This charge is spread over the period the employees' services are received, which is the vesting period. The fair value of options granted is determined using option pricing models.

(f) Pensions and other post-retirement benefits

Pension costs, based on actuarial assumptions, are calculated so as to allocate the cost of providing benefits over the average remaining service lives of the employees.

For defined benefit schemes, an actuarial valuation of the scheme obligation and the fair value of the plan assets are made annually and the difference between fair value of the plan assets and the present value of the defined benefit obligation at the balance sheet date, together with adjustments for any unrecognised actuarial losses and past service cost is recognised as a liability in the balance sheet.

Cumulative actuarial gains and losses in excess of the greater of 10% of the plan assets or 10% of the obligations of the plan are recognised in the income statement over the remaining average service lives of the employees of the related plan, on a straight-line basis.

At 1st January 2004, pension assets and liabilities have been recognised in full.

(g) Intangible assets other than goodwill

The Group writes off the cost of computer software unless the software is required to facilitate the use of new hardware. Capitalised amounts are included with the hardware within Fixed assets.

IFRS requires the capitalisation of both external and directly related internal costs where the software will result in a directly measurable Intangible asset. Amounts capitalised are amortised over their estimated useful lives. Computer software is amortised at a rate of 20-33% per year.

Where software developed is not integral to the related hardware, the costs are classified as an intangible asset.

At 1st January 2004, qualifying amounts previously written off under UK GAAP have been recognised as intangible assets and the 2004 income statement has been adjusted accordingly.

For acquisitions arising after 1st January 2004, intangible assets which are required to be recognised separately from goodwill in accordance with IFRS 3 have been transferred from goodwill to intangible assets as at the date of acquisition.

Intangible assets acquired before 1st January 2004 have been reclassified from goodwill to intangible assets.

(h) Financial guarantees

Credit related instruments (other than credit derivatives) are treated as contingent liabilities and these are not shown on the balance sheet unless, and until, the Group is called upon to make a payment under the instrument. Fees received for providing these instruments are taken to profit over the life of the instrument and reflected in fees and commissions receivable.

Financial guarantees (other than credit derivatives) are initially recognised in the financial statements at fair value on the date that the guarantee was given. Subsequent to initial recognition, the Group's liabilities under such guarantees are measured at the higher of the initial measurement, less amortisation calculated to recognise in the income statement the fee income earned over the period, and the best estimate of the expenditure required to settle any financial obligation arising as a result of the guarantees at the balance sheet date.

(i) Leasing

Group as Lessor

Assets leased to customers under agreements which transfer substantially all the risks and rewards of ownership other than legal title are classed as finance leases. All other leases are classified as operating leases.

Amounts due from lessees under finance leases are recorded as Loans and advances to customers at the amount of the Group's net investment in the lease.

Finance lease income is recognised so as to give a constant periodic rate of return on the net cash investment in the lease taking into account tax payments and receipts associated with the lease.

Group as Lessor

Assets leased to customers under agreements which transfer substantially all the risks and rewards of ownership other than legal title are classified as finance leases. All other leases are classified as operating leases.

Amounts due from lessees under finance leases are recorded as Loans and advances to customers at the amount of the Group's net investment in the lease.

Finance lease income is recognised so as to give a constant rate of return on the net cash investment, without taking account of tax payments and receipts ("the pre-tax actuarial method").

Rental income from operating leases is recognised on a straight-line basis over the term of the lease unless another systematic basis is more appropriate.

Group as Lessee

Assets held on finance leases are capitalised where the lease transfers the risks and rewards of ownership to the Group. This is achieved generally where the lease payments, when discounted at the rate of interest implicit in the lease, constitute substantially all, generally not less than 90%, of the fair value of the leased asset at the date of the inception of the lease, and the primary lease term equates to the useful life of the asset. Leases related to land and buildings do not qualify for capitalisation, since the useful life of land is not finite.

Lease incentives are spread over the period to the next rent review

(j) Dividends

Dividends declared after the period end are recorded in the period to which they relate.

(k) Deferred tax

Deferred tax is provided in full for all material timing differences that have not reversed at the balance sheet date. Provision is not made for specific items which are not expected to result in taxable income in the future, namely gains on the revaluation of property and the unremitted earnings of subsidiary and associated companies.

(l) Other credit risk provisions

Provision balances for bad and doubtful debts include provisions raised with respect to undrawn contractually committed facilities and guarantees.

(m) Property, plant and equipment

Property, plant and equipment is carried at either original cost or subsequent valuation, less depreciation calculated on the revalued amount where applicable. From 1st January 2000, following the introduction of FRS 15, the revalued book amounts were retained without subsequent revaluation subject to the requirement to test for impairment.

Depreciation is charged on the cost or revalued amounts of freehold and long leasehold properties over their estimated economic lives.

The assets held for operating leases are included within the Group's property, plant and equipment and depreciated over their useful economic lives. Lease income is recognised on a straight-line basis over the term of the lease unless another systematic basis is more appropriate.

Group as Lessee

Assets held on finance leases are capitalised where the lease transfers the risks and rewards of ownership to the Group. The conditions for capitalisation are the same as UK GAAP, except that IFRS requires the land and buildings elements of leases to be assessed separately to determine whether the buildings element should be capitalised. This has not resulted in any significant change to the classification or measurement of assets or liabilities arising from finance leases where the Group is lessee.

Lease incentives are spread over the term of the lease.

Dividends are recorded in the period in which they are approved by the Company's shareholders.

Deferred tax is provided in full based on the concept of temporary differences, including items such as the revaluation of property and the unremitted earnings of subsidiaries and associated companies where the Group is not able to control their distribution policies.

Provisions raised with respect to undrawn contractually committed facilities and guarantees (other credit risk provisions) are presented separately from impairment losses on loans and advances.

In 2004, the other credit risk provisions have been presented separately from provision balances for bad and doubtful debts. However, the measurement of these provisions is unchanged from UK GAAP.

The carrying value of property, plant and equipment included in the UK GAAP balance sheet at 1st January 2004 has been carried forward into the IFRS balance sheet without adjustment as deemed cost. Depreciation is charged in a manner consistent with UK GAAP.

(n) Derivatives and hedge accounting

Derivatives used for hedging purposes are measured on an accruals basis consistent with the assets, liabilities, positions or future cash flows being hedged. The gains and losses on these instruments (arising from changes in fair value) are not recognised in the profit and loss account immediately as they arise. Such gains are either not recognised in the balance sheet or are recognised and carried forward. When the hedged transaction occurs, the gain or loss is recognised in the profit and loss account at the same time as the hedged item.

Derivatives that are not hedge accounted are recorded at fair value, with changes in fair value recorded in the profit and loss account.

Products which contain embedded derivatives are valued with reference to the total product inclusive of the derivative element.

IAS 39 requires all derivatives to be recorded at fair value. Provided all hedge accounting conditions are met and the hedging relationship is deemed to be effective, the derivative may be designated as a fair value hedge, cash flow hedge or hedge of a net investment in a foreign operation. The change in value of the fair value hedge is recorded in income along with the change in fair value, relating to the hedged risk, of the hedged asset or liability. The change in value of a cash flow hedge is recorded in equity, to the extent it is effective and recycled to income as the hedged cash flows affect the income statement. The change in value of a net investment hedge is recorded in the translation reserve to the extent the hedge is effective and only released to the income statement when the underlying investment is sold.

As at 1st January 2005, all hedging derivatives have been recognised at fair value and adjustments have been made to hedged items where fair value hedge accounting will be applied. Hedges have been designated and documented in compliance with IFRS and, where possible, US GAAP with hedge accounting applied from that date. Where hedges were in place under UK GAAP that have not been designated as hedges under IFRS, adjustments have been made to the hedged item or equity to reflect the hedged position as at 31st December 2004.

Some hybrid contracts contain both a derivative and a non-derivative component. In such cases, the derivative component is termed an embedded derivative. Where the economic characteristics and risks of the embedded derivative are not closely related to those of the host contract, and the host contract itself is not carried at fair value, the embedded derivative is bifurcated and reported at fair value with gains and losses being recognised in the income statement.

At 1st January 2005, all embedded derivatives or the whole contracts containing embedded derivatives have been included on the balance sheet at fair value.

(o) Classification and measurement of financial instruments

Financial instruments are generally divided into banking book, which are carried at cost, and trading book, which are carried at fair value.

Positions in investment debt securities and investments in equity shares are stated at cost less provision for diminution in value. Investment securities are those intended for use on a continuing basis by the Group.

Classification	Measurement basis
Held to maturity	Amortised cost less impairment Amortised cost less
Loan or receivable	impairment
Available for sale	Fair value – gains and
Fair value through profit or loss	losses included in shareholders' equity until disposal or impairment
	Fair value – gains and losses included in the income statement

Financial liabilities are classified as held for trading or are carried at amortised cost.

In addition, in certain circumstances financial assets and liabilities may be designated as fair valued through profit and loss at initial acquisition.

Investment securities and equity shares are generally classified as available for sale.

The best evidence of the fair value of a financial instrument at initial recognition is the transaction price, unless the fair value of that instrument is evidenced by comparison with other observable current market transactions in the same instrument or is based on a valuation technique whose variables include only data from observable markets.

At 1st January 2005, financial instruments have been classified and measured in accordance with IAS 39. In general, financial instruments included in the trading book under UK GAAP have been classified as held for trading, banking book loans and receivables have been classified as loans or receivables and investment securities have been classified as available for sale.

In addition, the fair value of certain trading derivatives has been restated to eliminate any profits recognised that are not evidenced by reference to data from observable markets

(p) Netting

Under FRS 5, items are aggregated into a single item where there is a right to insist on net settlement and the debit balance matures no later than the credit balance.

Financial assets and liabilities are offset and the net amount reported in the balance sheet if, and only if, there is currently a legally enforceable right to set off the recognised amounts and there is an intention to settle on a net basis at all times, or to realise the asset and settle the liability simultaneously.

The application of IFRS has resulted in certain transactions that qualified for netting under UK GAAP, being presented on a gross basis from 1st January 2005. The primary differences include derivative assets and liabilities subject to master netting agreements, repurchase contracts and cash collateral balances.

(q) Capital instruments

Under FRS 4, capital instruments are classified as debt if they contain an obligation, including a contingent obligation, to transfer economic benefits to another party.

Issued financial instruments are classified as liabilities where the substance of the contractual arrangement results in the Group having a present obligation to either deliver cash or another financial asset to the holder. In the absence of such an obligation, the financial instrument is classified as equity.

The application of IFRS has resulted in certain funding instruments that were included in undated loan capital under UK GAAP being reclassified

(r) Loan impairment

Specific provisions are raised when the credit-worthiness of a borrower has deteriorated such that the recovery of the whole or part of an outstanding advance is in serious doubt. Specific provisions are generally raised on an individual basis, although specific provisions may be raised on a portfolio basis for homogeneous assets and where statistical techniques are appropriate. General provisions are raised to cover losses which are judged to be present in loans and advances at the balance sheet date, but which have not been specifically identified as such.

If collection of interest is doubtful, it is credited to a suspense account and excluded from interest income in the profit and loss account. The suspense account in the balance sheet is netted against the relevant loan.

(s) Effective interest

Interest is recognised in the income statement as it accrues. Fee income relating to loans and advances is recognised so as to match the cost of providing a continuing service, together with a reasonable profit margin. Where fees are charged in lieu of interest, it is recognised as interest receivable on a level yield basis over the life of the advance. Costs associated with the acquisition of financial assets are either spread over the anticipated life of the loans or recognised as incurred, depending on the nature of the cost.

as equity from 1st January 2005. Where the instruments have been reclassified, they have been remeasured to net proceeds at the date of issue and the subsequent foreign currency movements have been eliminated.

Impairment losses are recognised where there is evidence of impairment as a result of one or more loss events that have occurred after initial recognition, and where these events have had an impact on the estimated future cash flows of the financial asset or portfolio of financial assets. Impairment of loans and receivables is measured as the difference between the carrying amount and the present value of estimated future cash flows discounted at the financial asset's original effective interest rate. Impairment is measured individually for assets that are individually significant and on a collective basis for portfolios with similar risk characteristics.

Under IFRS, all impairment allowances are calculated in the same manner and there is no distinction between general and specific provisions.

The overall change in the total level of credit impairment is not material. The application of IFRS has resulted in reanalysis of UK GAAP general and specific provisions into IFRS impairment allowances and the reallocation of impairment allowances within the businesses.

Interest on impaired loans is recognised using the original effective interest rate, being the rate used to discount the estimated future cash flows for the purpose of calculating impairment.

The effective interest method is a method of calculating the amortised cost of a financial asset or liability (or group of assets and liabilities) and of allocating the interest income or interest expense over the relevant period. The effective interest rate is the rate that exactly discounts the expected future cash payments or receipts through the expected life of the financial instrument, or when appropriate, a shorter period, to the net carrying amount of the instrument. The method results in all fees relating to the origination or settlement of the loan that are in the nature of interest and all direct and incremental costs associated with origination being recognised over the expected life of the loan. The application of the method has the effect of recognising income (or expense) receivable (or payable) on an instrument evenly in proportion to the amount outstanding over the period to maturity or repayment.

(t) Insurance contracts

Certain products offered to institutional pension funds are accounted for as investment products when the substance of the investment is that of managed funds. The assets and related liabilities are excluded from the consolidated balance sheet in order to reflect this substance.

From 1st January 2005, life assurance products are divided into investment contracts and insurance contracts. Investment contracts are accounted for under IAS 39 and insurance contracts are accounted for under the Modified Statutory Solvency Basis. The income and expense and assets and liabilities that arise on the investment contracts are presented separately from those arising under insurance contracts.

Where the legal form of the asset management products offered to institutional pension funds is an insurance contract, the assets and corresponding liabilities associated with these products are recorded on the balance sheet as investment contracts.

(u) Derecognition and financial liabilities

Under IFRS 5, a liability is derecognised if an entity's obligation to transfer economic benefits is satisfied, removed or is no longer likely to occur.

A financial liability is extinguished when and only when the obligation is discharged, cancelled or expires. A financial asset can be removed from the balance sheet only where the derecognition conditions have been met, including a requirement to continue to recognise financial assets only to the extent of any continuing involvement in them after the transfer.

The application of IFRS has resulted in certain customer accounts being remeasured as at 1st January 2005 to reflect the entire legal obligation. In addition, certain customer loyalty provisions, which meet the definition of financial liabilities, have been reclassified from provisions to financial liabilities and remeasured accordingly.

Certain securitisation structures that qualified for linked presentation under UK GAAP in 2004, and which were presented on a gross basis under IFRS in 2004, qualified for derecognition on a "continuing involvement" basis under IFRS from 1st January 2005 and have been substantially removed from the balance sheet from that date.

Source: Barclays Bank Annual Report 2005

Key Takeaways

- The proposed move to the expected loss model in IFRS 9 could increase loan loss provisioning in banks and financial institutions.
- The treasury function in Banks deal in financial instruments on a regular basis. Fair Valuing unquoted investments could be a challenge.
- Banks and financial institutions are intricately linked with the state of the economy as they lend large amounts to borrowers. A downside in the economy would mean that these loans would have to be tested for impairment. Determining the point of time for this trigger of impairment could prove to be a challenge.

4.5 FAMILY CONTROLLED ENTERPRISES (FCES)

4.5.1 Overview

Though FCEs are not an industry in themselves, they are presented here separately due to the fact that they are generally not considered to be very proactive in an area where IFRS mandates proactiveness – detailed disclosures. FCEs normally undertake a lot of transactions between family-owned enterprises – they would have to choose which IFRS standard would apply to which transaction – consolidation under IFRS 10, significant influence under IAS 28, joint arrangement under IFRS 111 or just a related party disclosure under IAS 24.

It is a well-known fact that when China transitioned to IFRS, Chinese undertakings had no objection with any IFRS Standard save one: IAS 24 *Related Party Transactions* (RPTSs). RPTSs are the norm rather than the exception in China. Many companies gave out an oft-used excuse against providing these disclosures – that the costs of providing these disclosures far exceed the benefits being obtained. Though the IASB did a bit of tinkering with the disclosure requirements, they did not completely alter the requirements.

4.5.2 The IFRS Standard that could impact FCEs

4.5.2.1 IAS 24 Related Party Transactions

Shareholders and investors use financial statements to help them assess management's responsibilityto use assets efficiently and in the interests of shareholders and the future profitability of the enterprise. One of the fundamental presumptions underlying the value of financial statement information is that the transactions on which they are based take place between disinterested parties. If this were not the case, there is less assurance that transactions were negotiated to the maximum advantage of the shareholders of the enterprise, or that historic transactions can be validly extrapolated to predict the future. Though only a Disclosure Standard, IAS 24 would impact Family Controlled enterprises who deal with one another regularly.

The disclosure part comes later. The key issue in IAS 24 would be in identifying who is a related party. The Standard breaks up the definition into two possibilities – persons and entities.

Person	Entity
Has control or joint control over the reporting entity	The entity and the reporting entity are members of the same group
Has significant influence over the reporting entity	One entity is an associate or joint venture of the other entity
Is a member of the key management personnel of the reporting entity or of a parent of the reporting entity	Both entities are joint ventures of the same third party
	One entity is a joint venture of a third entity and the other entity is an associate of the third entity

> The entity is a post-employment defined benefit plan for the benefit of employees of either the reporting entity or an entity related to the reporting entity. If the reporting entity is itself such a plan, the sponsoring employers are also related to the reporting entity
>
> The entity is controlled or jointly controlled by a person identified as being in control
>
> A person identified has significant influence over the entity or is a member of the key management personnel of the entity (or of a parent of the entity)
>
> The entity, or any member of a group of which it is a part, provides key management personnel services to the reporting entity or to the parent of the reporting entity

While the concepts of control, joint control and significant influence have been explained in IFRS 10, IFRS 11 and IAS 28, proving that control or significant influence exists could prove knotty. Mathematical trigger points such as 20% to ascertain significant influence and 50% to ascertain control would be easy to identify and prove. It is the non-mathematical trigger points of control that could prove to be irksome – for instance proving control over the operating and financial policies. This could prove particularly tricky in a FCE due to the number of transactions between them.

FCEs would need to be transparent in their disclosures about related party transactions. This could have a impact on other areas such as Transfer Pricing. In some geographies, the tax department have enunciated laws by which they need even domestic transfer pricing to be at arm's length (I can state with authority that there is such a law in India). A detailed disclosure of related party transactions by FCEs could provide information to the tax department that they did not possess. Consequently, FCEs would need to ensure that transactions between their enterprises are not "artificial" and meet the arm's-length test.

Considering the principle focus of IFRS on Disclosures, FCEs should probably be more forthcoming and upfront in their Disclosures of all Related Party Transactions.

As we indicated China earlier, let us take an example of RPTs from a Chinese entity that presents its financial statements in IFRS.

China Mobile Limited (Disclosures on Related Party Transactions)

ACCOUNTING POLICIES

Related parties

(a) A person, or a close member of that person's family, is related to the Group if that person:
  (i) has control or joint control of the Group;
  (ii) has significant influence over the Group; or
  (iii) is a member of the key management personnel of the Group or the Group's parent.
(b) An entity is related to the Group if any of the following conditions applies:
  (i) The entity and the Group are members of the same group (which means that each parent, subsidiary and fellow subsidiary is related to the others);

(ii) One entity is an associate or joint venture of the other entity (or an associate or joint venture of a member of a group of which the other entity is a member);

(iii) Both entities are joint ventures of the same third party;

(iv) One entity is a joint venture of a third entity and the other entity is an associate of the third entity;

(v) The entity is a post-employment benefit plan for the benefit of employees of either the Group or an entity related to the Group;

(vi) The entity is controlled or jointly controlled by a person identified in note 2(z)(a); or

(vii) A person identified in note 2(z)(a)(i) has significant influence over the entity or is a member of the key management personnel of the entity (or of a parent of the entity).

Close members of the family of a person are those family members who may be expected to influence, or be influenced by, that person in their dealings with the entity.

FINANCIAL STATEMENTS

(a) Transactions with CMCC Group

The following is a summary of principal related party transactions entered into by the Group with CMCC and its subsidiaries ("CMCC Group"), other than transactions disclosed in note 26, for the years ended 31 December 2014 and 31 December 2013. The majority of these transactions also constitute continuing connected transactions as defined under Chapter 14A of Listing Rules. Further details of these continuing connected transactions are disclosed under the paragraph "Connected Transactions" in the Report of Directors.

	2014	*2013*
Telecommunications Services Revenue	885	1590
Telecommunications Services Charges	4602	2843
Property Leasing and Management Service Charges	803	808
Interest Expenses	-	103
Interconnection Revenue	216	241
Interconnection Charges	425	500
Network assets leasing revenue	95	109
Network assets leasing charges	11,062	9837
Network capacity leasing charges	5012	3876
Revenue derived from cooperation of telecommunication services	481	494
Charges for cooperation of telecommunication services	2567	2232

Note:

(i) The amounts represent telecommunications services settlement received/receivable from or paid/payable to CMCC Group for the telecommunications project planning, design and construction services, telecommunications line and pipeline construction services, telecommunications line maintenance services, and installation and maintenance services in respect of transmission towers.

(ii) The amount represents the rental and property management fees paid/payable to CMCC Group in respect of business premises and offices, retail outlets and warehouses.

(iii) The amount represents the interest expenses paid to China Mobile Hong Kong (BVI) Limited, the Company's immediate holding company, in respect of the balance of purchase consideration for acquisitions of subsidiaries.

(iv) The amounts represent settlement received/receivable from or paid/payable to CMCC Group, in respect of interconnection settlement revenue and charges.

(v) The amounts represent the network assets leasing settlement received/receivable from or paid/payable to CMCC Group and the TD-SCDMA network capacity charges paid/payable to CMCC Group. On 29 December 2008, the Company entered into a network capacity leasing agreement (the "Network Capacity Leasing Agreement") with CMCC Group for the provision of TD-SCDMA related services. The lease was effective from 1 January 2009 to 31 December 2009 and is automatically renewed for successive one-year periods unless otherwise notified by one party to the other party. The Group is permitted to terminate the lease by giving 60 days advance written notice to CMCC Group. No penalty will be imposed in the event of a lease termination. Pursuant to the Network Capacity Leasing Agreement, the Group leases TD-SCDMA network capacity from CMCC Group and pays leasing fees to CMCC Group. The leasing fees are determined on a basis that reflects the actual usage of CMCC Group's TD-SCDMA network capacity and compensates CMCC Group for the costs of such network capacity. At the end of the lease terms, there is no purchase option granted to the Group to purchase the leased network assets. The Group also does not bear any gains or losses in the fluctuation in the fair value of the leased network assets at the end of the lease terms. As a result, the Group does not bear the risks associated with the ownership of the leased network assets, and accordingly the Group accounts for the network assets leasing and the network capacity leasing as operating leases.

(vi) The amounts represent the services fee received/receivable from or paid/payable to CMCC Group for providing customer development services and cooperation in the provision of basic and value added telecommunications service.

(b) Amounts due from/to CMCC Group

Amounts due from/to CMCC Group, other than amount due from/to ultimate holding company, are included in the following accounts captions summarised as follows:

	2014	2013
Accounts Receivable	1037	1162
Other Receivables	5	6
Prepayments and other current assets	146	109
Accounts Payable	5693	4036
Accrued Expenses and other payables	309	145

(c) Significant transactions with associates of the Group and of CMCC Group

The Group has entered into transactions with associates over which the Group or CMCC Group can exercise significant influence. The major transactions entered into by the Group and the associates and amount due from/to the associates are follows:

	2014	2013
Bank Deposits	42660	42752
Available for sale financial assets	1000	-
Interest receivable	934	664
Accounts Payable	513	208
Interest Income	1653	1355
Mobile telecommunications revenue	127	84
Mobile telecommunications services charges	1837	2261
Dividend Income	2476	2062

Note:

(i) Interest income represents interest earned from deposits placed with SPD Bank. The applicable interest rate is determined in accordance with the benchmark interest rate published by PBOC.

(ii) The amount represents the mobile telecommunications services revenue received/receivable from SPD Bank.

(iii) The amount represents the mobile telecommunications services charges paid/payable to Union Mobile Pay Co., Ltd., an associate of CMCC Group.

(d) Transactions with other government-related entities in the PRC

The Group is a government-related enterprise and operates in an economic regime currently dominated by entities directly or indirectly controlled by the PRC government through government authorities, agencies, affiliations and other organisation (collectively referred to as "government-related entities").

Apart from transactions with CMCC Group (notes 26 and 36(a)) and an associate (note 36(c)) and the transaction to establish Tower Company (note 19), the Group has collectively, but not individually, significant transactions with other government-related entities which include but not limited to the following:

– rendering and receiving telecommunications services, including interconnection revenue/charges
– purchasing of goods, including use of public utilities
– placing of bank deposits

These transactions are conducted in the ordinary course of the Group's business on terms comparable to the terms of transactions with other entities that are not government-related. The Group prices its telecommunications services and products in accordance with rules and regulations stipulated by related authorities of the PRC Government, where applicable, or based on commercial negotiations. The Group has also established its procurement policies and approval processes for purchases of products and services, which do not depend on whether the counterparties are government-related entities or not.

http://www.chinamobileltd.com/en/ir/reports/ar2014.pdf

Key Takeaway

We have discussed elsewhere that one of the criticisms of IFRS is that there are too many disclosures – many use the term "death by disclosures." FCEs should start getting used to the mantra "When in doubt, disclose." They may not earn any credits for disclosing more, but it is a fact that in some geographies, regulators levy fines and penalties for not disclosing facts.

4.6 FAST-MOVING CONSUMER GOODS (FMCG)

4.6.1 Overview

The use of the words "fast-moving" summarises what the industry is all about: they manufacture, trade and deal in goods with short shelf lives. Revenue realisations are quick but so are inventory pile-ups and losses. Trends in this industry change at the blink of an eyelid – yet the industry manages to generate brands on a regular basis.

4.6.2 IFRS Standards that could impact the industry

4.6.2.1 Revenue

A major portion of the sales of FMCG companies are to retailers who front-end the products of these companies. This could mean that there could be varying terms and conditions for different retailers. Recognising Revenue as per the existing guidelines of IAS 18 or the five-step approach enunciated by IFRS 15 would involve a lot of careful consideration and judgement. Some typical questions that need to be answered are:

1. How are product returns to be estimated?
2. Should there be a "cooling period" to estimate product returns for new product launches?
3. How are rebates and discounts to be accounted? FMCG companies typically offer rebates and discounts on a daily basis. Capturing the effects of this on an ERP system could be challenging?
4. How are sales incentives to be estimated? It would not be out of place to indicate here that what Tesco did was to overestimate the sales incentives that FMCG companies offered.
5. IAS 18 makes a categorical statement that amounts collected on behalf of others would not constitute Revenue. FMCG companies collect a variety of taxes levied by local tax authorities. The nature of the levy would need to be looked into to ascertain its accounting treatment.

REVENUE RECOGNITION

Turnover comprises sales of goods after the deduction of discounts, sales taxes and estimated returns. It does not include sales between group companies. Discounts given by Unilever include rebates, price reductions and incentives given to customers, promotional couponing and trade communication costs.

Turnover is recognised when the risks and rewards of the underlying products have been substantially transferred to the customer. Depending on individual customer terms, this can be at the time of dispatch, delivery or upon formal customer acceptance.

Unilever Annual Report 2013, page 99

4.6.2.2 *Intangible Assets*

Though the products of FMCG companies live life in the fast lane, they still manage to create brands along the way. For instance, Oreo cookies can be considered to be a brand as they have are not only instantly identified with the sandwich cookie but also because it is used in many other food products. Trade-marks are an extension of brands and are significant in the FMCG sector. Accounting for intangible assets involves significant judgements, such as determining whether these assets could be recognised or not, whether they have finite or indefinite useful lives, how long they should be amortised for and whether they show any signs of impairment.

GOODWILL

Goodwill is initially recognised based on the accounting policy for business combinations. Goodwill is subsequently measured at cost less amounts provided for impairment. The Group's cash generating units (CGUs) are based on the four product categories and the three geographical areas.

Goodwill acquired in a business combination is allocated to the Group's CGUs, or groups of CGUs, that are expected to benefit from the synergies of the combination. These might not always be the same as the CGUs that include the assets and liabilities of the acquired business. Each unit or group of units to which the goodwill is allocated represents the lowest level within the Group at which the goodwill is monitored for internal management purposes, and is not larger than an operating segment.

INTANGIBLE ASSETS

Separately purchased intangible assets are initially measured at cost. On acquisition of new interests in group companies, Unilever recognises any specifically identifiable intangible assets separately from goodwill. Intangible assets are initially measured at fair value as at the date of acquisition.

Finite-life intangible assets mainly comprise patented and non-patented technology, know-how and software. These assets are capitalised and amortised on a straight-line basis in the income statement over the period of their expected useful lives, or the period of legal rights if shorter. None of the amortisation periods exceeds ten years. Indefinite-life intangibles mainly comprise trademarks and brands. These assets are capitalised at cost but are not amortised. They are subject to a review for impairment annually; or more frequently if events or circumstances indicate this is necessary. Any impairment is charged to the income statement as it arises.

IMPAIRMENT CHARGES

We have tested all material goodwill and indefinite-life intangible assets for impairment. No impairments were identified.

SIGNIFICANT CGUS

The goodwill and indefinite-life intangible assets held in the three CGUs relating to Foods across the geographical areas are considered significant within the total carrying amounts of goodwill and indefinite-life intangible assets at 31 December 2013 in terms of size, headroom and sensitivity to assumptions used. No other CGUs are considered significant in this respect.

Value in use has been calculated as the present value of projected future cash flows. A pre-tax discount rate of 7.4% was used.

The growth rates and margins used to estimate future performance are based on past performance and our experience of growth rates and margins achievable in our key markets.

The projections covered a period of five years, as we believe this to be the most appropriate timescale over which to review and consider annual performances before applying a fixed terminal value multiple to the final year cash flows.

The growth rates used are consistent with our annual planning and strategic planning processes.

We have performed sensitivity analyses around the base assumptions and have concluded that no reasonable possible changes in key assumptions would cause the recoverable amount of the significant CGUs to be less than the carrying value.

Source: Unilever Annual Report 2013, pages 112–14

4.6.2.3 Inventory

As indicated earlier, as the products are supposed to be fast-moving, one of the principal risks of FMCG companies are slow and non-moving inventory which would necessitate their testing for impairment/write-off. Since inventory is valued at cost or net realisable value (NRV) whichever is lower as per IAS 2, ascertaining the NRV for a product that has not moved for months is tricky.

Inventories are valued at the lower of weighted average cost and net realisable value. Cost comprises direct costs and, where appropriate, a proportion of attributable production overheads. Net realisable value is the estimated selling price less the estimated costs necessary to make the sale.

Inventories with a value of €204 million (2012: €143 million) are carried at net realisable value, this being lower than cost. During 2013, €198 million (2012: €131 million) was charged to the income statement for damaged, obsolete and lost inventories. In 2013, €155 million (2012: €71 million) was utilised or released to the income statement from inventory provisions taken in earlier years.

Source: Unilever Annual Report 2013, page 116

4.6.2.4 Property, Plant and Equipment (PPE)

In a FMCG company, production of the goods is a critical task. FMCG companies invest heavily in PPE to produce goods at the speed and accuracy that the market demands. There are a few challenging issues in respect of accounting for property, plant and equipment:

1. Do the Assets meet the definition of an Asset as per the Framework?
2. In some instances, the containers in which the goods are shipped are returnable to the supplier. The goods (and thereby the container) would remain with the FMCG company for a long time. This could pose an accounting challenge as to whether the company should account for the container as an Asset. In the absence of a specific mandate in IAS 16 or if the provisions are unclear, it is recommended to fall back on the Framework for clarity. If the container meets the definition of an Asset as per the Framework, (which would obviously depend on its manner of use) it should be accounted for accordingly.
3. Due to numerous products being manufactured by an FMCG company en-masse, ascertaining the useful lives of Assets as per the component approach suggested by IAS 16 could be tricky.
4. The economic turmoil of the last few years has seen particular pressure on impairment testing, and part of the challenge that companies face these days is whether any of those previously recorded impairment losses should be reversed.

Impairment testing requires significant judgement, and relies heavily on discounted cash flow projections as well as on the appropriate determination of cash-generating units.

4.6.2.5 Provisions

IAS 37 defines a provision to be a current liability from a past event which would lead to an outflow of economic resources at some point of time in the future. Over the past few years, some entities operating in the FMCG sector have been receiving legal notices from irate customers who have filed claims for compensation. Whether this triggers a Provision as per the requirements of IAS 37 needs to be carefully thought out.

4.6.2.6 Financial Instruments

FMCG companies are normally conglomerates that are subject to a great variety of risks. These risks include credit risk, market risk (foreign currency risk, interest rate risk, and commodity price risk) and liquidity risk. Derivatives are frequently used to manage these risks. Various factors influence a FMCG company's hedging strategy, including the company's risk management objective, the nature of risks being hedged, the company's risk appetite, the nature of its selling arrangements, the general economic outlook, and the company's funding structure. The impact of these factors could be significant.

4.6.3 First time conversion

This extract is from the Annual Report of Reckitt Benckiser for the year ended 2005 when they converted to IFRS.

Explanation of Adjustments from UK GAAP to IFRS

(A) IFRS 2: SHARE-BASED PAYMENT

In accordance with IFRS 2, the Group has recognised an expense representing the fair value of outstanding share awards based on a Black-Scholes calculation at date of grant, spread over the vesting period. The Group has also adopted the transitional arrangement which allows companies that have previously disclosed the fair value charge to apply IFRS 2 retrospectively to all grants not vested at 1 January 2005. This approach is encouraged by the standard and gives consistency across reporting periods.

As a result of the above, an incremental charge to net income of £11m has been included in 2004. The Group has recognised a share award reserve within the profit and loss reserve in the balance sheet to reflect the cumulative charge under IFRS 2 in respect of outstanding share awards. The deferred tax impact is a debit to deferred tax of £8m at 1 January 2004, a debit of £16m at 31 December 2004, and a £2m credit to the income statement for 2004.

(B) IAS 19: EMPLOYEE BENEFITS

The Group has adopted IAS 19 by recognising in full the surplus/deficit on defined benefit schemes and other employee related liabilities in the Group balance sheet at the date of transition. The Group has included movements in the surplus/deficit within the income statement and statement of movement in equity as required by IFRS. The Group has also adopted early the amendment to IAS 19 issued on 16 December 2004 allowing all actuarial gains and losses to be taken to the SORIE in the year in which they arise.

In reversing the SSAP 24 accounting treatment and adopting IAS 19, the Group balance sheet is credited with £84m (being £109m less deferred tax of £25m) at 1 January 2004 and £130m (being £184m less deferred tax of £54m) at 31 December 2004. The impact on the income statement from reversing the SSAP 24 charge and including the IAS 19 charges is £2m in 2004, which is included within operating costs. Actuarial losses of £76m less tax of £22m are shown in the statement of movement in equity.

(C) IAS 32: FINANCIAL INSTRUMENTS: DISCLOSURE AND PRESENTATION

IAS 32 requires that where financial instruments contain both liability and equity components, the components are classified separately on the balance sheet. The Group's Convertible Capital Bond is such an instrument and accordingly £45m and £9m representing the split between debt and equity components has been reclassified from debt to equity in the balance sheets of 1 January 2004 and 31 December 2004 respectively. These amounts are based on the fair value of the components on issue.

Additionally under IAS 32, the Group's 5% cumulative preference shares fall to be classified as debt in the balance sheet and the dividends classified as financial expense in the income statement. Accordingly, a balance sheet adjustment of £5m is reflected at 1 January 2004 and 31 December 2004, while £0.2m is reclassified in the income statement from dividends to net financial income.

(D) IFRS 3: BUSINESS COMBINATIONS

IFRS prohibits the amortisation of goodwill, requiring at least annual impairment reviews to be undertaken. Accordingly, goodwill balances at 1 January 2004 are no longer subject to amortisation, resulting in a credit to net operating expenses in 2004 of £4m (£2m after tax) and an equivalent debit to goodwill at 31 December 2004.

(E) IAS 39: FINANCIAL INSTRUMENTS: RECOGNITION AND MEASUREMENT

Under IAS 39 and IFRS 1, the Group's policy is to recognise the fair value of financial derivative instruments on the balance sheet with effect from 1 January 2004. Accordingly, financial assets of £1m and financial liabilities of £3m have been recognised on the balance sheet as at 1 January 2004. As at 31 December 2004, financial liabilities of £4m were recognised, resulting in a £2m (£1m after tax) charge to financial income in 2004.

(F) IAS 17: LEASES

The Group has applied the requirements of IAS 17 to its leases and accordingly has reclassified certain leases from operating to finance leases to reflect the substance of the transaction according to IFRS. The total amount of assets and liabilities added to the balance sheet in respect of finance leases is £10m each, at both 1 January 2004 and 31 December 2004.

(G) IAS 38: INTANGIBLE ASSETS

Computer software that is not an integral part of related hardware is classified as an intangible asset under IFRS, whereas such assets were classified under tangible assets under UK GAAP. Reclassifications of £4m and £2m have been made between tangible and intangible assets at 1 January 2004 and 31 December 2004 respectively.

(H) IAS 10: EVENTS AFTER THE BALANCE SHEET DATE

In accordance with IAS 10, dividends declared after the balance sheet date are not recognised as a liability in the financial statements, as there is no present obligation at the balance sheet date, as defined by IAS 37: Provisions, Contingent Liabilities and Contingent Assets. Accordingly the final dividends for 2003 of £99m and for 2004 of £131m are de-recognised in the balance sheets for 2003 and 2004 respectively. Dividends (Note 8) for 2004 are adjusted by £32m to reflect these timing adjustments.

(I) IAS 14: SEGMENT REPORTING

In accordance with IAS 14, the Group has defined its primary segment as geographical and its secondary segment as product group. Analysis of net revenues and operating profit by geographical area (primary segment) and of net revenues by product group (secondary segment) are set out separately.

(J) IAS 7: CASH FLOW STATEMENTS

The Cash Flow Statement is presented in accordance with IAS 7. The Group's cash and investments balances are not impacted by the change of accounting basis. However, the

Group has presented short-term investments separately from cash and cash equivalents as required by IAS 7. Short-term investments represent those deposits with a maturity of over three months from inception. The other adjustments do not impact the movement of cash in and out of the Group and so there are no material effects on the cash flow aside from the presentation format required by IAS 7.

(K) IAS 12: DEFERRED TAX

Under IAS 12, deferred tax is recognised in respect of nearly all taxable temporary timing differences arising between the tax base and the book value of most balance sheet items. The application of this principle may result in the recognition of additional temporary differences when compared to UK GAAP. Accordingly the Group now recognises a net deferred tax liability of £122m at 1 January 2004, the date of transition. This adjustment does not impact the income statement.

(L) OTHER ADJUSTMENTS

Under IFRS, provisions are required to be analysed as those expected to be utilised within one year and after more than one year. Accordingly, £4m are reclassified from non-current liabilities to current liabilities as at 1 January 2005 and 31 December 2005 respectively.

For presentational purposes, the minority interest has been reclassified to equity on the face of the balance sheet. Taxation is provided on the conversion adjustments at the appropriate rate and is separately described above where material.

Key Takeaways

- Timing of Revenue and its quantum need to be carefully considered.
- Assets need to be tested for Impairment.
- Recognising a provision needs to be carefully thought out.

4.7 GOVERNMENT OWNED INDUSTRY

4.7.1 Overview

Though IFRS is supposed to solve the requirement and need of a single universal accounting language, it may not be able to solve all pieces of the puzzle. This is due to the fact that the eclectic types of businesses the world over with different methods of control demand distinguished accounting treatment. Entities that are controlled by the government – popularly known as the public sector – are a case in point. In most instances, they are controlled and run by the government and are in areas that could be sensitive or the prerogative of the government e.g. defence. Applying the fair value concept without looking into the sensitivities of the sector can lead to skewed results.

Thankfully, the problem is being solved by a Board known as the International Public Sector Accounting Standards Board (IPSASB). The IPSASB has formulated accounting standards that have to be followed by public sector entities. Though these Standards are modelled on IFRS Standards, there are some differences between the two. The summary of these standards is not being reproduced here due to the focus of this book on IFRS as well as space constraints. It would suffice if we understood the differences between IPSAS and IFRS to assess IPSAS standards would have on entities that present their financial statements as per IPSAS standards and not IFRS.

These differences are summarised below.

4.7.2 Differences between IFRS and IPSAS

4.7.2.1 Service potential as part of the definitions and recognition criteria

Many of the assets and liabilities of entities within the public sector are acquired or incurred as a result of the entity's service delivery mandate, for example, heritage assets and parks maintained for public access. IPSAS introduces the concept of service potential into the definition of assets, liabilities, revenue and expenses. Service potential is also a supplementary recognition criterion to account for items that do not result in the inflow or outflow of economic benefits, where an item either contributes to or detract from the entity's ability to deliver its services.

4.7.2.2 Exchange vs non-exchange transactions

Non-exchange transactions are those transactions where an entity either receives value from another entity without directly giving approximately equal value in exchange, or gives value to another entity without directly receiving approximately equal value in exchange. Within the public sector non-exchange transactions are prevalent. IPSAS provides principles to guide the measurement and recognition of non-exchange transactions, whereas IFRS is generally silent on the matter.

4.7.2.3 Recognition of revenue from government grants

IPSAS focuses on whether there is entitlement to the revenue from government grants (even though there may be restrictions on how the funds are spent), or an obligation to meet certain conditions, which is recorded as liability. The distinction between restrictions and conditions is crucial in determining whether or not to recognise revenue from a non-exchange transaction. As a result, government grants are generally fully released to income earlier under IPSAS than under IFRS.

4.7.2.4 Income tax

IPSAS presumes that entities that operate within the public sector are generally exempt from income taxes and therefore does not cater for the accounting of income taxes. In the unlikely event that an entity reports using IPSAS but is liable for tax, reference should be made to IFRS (IAS 12 Income Taxes) for guidance.

4.7.2.5 Consolidations and interests in associates and joint ventures

With the introduction of IFRS 10 *Consolidated Financial Statements*, IFRS 11 *Joint Arrangements* and IFRS 12 *Disclosures of Interests in Other Entities*, there are significant differences between IFRS and IPSAS. IPSAS is still based on IAS 27 *Consolidated and Separate Financial Statements*, IAS 28 *Investments in Associates* and IAS 31 *Interest in Joint Ventures*. The main difference that arises with the introduction of IFRS 10, IFRS 11 and IFRS 12 is the manner in which control is determined for the purpose of consolidation. Until the IPSASB finalises its project to consider these new developments in IFRS, this could become a major source of difference between the two frameworks.

4.7.2.6 Financial instruments classification and measurement

With the introduction and ongoing development of IFRS 9 *Financial Instruments*, the classification and measurement of financial instruments under IFRS is changing from IAS 39. Prior to IFRS 9, the recognition and measurement of financial instruments were similar under IFRS and IPSAS. Until the IPSASB finalises its project to consider these new developments in IFRS, this could become a major source of difference between the two frameworks.

4.7.2.7 Reporting of budgets vs actual

With the increased focus on stewardship, service delivery and budget management in the public sector, IPSAS requires a comparison of the actual financial performance of an entity with the approved budget of that entity, where the budget is publicly available. IPSAS 24 *Presentation of Budget Information in Financial Statements* requires a presentation of Budget and Actual amounts. There is no equivalent requirement in IFRS.

4.7.2.8 Impairment of non-cash-generating assets

In light of the assets recognised based purely on their service potential (as opposed to economic benefits), IPSAS also caters specifically for impairment considerations for non-cash-generating assets. IFRS assumes that all assets will be cash-generating, whereas IPSAS assumes that the majority of a public sector entity's assets are likely to be non-cash generating. IPSAS 21 *Impairment of Non-cash-generating Assets* provides specific guidance on how to determine the value-in-use of such assets.

4.7.2.9 Elimination of private sector specific concepts

IFRS provides principles for certain economic phenomena that are irrelevant to the operations of a public sector entity, such as accounting for share-based payments and earnings per share disclosures. IPSAS excludes such guidance and refers reporting entities back to IFRS if and when applicable.

4.7.2.10 Growing divergence in the conceptual framework of the IPSASB and IASB

The IPSASB is in the process of developing its own conceptual framework, proposing concepts that may be more suitable in the public sector context. We may see further differences in the outlook and focus of the IPSASB and IASB in the future.

Key Takeaways

- Public Sector entities would be bound by IPSAS and not IFRS. They would need to understand the differences between the two in detail.
- There are no IPSAS equivalents for all IFRS Standards. In such instances, public sector entities will need to look up to IFRS for guidance which could result in additional administrative work.

4.8 INSURANCE

4.8.1 Overview

Though very different, in an indirect manner, the insurance industry can be compared to the banking industry. A bank takes money from depositors and lends it to borrowers. An Insurance company gets premium from the insuree to pay them a sum of money when an event occurs in the future. The premium is normally received over a period of time while the payout is normally one-time. Thus, it is critical that an insurance company always keeps enough assets to meets its liabilities – any mismatch either in the quantity or value could impact the financial statements of the insurer.

4.8.2 IFRS Standards that could impact the industry

Just like the project for Financial Instruments, the IASB/FASB combine embarked on a similar project for Insurance Contracts. The IFRS 4 that is on the statute book today is the result of Phase 1 of the Project. Phase 2 of the project has gone through various stages but in February 2014 the FASB decided not to pursue the project with the IASB for the present. However, the IASB has issued an Exposure Draft which is expected to be deliberated upon this year 2015.

4.8.2.1 IFRS 4

Product Classification and Significant risks

IFRS 4 is the first Standard from the International Accounting Standards Board (IASB) on insurance contracts. The Standard is designed to make limited improvements to accounting practices and to provide users with an insight into the key areas that relate to accounting for *insurance contracts*. All entities that issue policies that meet the definition of *an insurance contract* under IFRS 4 have to apply this Standard. The Standard does not apply to other assets and liabilities of the insurance companies, such as financial assets and financial liabilities, which fall within the scope of IAS 39.

Classification of products into insurance products and other than insurance products is thus a *pre-requisite* for applying IFRS 4.

Basis of classification of Insurance Contract

The conceptual basis of an insurance contract is the presence of significant insurance risk and insurance risk is defined as a transferred risk other than financial risk.

> IFRS 4 defines an insurance contract as a contract under which one party (the insurer) accepts significant insurance risk from another party (the policyholder) by agreeing to compensate the policyholder if a specified uncertain future event (the insured event) adversely affects the policyholder.

Various aspects viz. financial risk, insurance risk, transferred risk, significance of insurance risk and uncertainty of future event, need to be considered while determining whether a contract or product would classify as Insurance contract. There could be some contracts that do not meet the definition of an insurance contract. IFRS 4 requires that the insurable interest is embodied in the contract as a precondition for providing benefits. IFRS 4 also clarifies that survival risk, which reflects uncertainty about the required overall cost of living, qualifies as insurance risk.

Contracts issued that do not meet the definition of an insurance contract contained in IFRS 4 (also referred to as investment contracts) will be accounted for as financial instruments under IAS 39. Such contracts would be accounted at fair value or on amortised cost basis, based on classification of such contracts done by the company.

Accounting for insurance contracts under IFRS

IFRS 4 permits the company to continue with its existing accounting policies on Insurance contracts except for the following:

(a) measuring insurance liabilities on an undiscounted basis;
(b) measuring contractual rights to future investment management fees at an amount that exceeds their fair value as implied by a comparison with current fees charged by other market participants for similar services;
(c) using non-uniform accounting policies for the insurance liabilities of subsidiaries.

It further,

(a) prohibits provisions for possible claims under contracts that are not in existence at the reporting date (such as catastrophe and equalisation provisions);
(b) requires a test for the adequacy of recognised insurance liabilities and an impairment test for reinsurance assets;
(c) requires an insurer to keep insurance liabilities in its balance sheet until they are discharged or cancelled, or expire, and to present insurance liabilities without offsetting them against related reinsurance assets.

Further the standard requires deposit element (if any) inherent in the insurance contract to be separated (unbundled) in case certain conditions are satisfied, as failure to separately account for the deposit element inherent in an insurance contract may result in material liabilities and assets not being fully recognised on the balance sheet of an entity, under the existing accounting policies which continue to apply in terms of IFRS 4.

Unbundling of deposit component is mandated if:

• the deposit component can be measured separately and the insurer's accounting policies do not otherwise require recognition of all obligations and rights arising from the deposit component;
• it is permitted but not required, if the deposit component can be measured separately and the insurer's accounting policies require recognition of all obligations and rights arising from the deposit component;
• it is prohibited if the deposit component cannot be measured separately.

If unbundled, the insurance component is accounted for under IFRS 4 and the deposit component under IAS 39 Financial instruments: recognition and measurement.

The impact of unbundling would mean that only the net revenue for the company being recognised as top line (premium income) thereby eroding the top line to the extent of unbundling.

4.8.2.2 IFRS 9 Financial Instruments

Financial Instruments are an integral part of an insurers financial statements. Ensuring financial assets are classified appropriately under IFRS 9 will require insurers to: determine the objective of the business model in which financial assets are managed; and where relevant, analyse the contractual cash flow characteristics of financial assets (e.g. whether the contractual cash flows give rise, on specified dates, to cash flows that are solely payments of principal and interest).

Applying the expected credit loss model to calculate impairment for debt instruments measured at amortised cost or FVOCI and certain financial guarantees and loan commitments will require robust estimates of expected credit losses; identification of the point at which there is a significant increase in credit risk since initial recognition of an asset; and decisions as to how key terms will be defined in the context of their financial assets.

Volatility in profit or loss and equity may arise as a result of mismatches between the measurement bases for financial assets and insurance contract liabilities and from the presentation of gains and losses in the statement of profit or loss and OCI. The effects of changes in discount rates may cause these mismatches; changes in other market factors (e.g. equity prices); or timing or accounting differences between the settlement or disposal of assets and liabilities.

The expected credit loss model is likely to lead to larger and more volatile charges for credit losses on financial assets, but an insurer's own credit risk is not intended to be reflected in the measurement of insurance contract liabilities under the forthcoming standard – limiting any significant offsetting impact.

For insurers with significant portfolios of financial assets measured at amortised cost, initial application of the expected credit loss model may result in a potentially large negative impact on equity, as equity will incorporate not only incurred credit losses but also expected credit losses.

Where regulatory capital resources and requirements are based on an entity's IFRS financial statements, the classification of an insurer's financial assets under IFRS 9 may affect those calculations.

4.8.3 Presentation of Financial Statements

Being a specialised business, Insurance companies may have their own way of presenting their financial statements. In many geographies, the insurance regulator gives a format for the financial statements of an Insurance Company. The provisions of IFRS 4 only provide some guidance on how insurance companies should present Assets and Liabilities in their Balance-Sheet and Income and Expenses in their Profit or Loss Account. For additional guidance, insurance companies would need to seek guidance from IAS 1.

Presented below are extracts from the Financial Statements of Aegon

INSURANCE CONTRACTS

Insurance contracts are accounted for under IFRS 4 *Insurance Contracts*. In accordance with this standard, Aegon continues to apply the existing accounting policies that were applied prior to the adoption of IFRS, with certain modifications allowed by IFRS 4 for standards effective subsequent to adoption. Aegon applies non-uniform accounting policies for insurance liabilities and related deferred policy acquisition costs and intangible assets to the extent that it was allowed under Dutch Accounting Principles. As a result, specific methodologies applied may differ between Aegon's operations as they may reflect local regulatory requirements and local practices for specific product features in these local markets. At the time of IFRS adoption, Aegon was applying US GAAP for its United States operations whereas in the Netherlands and the United Kingdom, Aegon was applying Dutch Accounting Principles. Since adoption of IFRS, Aegon has considered new and amended standards in those GAAPs which have become effective subsequent to the date of transition to IFRS.

Insurance contracts are contracts under which the Group accepts a significant risk – other than a financial risk – from a policyholder by agreeing to compensate the beneficiary on the occurrence of an uncertain future event by which he or she will be adversely affected. Contracts that do not meet this definition are accounted for as investment contracts. The Group reviews homogeneous books of contracts to assess whether the underlying contracts transfer significant insurance risk on an individual basis. This is considered the case when at least one scenario with commercial substance can be identified in which the Group has to pay significant additional benefits to the policyholder. Contracts that have been classified as insurance are not reclassified subsequently.

Insurance liabilities are recognised when the contract is entered into and the premiums are charged. The liability is derecognised when the contract expires, is discharged or is cancelled.

Insurance assets and liabilities are valued in accordance with the accounting principles that were applied by the Group prior to the transition to IFRS and with consideration of standards effective subsequent to the date of transition to IFRS, as further described in the following paragraphs. In order to reflect the specific nature of the products written, subsidiaries are allowed to apply local accounting principles to the measurement of insurance contracts. All valuation methods used by the subsidiaries are based on the general principle that the carrying amount of the net liability must be sufficient to meet any reasonably foreseeable obligation resulting from the insurance contracts.

Included under insurance contracts are interest rate rebates. Interest rate rebate is a form of profit sharing whereby the Group determines the premium based on the expected interest that will be earned on the contract. The expected interest is calculated with reference to a portfolio of government bonds. Interest rate rebates that are expected to be recovered in future periods are deferred and amortised as the interest is realised. The amortisation is recognised in Aegon's income statement. They are considered in the liability adequacy test for insurance liabilities. Deferred interest rebates are derecognised when the related contracts are settled or disposed of.

(a) Life insurance contracts

Life insurance contracts are insurance contracts with guaranteed life-contingent benefits. The measurement of the liability for life insurance contracts varies depending on the nature of the product.

Some products, such as traditional life insurance products in continental Europe and products in the United States, for which account terms are fixed and guaranteed, are measured using the net premium method. The liability is determined as the sum of the discounted value of the expected benefits and future administration expenses directly related to the contract, less the discounted value of the expected theoretical premiums that would be required to meet the future cash outflows based on the valuation assumptions used. The liability is either based on current assumptions or calculated using the assumptions established at the time the contract was issued, in which case a margin for risk and adverse deviation is generally included. A separate reserve for longevity may be established and included in the measurement of the liability. Furthermore, the liability for life insurance comprises reserves for unearned premiums and accrued annuity benefits payable.

Other products with account terms that are not fixed or guaranteed are generally measured at the policyholder's account balance. Depending on local accounting principles, the liability may include amounts for future services on contracts where the policy administration charges are higher in the initial years than in subsequent years. In establishing the liability, guaranteed minimum benefits issued to the policyholder are measured as per IFRS 4 or, if bifurcated from the host, as a derivative.

One insurance product in the United States is carried at fair value through profit or loss as it contains an embedded derivative that could not be reliably bifurcated. The fair value of the contract is measured using market consistent valuation techniques.

(b) Life insurance contracts for account of policyholders

Life insurance contracts under which the policyholder bears the risks associated with the underlying investments are classified as insurance contracts for account of policyholders.

The liability for the insurance contracts for account of policyholders is measured at the policyholder account balance. Contracts with unit-denominated payments are measured at current unit values, which reflect the fair values of the assets of the fund. If applicable, the liability representing the nominal value of the policyholder unit account is amortised over the term of the contract so that interest on actuarial funding is at an expected rate of return.

(c) Embedded derivatives and participation features

Life insurance contracts typically include derivative-like terms and conditions. With the exception of policyholder options to surrender the contract at a fixed amount, contractual features that are not closely related to the insurance contract and that do not themselves meet the definition of insurance contracts are accounted for as derivatives.

Other terms and conditions, such as participation features and expected lapse rates, are considered when establishing the insurance liabilities. Where the Group has discretion over the amount or timing of the bonuses distributed resulting from participation features, a liability is recognised equal to the amount that is available at the balance sheet date for future distribution to policyholders.

Guaranteed minimum benefits

The Group issues life insurance contracts, which do not expose the Group to interest rate risk as the account terms are not fixed or guaranteed or because the return on the investments held is passed on to the policyholder. Some of these contracts, however, may contain guaranteed minimum benefits. Bifurcated guaranteed minimum benefits are classified as derivatives.

In the United States, the additional liability for guaranteed minimum benefits that are not bifurcated is determined each period by estimating the expected value of benefits in excess of the projected account balance and recognising the excess over the accumulation period based on total expected assessments. The estimates are reviewed regularly and any resulting adjustment to the additional liability is recognised in the income statement. The benefits used in calculating the liabilities are based on the average benefits payable over a range of stochastic scenarios. Where applicable, the calculation of the liability incorporates a percentage of the potential annuitisations that may be elected by the contract holder.

In the Netherlands, an additional liability is established for guaranteed minimum benefits that are not bifurcated on group pension plans with profit sharing and on traditional insurance contracts with profit sharing based on an external interest index. These guarantees are measured at fair value.

(d) Shadow accounting

Shadow accounting ensures that all gains and losses on investments affect the measurement of the insurance assets and liabilities in the same way, regardless of whether they are realised or unrealised and regardless of whether the unrealised gains and losses are recognised in the income statement or directly in equity in the revaluation reserve. In some instances, realised gains or losses on investments have a direct effect on the measurement of the insurance assets and liabilities. For example, some insurance contracts include benefits that are contractually based on the investment returns realised by the insurer. In addition, realisation of gains or losses on available-for-sale investments can lead to unlocking of VOBA or DPAC and can also affect the outcome of the liability adequacy test to the extent that it considers actual future investment returns. For similar changes in unrealised gains and losses, shadow accounting is applied. If an unrealised gain or loss triggers a shadow accounting adjustment to VOBA, DPAC or the insurance liabilities, the corresponding adjustment is recognised through other comprehensive income in the revaluation reserve, together with the unrealised gain or loss.

Some profit sharing schemes issued by the Group entitle the policyholder to a bonus which is based on the actual total return on specific assets held. To the extent that the bonus relates to gains or losses on available-for-sale investments for which the unrealised gains or losses are recognised in the revaluation reserve in equity, shadow accounting is applied. This means that the increase in the liability is also charged to equity to offset the unrealised gains rather than to the income statement.

(e) Non-life insurance contracts

Non-life insurance contracts are insurance contracts where the insured event is not life-contingent. For non-life products the insurance liability generally includes reserves for unearned premiums, unexpired risk, inadequate premium levels and outstanding claims and benefits. No catastrophe or equalisation reserves are included in the measurement of the liability.

The reserve for unearned premiums includes premiums received for risks that have not yet expired. Generally, the reserve is released over the coverage period of the premium and is recognised as premium income.

The liability for outstanding claims and benefits is established for claims that have not been settled and any related cash flows, such as claims handling costs. It includes claims that have been incurred but have not been reported to the Group. The liability is calculated at the reporting date using statistical methods based on empirical data and current assumptions that may include a margin for adverse deviation. Liabilities for claims subject to periodic payment are calculated using actuarial methods consistent with those applied to life insurance contracts. Discounting is applied if allowed by the local accounting principles used to measure the insurance liabilities. Discounting of liabilities is generally applied when there is a high level of certainty concerning the amount and settlement term of the cash outflows.

(f) Liability adequacy testing

At each reporting date, the adequacy of the life insurance liabilities, net of VOBA and DPAC, is assessed using a liability adequacy test. Additional recoverability tests for policies written in the last year may also result in loss recognition.

Life insurance contracts for account of policyholders and any related VOBA and DPAC are considered in the liability adequacy test performed on insurance contracts. To the extent that the account balances are insufficient to meet future benefits and expenses, additional liabilities are established and included in the liability for life insurance.

All tests performed within the Group are based on current estimates of all contractual future cash flows, including related cash flows from policyholder options and guarantees. A number of valuation methods are applied, including discounted cash flow methods, option pricing models and stochastic modelling. Aggregation levels are set either on geographical jurisdiction or at the level of portfolio of contracts that are subject to broadly similar risks and managed together as a single portfolio. Specifically, in the Netherlands and the UK the liability adequacy test is performed on a consolidated basis for all life and non-life business, whereas in the Americas it is performed at the level of the portfolio of contracts. To the extent that the tests involve discounting of future cash flows, the interest rate applied is based on market rates or is based on management's expectation of the future return on investments. These future returns on investments take into account management's best estimate related to the actual investments and, where applicable, reinvestments of these investments at maturity. The fair value of the assets carried at amortised cost is considered in determining any liability adequacy surplus or deficit.

Any resulting deficiency is recognised in the income statement, initially by impairing the DPAC and VOBA and subsequently by establishing an insurance liability for the remaining loss, unless shadow loss recognition has taken place.

The adequacy of the non-life insurance liability is tested at each reporting date. Changes in expected claims that have occurred, but that have not been settled, are reflected by adjusting the liability for claims and future benefits. The reserve for unexpired risk is increased to the extent that the future claims and expenses in respect of current insurance contracts exceed the future premiums plus the current unearned premium reserve.

INVESTMENT CONTRACTS

Contracts issued by the Group that do not transfer significant insurance risk, but do transfer financial risk from the policyholder to the Group are accounted for as investment contracts. Depending on whether the Group or the policyholder runs the risks associated with the investments allocated to the contract, the liabilities are classified as investment contracts or as investment contracts for account of policyholders. Investment contract liabilities are recognised when the contract is entered into and are derecognised when the contract expires, is discharged or is cancelled.

(a) Investment contracts with discretionary participation features

Some investment contracts have participation features whereby the policyholder has the right to receive potentially significant additional benefits which are based on the performance of a specified pool of investment contracts, specific investments held by the Group or on the issuer's net income. If the Group has discretion over the amount or timing of the distribution of the returns to policyholders, the investment contract liability is measured based on the accounting principles that apply to insurance contracts with similar features.

Some unitised investment contracts provide policyholders with the option to switch between funds with and without discretionary participation features. The entire contract is accounted for as an investment contract with discretionary participation features if there is evidence of actual switching resulting in discretionary participation benefits that are a significant part of the total contractual benefits.

(b) Investment contracts without discretionary participation features

At inception, investment contracts without discretionary features are carried at amortised cost.

Investment contracts without discretionary participation features are carried at amortised cost based on the expected cash flows and using the effective interest rate method. The expected future cash flows are re-estimated at each reporting date and the carrying amount of the financial liability is recalculated as the present value of estimated future cash flows using the financial liability's original effective interest rate. Any adjustment is immediately recognised in the income statement.

The consolidated financial statements provide information on the fair value of all financial liabilities, including those carried at amortised cost. As these contracts are not quoted in active markets, their value is determined by using valuation techniques, such as discounted cash flow methods and stochastic modeling. For investment contracts that can be cancelled by the policyholder, the fair value cannot be less than the surrender value.

(c) Investment contracts for account of policyholders

Investment contracts for account of policyholders are investment contracts for which the actual return on investments allocated to the contract is passed on to the policyholder. Also included are participations held by third parties in consolidated investment funds that meet the definition of a financial liability.

Investment contracts for account of policyholders are designated at fair value through profit or loss. Contracts with unit-denominated payments are measured at current unit values, which reflect the fair values of the assets of the fund.

For unit-linked contracts without discretionary participation features and subject to actuarial funding, the Group recognises a liability at the funded amount of the units. The difference between the gross value of the units and the funded value is treated as an initial fee paid by the policyholder for future asset management services and is deferred. It is subsequently amortised over the life of the contract or a shorter period, if appropriate.

Source: Aegon Annual Report 2013

Key Takeaways

- The specific provisions of IFRS 4 regarding Unbundling of Deposits, Liability Adequacy etc. need to be taken into account
- The provisions of IAS 39/IFRS 9 would apply to the Financial Instrument part of Insurance Contracts
- Insurance companies would need to seek Guidance from IAS 1 on Presentation of Financial Statements for guidance not provided in IFRS 4. This becomes all the more important due to the delay in the issue of a comprehensive Standard on Insurance Contracts

4.9 PHARMACEUTICALS

4.9.1 Overview

The pharmaceutical industry develops, produces, and markets drugs or pharmaceuticals licensed for use as medications. Pharmaceutical companies are allowed to deal in generic or brand medications and medical devices. They are subject to a variety of laws and regulations regarding the patenting, testing and ensuring safety and efficacy and marketing of drugs. The global pharmaceuticals market is worth US$300 billion a year, a figure expected to rise to US$400 billion within three years. Companies currently spend one-third of all sales revenue on marketing their products – roughly twice what they spend on research and development. The private sector dominates R&D, spending millions of dollars each year developing new drugs for the mass market. The profit imperative ensures that the drugs chosen for development are those most likely to provide a high return on the company's investment.

4.9.2 IFRS Standards that could impact the industry

4.9.2.1 Research & Development Expenditure

The chart below depicts a typical drug development process. Considering the number of processes involved, the time-frame from Target ID to Market approval could take up to six years – and in some instances even a decade. Assuming that a drug manufacturer incurs the expenditure all through this period, the immediate question that arises is: which of these expenses would be expensed and which would be capitalised under IFRS?

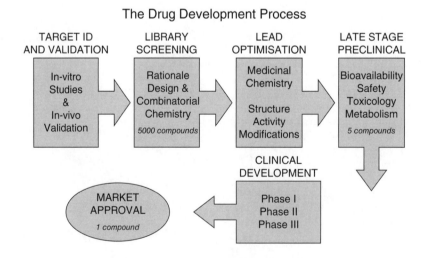

The Drug Development Process

IFRS has ensured that there is no separate standard to deal with Research and Development Expenditure – the provisions are contained in IAS 38 *Intangible Assets*.

In other words, if the expenditure meets the definition of an Asset as per IAS 38, it can be treated as an Intangible Asset – otherwise it has to be expensed.

Recognition

IAS 38 states that an intangible asset is to be recognised if, and only if, the following criteria are met:

- it is probable that future economic benefits from the asset will flow to the entity; and
- the cost of the asset can be reliably measured.

The above recognition criteria look straightforward enough, but in reality it can prove to be very difficult to assess whether or not these have been met. In order to make the recognition of internally-generated intangibles more clear-cut, IAS 38 separates an R&D project into a research phase and a development phase.

Research phase

It is impossible to demonstrate whether or not a product or service at the research stage will generate any probable future economic benefit. As a result, IAS 38 states that all expenditure incurred at the research stage should be written off to the income statement as an expense when incurred, and will never be capitalised as an intangible asset.

Development phase

Under IAS 38, an intangible asset arising from development must be capitalised if an entity can demonstrate all of the following criteria:

- the technical feasibility of completing the intangible asset (so that it will be available for use or sale),
- intention to complete and use or sell the asset,
- ability to use or sell the asset,
- existence of a market or, if to be used internally, the usefulness of the asset,
- availability of adequate technical, financial, and other resources to complete the asset, and
- the cost of the asset can be measured reliably.

If any of the recognition criteria are not met then the expenditure must be charged to the income statement as incurred. Note that if the recognition criteria have been met, capitalisation must take place.

Treatment of capitalised development costs

Once development costs have been capitalised, the asset should be amortised in accordance with the accruals concept over its finite life. Amortisation must only begin when commercial production has commenced (hence matching the income and expenditure to the period in which it relates). Each development project must be reviewed at the end of each accounting period to ensure that the recognition criteria are still met. If the criteria are no longer met, then the previously capitalised costs must be written off to the income statement immediately.

In view of the above, pharmaceutical companies would need to be extremely careful in segregating their costs into research costs and development costs. There can be no single formula to do this segregation and it would depend on a case to case basis. The trigger point to decide whether to stop expensing costs and capitalising them would be when the entity is certain that there are future economic benefits available.

There could also be some issues related to what type of expenditure can be capitalised in case the expenditure meets the definition of an Intangible Asset. If the Asset meets the definition of a Qualifying Asset detailed in IAS 23, borrowing costs can be capitalised. Patent protection costs that are specific to the drug being developed can also be capitalised as there would be future economic benefits. As a general rule, advertisement and promotional expenditure would be expensed unless the future economic benefit test can be satisfied for it to meet the definition of an asset.

Once recognised as an Intangible Asset, the next step would be to identify its useful life. Unlike other products, certain drugs may not have limited shelf-lives. Since IFRS necessitates doing a useful life test every year besides mandating an Impairment Test, initial estimates of useful lives made by pharmaceutical companies can be trued up every year.

Bayer

RESEARCH AND DEVELOPMENT EXPENSES

For accounting purposes, research expenses are defined as costs incurred for current or planned investigations under – taken with the prospect of gaining new scientific or technical knowledge and understanding. Development expenses are defined as costs incurred for the application of research findings or specialist knowledge to plans or designs for the production, provision or development of new or substantially improved products, services or processes, respectively, prior to the commencement of commercial production or use.

Research and development expenses are incurred in the Bayer Group for in-house research and development activities as well as numerous research and development collaborations and alliances with third parties.

Research and development expenses mainly comprise the costs for active ingredient discovery, clinical studies, research and development activities in the areas of application technology and engineering, field trials, regulatory approvals and approval extensions.

Research costs cannot be capitalised. The conditions for capitalisation of development costs are closely defined: an intangible asset must be recognised if, and only if, there is reasonable certainty of receiving future cash flows that will cover an asset's carrying amount. Since our own development projects are often subject to regulatory approval procedures and other uncertainties, the conditions for the capitalisation of costs incurred before receipt of approvals are not normally satisfied.

In the case of research and development collaborations, a distinction is generally made between payments on contract signature, upfront payments, milestone payments and cost reimbursements for work performed. If an intangible asset (such as the right to the use of an active ingredient) is acquired in connection with any of these payment obligations, the respective payment is capitalised even if it is uncertain whether further development work will ultimately lead to the production of a saleable product. Reimbursements of the cost of research or development work are recognised in profit or loss.

Source: Bayer Annual Report 2013, page 248

4.9.2.2 *Revenue Recognition*

Revenue Recognition from sale of pharmaceutical products does not pose much of a challenge – they are recognised when the products are sold. Discounts and rebates are knocked off and the sales revenue is presented net of these incentives.

In many instances, pharmaceutical companies enter into in-licensing and out-licensing arrangements. Licensing, as is understood in plain terms, is the transfer of rights to a third party (the Licensee) to use the Intellectual Property owned by a party (the Licensor) for a fixed duration of time and under defined terms and conditions. The said terms and conditions may be, for example, manufacturing and/or marketing rights in select geography, etc. Depending from whose perspective you see it, a licensing deal can be called an Out-Licensing deal or an In-Licensing deal. Out-Licensing means that the Licensor is "out"-licensing his Intellectual Property to a third party. For the third party, the Licensee, who takes "In" the Intellectual Property, it becomes an In-Licensing deal. The Licensing Agreements normally specify royalty, or royalty-based, payment schedules which are dependent on achieving certain milestones. Revenue in such cases is normally recognised as per the terms of the Licensing Agreement – there could be certain upfront payments as well as certain milestone and similar conditional payments.

Bayer

NET SALES AND OTHER OPERATING INCOME

All revenues derived from the selling of products or rendering of services or from licensing agreements are recognised as sales. Other operational revenues are recognised as other operating income. Sales are recognised in profit or loss when the significant risks and rewards of ownership of the goods have been transferred to the customer, the company retains neither continuing managerial involvement to the degree usually associated with ownership nor effective control over the goods sold, the amount of revenue and costs incurred or to be incurred can be measured reliably, and it is sufficiently probable that the economic benefits associated with the transaction will flow to the company.

Sales are stated net of sales taxes, other taxes and sales deductions at the fair value of the consideration received or to be received. Sales deductions are estimated amounts for rebates, cash discounts and product returns. They are deducted at the time the sales are recognised, and appropriate provisions are recorded. Sales deductions are estimated primarily on the basis of historical experience, specific contractual terms and future expectations of sales development. It is unlikely that factors other than these could materially affect sales deductions in the Bayer Group. Adjustments to provisions made in prior periods for rebates, cash discounts or product returns were of secondary importance for income before income taxes in the years under report.

Provisions for rebates in 2013 amounted to 2.8% of total net sales (2012: 2.4%). In addition to rebates, Group companies offer cash discounts for prompt payment in some countries. Provisions for cash discounts as of December 31, 2013 and December 31, 2012 were less than 0.1% of total net sales for the respective year.

Sales are reduced by the amount of the provisions for expected returns of defective goods or of saleable products that may be returned under contractual arrangements. The net sales are reduced on the date of sale or on the date when the amount of future returns can be reasonably estimated. Provisions for product returns in 2013 amounted to 0.3% of total net sales (2012: 0.3%). If future product returns cannot be reasonably estimated and are significant to a sales transaction, the revenues and the related cost of sales are deferred until a reasonable estimate can be made or the right to return the goods has expired.

Some of the Bayer Group's revenues are generated on the basis of licensing agreements under which third parties have been granted rights to products and technologies. Payments received, or expected to be received, that relate to the sale or out licensing of technologies or technological expertise are recognised in profit or loss as of the effective date of the respective agreement if all rights relating to the technologies and all obligations resulting from them have been relinquished under the contract terms. However, if rights to the technologies continue to exist or obligations resulting from them have yet to be fulfilled, the payments received are deferred accordingly. Upfront payments and similar non-refundable payments received under these agreements are recorded as other liabilities and recognised in profit or loss over the estimated performance period stipulated in the agreement.

License or research and development collaboration agreements may consist of multiple elements and provide for varying consideration terms, such as upfront payments and milestone or similar payments. They therefore have to be assessed to determine whether sales revenues should be recognised for individually delivered elements of such arrangements, i.e. for more than one unit of account. The condition for separate revenue recognition for individual units of account is that each element has value to the customer on a stand-alone basis, the fair value of the undelivered goods or unrendered services can be reliably determined, and delivery or performance of the as yet undelivered element(s) is probable and substantially within the control of the Bayer Group.

Other operating income may also arise from the exchange of intangible assets. The amount recognised is generally based on the fair value of the assets given up, calculated using the discounted cash flow method. If the assets given up are internally generated, the gain from the exchange generally equals their fair value.

Source: Bayer Annual Report 2013, pages 247 and 248

4.9.2.3 Other Intangible Assets

As a part of their drug discovery, process, it is common for pharmaceutical companies to apply for patents for every major drug that they manufacture.

Mergers and Acquisitions are common in the Pharmaceutical industry. Many a time, mergers are entered into only for the purchase of brands that have become blockbusters. The recognition, measurement and disclosure norms stipulated in IAS 38 would need to be applied. An area where a lot of judgement would be needed to be applied is the determination of the useful lives of Intangible Assets.

Bayer

INTANGIBLE ASSETS

Goodwill

In a business combination, goodwill is capitalised at the acquisition date. It is measured at its cost of acquisition, which is the excess of the acquisition price for shares in a company over the acquired net assets. The net assets are the balance of the fair values of the acquired identifiable assets and the assumed liabilities and contingent liabilities.

Goodwill is not amortised, but tested annually for impairment. Details of the annual impairment tests are given under "Procedure used in global impairment testing and its impact." Once an impairment loss has been recognised on goodwill, it is not reversed in subsequent periods.

Other Intangible Assets

An "other intangible asset" is an identifiable non-monetary asset without physical substance, other than goodwill (such as a patent, a trademark or a marketing right). It is capitalised if the future economic benefits attributable to the asset will probably flow to the company and the cost of acquisition or generation of the asset can be reliably measured.

Other intangible assets are recognised at the cost of acquisition or generation. Those with a determinable useful life are amortised accordingly on a straight-line basis over a period of up to 30 years, except where their actual depletion demands a different amortisation pattern. Determination of the expected useful lives of such assets and the amortisation patterns is based on estimates of the period for which they will generate cash flows. An impairment test is performed if there is an indication of possible impairment.

Other intangible assets with an indefinite life (such as the Bayer Cross trademark) and intangible assets not yet available for use (such as research and development projects) are not amortised, but tested annually for impairment.

Any impairment losses are recognised in profit or loss. If the reasons for a previously recognised impairment loss no longer apply, the impairment loss is reversed provided that the reversal does not cause the carrying amount to exceed the (amortised) cost of acquisition or construction.

Source: Bayer Annual Report 2013, pages 248 and 249

Provisions, Contingent Liabilities and Contingent Assets

It is probably impossible to find a pharmaceutical company that has not been fined by the Food and Drug Administration (FDA) in the United States. This is due to the strict quality control measures and policing that the FDA exercises over pharmaceutical companies. The fines have been levied for an eclectic variety of reasons:

- misbranding the painkiller ... with "the intent to defraud or mislead", promoting the drug to treat acute pain at dosages the FDA had previously deemed dangerously high;

- illegal promotion of the painkiller .. which was withdrawn from the market in 2004 after studies found the drug increased the risk of heart attacks;
- misbranding the drug …. for treating depression in patients under 18, even though the drug had never been approved for that age group;
- the company gave doctors free units of an injection to relieve knee pain to encourage those doctors to buy their product. They lowered the effective price by promising these free samples to doctors, but at the same time got inflated prices from government programmes by submitting false price reports;
- promoted these drugs for uses not approved as safe and effective by the FDA, targeted elderly dementia patients in nursing homes, and paid kickbacks to physicians and to the nation's largest long-term care pharmacy provider; and
- the drug was approved for treating schizophrenia and later for bipolar mania, but the government alleged that the company promoted the drug or a variety of unapproved uses, such as aggression, sleeplessness, anxiety, and depression.

It can be observed from the above that it is possible for pharmaceutical companies to pay fines to the FDA and other regulators for a wide variety of reasons. It is obvious that a pharma company will not provide for these fines in the normal course unless there is a triggering event. The triggering event could be a notice of demand from the FDA or an inspection by the FDA of the manufacturing facilities of the company. The time-line between the discovery of an infraction by a company and the ultimate penalty imposed could spread over a couple of years. Thus, it is possible that the company initially discloses this amount as a Contingent Liability and moves it to a Liability in the books on crystallisation of the liability.

Patent Protection Costs

Patents guarantee the protection of intellectual property. In the event of successful commercialisation, profits can be invested to enable continued, sustainable research and development. Due to the long period of time between the patent application and the market launch of a product, companies generally have only a few years in which to earn an adequate return on its intellectual property. This makes effective and reliable patent protection all the more important. Generic manufacturers and others attempt to contest patents prior to their expiration. Sometimes a generic version of a product may even be launched "at-risk" prior to the issuance of a final patent decision. This could result in legal proceedings. When a patent defense is unsuccessful, or it expires, prices are likely to come under pressure because of increased competition from generic products entering the market. Legal action by third parties for alleged infringement of patent or proprietary rights may impede or even halt the development or manufacturing of certain products or require payment of monetary damages or royalties to third parties. Large pharmaceutical companies have patent departments that keep themselves up to date with the developments.

Finance would need to interact with Patents Department to ascertain if either a Contingent Liability or Contingent Asset should be disclosed or a Liability provided for.

Roche

Legal provisions: Group companies are party to various legal proceedings and the most significant matters are described. Legal provisions at 31 December 2006 total 1,320 million Swiss francs, as disclosed in Note 28. Additional claims could be made which might not be covered by existing provisions or by insurance. There can be no assurance that there will not be an increase in the scope of these matters or that any future lawsuits, claims, proceedings or investigations will not be material. Such changes that arise could impact the provisions recognised in the balance sheet in future periods.

Environmental provisions: The Group has provisions for environmental remediation costs, which at 31 December 2006 total 186 million Swiss francs, as disclosed in Note 28. The material components of the environmental provisions consist of costs to fully clean and refurbish contaminated sites and to treat and contain contamination at certain other sites. Future remediation expenses are affected by a number of uncertainties that include, but are not limited to, the detection of previously unknown contaminated sites, the method and extent of remediation, the percentage of waste material attributable to the Group at the remediation sites relative to that attributable to other parties, and the financial capabilities of the other potentially responsible parties.

Management believes that the total provisions for environmental matters are adequate based upon currently available information. However, given the inherent difficulties in estimating liabilities in this area, it cannot be guaranteed that additional costs will not be incurred beyond the amounts accrued. The effect of the resolution of environmental matters on the results of operations cannot be predicted due to uncertainty concerning both the amount and the timing of future expenditures. Such changes that arise could impact the provisions recognised in the balance sheet in future periods.

Roche Annual Report 2006

4.9.2.4 *Business Combinations*

Over the last decade, the pharmaceutical industry has witnessed major business combinations. Some have been successful, some have not been successful and some have failed.

Acquired businesses are accounted for using the acquisition method, which requires that the assets acquired and liabilities assumed be recorded at their respective fair values on the date the acquirer obtains control. Ancillary acquisition costs are recognised as expenses in the periods in which they occur. The application of the acquisition method requires certain estimates and assumptions to be made, especially concerning the fair values of the acquired intangible assets, property, plant and equipment and the liabilities assumed at the acquisition date, and the useful lives of the acquired intangible assets, property, plant and equipment.

Measurement is based to a large extent on anticipated cash flows. In particular, the estimation of discounted cash flows from intangible assets under development, patented and non-patented technologies and brands could be based on the following assumptions:

- the outcomes of research and development activities regarding compound efficacy, results of clinical trials, etc.,
- the probability of obtaining regulatory approvals in individual countries,
- long-term sales trends,
- possible selling price erosion due to generic competition in the market following patent expirations,
- the behaviour of competitors (launch of competing products, marketing initiatives, etc.).

For significant acquisitions, the purchase price allocation is normally carried out with assistance from independent third-party valuation specialists. The valuations are based on the information available at the acquisition date. In step acquisitions, the fair values of the acquired entity's assets and liabilities are measured at the date on which control is obtained. Any resulting adjustments to the fair value of the existing interest are recognised in profit or loss. The carrying amount of the assets and liabilities already recognised in the statement of financial position is then adjusted accordingly.

4.9.2.5 Impairment of Assets

Considering the hectic world of a pharmaceutical company, Impairment of Assets are but to be expected. Bayer gives a good description of their Impairment method.

Bayer

PROCEDURE USED IN GLOBAL IMPAIRMENT TESTING AND ITS IMPACT

Impairment tests are performed not only on individual items of intangible assets, property, plant and equipment, but also at the level of cash-generating units or groups of cash-generating units. A cash-generating unit is the smallest identifiable group of assets that generates cash inflows that are largely independent of the cash inflows from other assets or groups of assets. The Bayer Group regards its strategic business entities or groups of strategic business entities, as well as certain product families, as cash-generating units and subjects them to global impairment testing. The strategic business entities constitute the second financial reporting level below the segments. Cash-generating units and unit groups are globally tested if there is an indication of possible impairment. Those to which goodwill is allocated are tested at least annually. Impairment testing involves comparing the carrying amount of each cash-generating unit, unit group or item of intangible assets, property, plant or equipment to the recoverable amount, which is the higher of its fair value less costs to sell or value in use. If the carrying amount exceeds the recoverable amount, an impairment loss must be recognised for the difference. If a strategic business entity or entity group is found to be impaired, an impairment loss is first recognised on any goodwill allocated to it. Any remaining part of the impairment loss is then allocated among the other assets of the strategic business entity or entity group in proportion to their carrying amounts. The resulting expense is reflected in the same functional item of the income statement as the depreciation or amortisation of the respective assets. If the criteria for a special item are satisfied, the impairment loss is recognised in profit or loss under other operating expenses. Income from impairment loss reversals is recognised in other operating income.

The recoverable amount is generally determined on the basis of the fair value less costs to sell, taking into account the present value of the future net cash flows as market prices for the individual units are not normally available. These are forecasted on the basis of the Bayer Group's current planning, the planning horizon normally being three to five years. Forecasting involves making assumptions, especially regarding future selling prices, sales volumes and costs. Where the recoverable amount is the fair value less costs to sell, the cash-generating unit or unit group is measured from the viewpoint of an independent market participant. Where the recoverable amount is the value in use, the cash-generating unit, unit group or individual asset is measured as currently used. In either case, net cash flows beyond the planning period are determined on the basis of long-term business expectations using the respective individual growth rates derived from market information. The measurement of fair value less costs to sell is based on unobservable inputs (Level 3).

The net cash inflows are discounted at a rate equivalent to the weighted average cost of equity and debt capital. To allow for the different risk and return profiles of the Bayer Group's principal businesses, the after-tax cost of capital is calculated separately for each subgroup and a subgroup-specific capital structure is defined by benchmarking against comparable companies in the same industry sector. The cost of equity corresponds to the return expected by stockholders, while the cost of debt is based on the conditions on which comparable companies can obtain long-term financing. Both components are derived from capital market information.

The growth rates are separately disclosed.

No impairment losses were recognised on goodwill on the basis of the global annual impairment testing of the cash-generating units and unit groups in 2013 or 2012. Taking into account impairment loss reversals of €13 million (2012: €21 million), net impairment losses on intangible assets, property, plant and equipment amounted to €285 million (2012: €347 million).

Although the estimates of the useful lives of certain assets, assumptions concerning the macroeconomic environment and developments in the industries in which the Bayer Group operates, and estimates of the discounted future cash flows are believed to be appropriate, changes in assumptions or circumstances could require changes in the analysis. This could lead to additional impairment losses in the future or – except in the case of goodwill – to reversals of previously recognised impairment losses if developments are contrary to expectations.

The sensitivity analysis for cash-generating units and unit groups to which goodwill is allocated was based on a 10% reduction in future cash flows, a 10% increase in the weighted average cost of capital and a one-percentage-point reduction in the long-term growth rate. Bayer concluded that under these conditions the only cash-generating unit in which an impairment loss would need to be recognised would be Diphenylmethane Diisocyanate (MDI).

Key Takeaways

- Clear demarcation of costs into Research Costs and Development Costs
- Accounting for the impact of in-licensing and out-licensing agreements. Impact on Revenues, Costs and Recognition of PPE
- Provisions for legal claims, patent protection costs and other provisions
- Testing for Impairment of Assets judiciously

4.10 PRIVATE EQUITY

4.10.1 Overview

If you want to know the meaning of risk capital, you only need to look at the PE industry. To many technology companies, start-ups and budding entrepreneurs, the private equity players are the new-age bankers. Across the globe, the number of start-ups is mushrooming – these ventures need funds during their early years and growth years. This is where angel investors and private equity funds step in. This discussion is restricted to a fund that invests in a company and not a fund that consolidates all its funds.

4.10.2 IFRS Standards that could impact the industry

IAS 32, 39, IFRS 7 & IFRS 9	*Financial Instruments – Recognition, Measurement, Derecognition and Disclosures & Hedge Accounting*
IAS 36	*Impairment of Assets*
IFRS 10	*Consolidated Financial Statements*

4.10.2.1 IFRS 10

Consolidated Financial Statements

It is often felt that private equity funds control the entities they invest in. This would depend on the facts and circumstances of each case. IFRS 10 mandates consolidation of all subsidiaries that are controlled by the entity but provides an exemption to investment entities.

IFRS 10 states that an investor controls an investee when the investor is exposed, or has rights, to variable returns from its involvement with the investee and has the ability to affect those returns through its power over the investee. An investment entity has been defined by IFRS 10 to mean an entity that:

1. obtains funds from one or more investors for the purpose of providing those investor(s) with investment management services,
2. commits to its investor(s) that its business purpose is to invest funds solely for returns from capital appreciation, investment income, or both, and
3. measures and evaluates the performance of substantially all of its investments on a fair value basis.

Most private equity funds would meet all the three requirements to qualify as an investment entity. It is advisable however to maintain adequate and sufficient documentation in support of these.

Often it is seen that private equity firms "demonstrate" that they have power over the investee. Often, this is achieved through the PE firms removing the Chief Executive Officer and/or the key management of the investee. In such situations where control has been demonstrated, the decision whether to consolidate the investee or not could prove to be tricky. The solution probably lies in the PE firm proving that the control that they demonstrated was with the sole intention of improving the capital appreciation for the ultimate investors. This could be proved by tangible evidence such as performance metrics and intangible parameters such as a "good feeling" about the change.

Special Purpose Entities

Enron showed the world what not to do with Special Purpose entities. IFRS 10 consolidates all the requirements of Consolidation including SIC 12 *Special Purpose Entities*. PE Investors normally set up various SPE's for tax and other purposes. They should carefully evaluate whether they meet the definition of an investment entity as mentioned in IFRS 10 or whether they control the SPE. The results of this evaluation will drive the accounting for these investments.

4.10.2.2 IAS 32, 39, IFRS 7 and IFRS 9

Financial Instruments

IFRS 10 states that if it were proved that an entity is an investment management entity, then IAS39/IFRS 9 would apply.

Financial instruments are recognised on the statement of financial position when the entity becomes party to the contractual provisions of the instrument.

All financial instruments are measured initially at fair value, directly attributable transaction costs are added to or deducted from the carrying value of those financial instruments that are not subsequently measured at fair value through profit or loss. Subsequent Measurement would depend on the category in which the Financial Instrument is classified:

- Fair Value through Profit and Loss Account
- Held to Maturity (HTM)
- Available for Sale (AFS)
- Loans and Receivables.

The HTM and the Loans and Receivables category can be ruled out due to the nature of the investment of the PE firm. As the Available for Sale category is a residual category, PE firms should probably classify the investment in the first category – Fair Value through Profit and Loss Account. This would appear to meet one of the requirements of IFRS 10 to determine investment management entity – measures and evaluates the performance of substantially all its returns on a Fair Value basis.

The financial instrument is measured at Fair Value. All gains and losses would be recognised in Profit or Loss Account.

4.10.2.3 IAS 36 Impairment of Assets

The "hit-rate" of PE firms is not very high. Not all the firms they invest in turn out to be showstoppers. Quite a few do not make the grade and go kaput taking the investment of the PE with them. In the brand-new IFRS 9, the IASB has moved over from the incurred loss model (which IAS 39 required) to the expected loss model to recognize impairment of financial instruments (which IFRS 9 requires). The difference between these two approaches has been demonstrated through an illustration in the Impact of IFRS on the Banking Sector. If PE firms present their financial statements in IFRS, they would need to provide for bad investments earlier instead of waiting for the bad news.

The financial statements of Blackstone demonstrate how the ultimate fund consolidates all its investment funds. (Note: This has been prepared under US GAAP and not IFRS. This has been provided here for illustrative purposes only.)

Blackstone

SUMMARY OF SIGNIFICANT ACCOUNTING POLICIES

The Blackstone Funds are, for GAAP purposes, investment companies under the AICPA Audit and Accounting Guide Investment Companies. For those funds which the Partnership consolidates, such funds reflect their investments, including Securities Sold, Not Yet Purchased, on the Condensed Consolidated Statements of Financial Condition at fair value, with unrealized gains and losses resulting from changes in fair value reflected as a component of Net Gains (Losses) from Fund Investment Activities in the Condensed Consolidated and Combined Statements of Income. Fair value is the amount that would be received to sell an asset or paid to transfer a liability, in an orderly transaction between market participants at the measurement date (i.e., the exit price). Additionally, the majority-owned and controlled investments of the Blackstone Funds (the "Portfolio Companies") are not consolidated by these funds. The Partnership has retained the specialized accounting for the Blackstone Funds pursuant to EITF Issue No. 85–12, *Retention of Specialized Accounting for Investments in Consolidation*.

The fair value of the Partnership's Investments and Securities Sold, Not Yet Purchased are based on observable market prices when available. Such prices are based on the last sales price on the measurement date, or, if no sales occurred on such date, at the "bid" price at the close of business on such date and if sold short, at the "ask" price at the close of business on such date. Futures and options contracts are valued based on closing market prices. Forward and swap contracts are valued based on market rates or prices obtained from recognized financial data service providers.

A significant number of the investments, including our carry fund investments, have been valued by the Partnership, in the absence of observable market prices, using the valuation methodologies described below. Additional information regarding these investments is provided in Note 4 to the condensed consolidated and combined financial statements. For some investments, little market activity may exist; management's determination of fair value is then based on the best information available in the circumstances and may incorporate management's own assumptions. The Partnership estimates the fair value of investments when market prices are not observable as follows.

Corporate private equity, real estate and debt investments – For investments for which observable market prices do not exist, such investments are reported at fair value as determined by the Partnership. Fair value is determined by reference to projected net earnings, earnings before interest, taxes, depreciation and amortisation ("EBITDA") and balance sheets, public market or private transactions, valuations for comparable companies and other measures. With respect to real estate investments, in determining fair values management considered projected operating cash flows and balance sheets, sales of comparable assets and replacement costs among other measures. Analytical methods used to estimate the fair value of private investments include the discounted cash flow method and/or capitalisation rates ("cap rates") analysis. Valuations may also be derived by reference to observable valuation measures for comparable companies or assets (e.g., multiplying a key performance metric of the investee company or asset, such as EBITDA, by a relevant valuation multiple observed in the range of comparable companies or transactions), adjusted by management for differences between the investment and the referenced comparables and in some instances by reference to option pricing models or other similar methods. Corporate private equity and real estate investments may also be valued at cost for a period of time after an acquisition as the best indicator of fair value. These valuation methodologies involve a significant degree of management judgment.

Funds of hedge funds—Blackstone Funds' direct investments in hedge funds ("Investee Funds") are stated at fair value, based on the information provided by the Investee Funds which reflects the Partnership's share of the fair value of the net assets of the investment fund. If the Partnership determines, based on its own due diligence and investment procedures, that the valuation for any Investee Fund based on information provided by the Investee Fund's management does not represent fair value, the Partnership will estimate the fair value of the Investee Fund in good faith and in a manner that it reasonably chooses.

Certain Blackstone Funds sell securities that they do not own, and will therefore be obligated to purchase such securities at a future date. The value of an open short position is recorded as a liability, and the fund records unrealized appreciation or depreciation to the extent of the difference between the proceeds received and the value of the open short position. The applicable Blackstone Fund records a realized gain or loss when a short position is closed. By entering into short sales, the applicable Blackstone Fund bears the market risk of increases in value of the security sold short. The unrealized appreciation or depreciation as well as the realized gain or loss associated with short positions is included in the Condensed Consolidated and Combined Statements of Income as Net Gains from Fund Investment Activities.

Source: http://www.wikinvest.com/stock/Blackstone_Group_%28BX%29/Summary_Significant_Accounting_Policies

Key Takeaways

- Ascertaining whether the fund is an investment management entity or controls the investee
- Accounting for the financial instrument
- Provide for Impairment Losses

4.11 REAL ESTATE AND INFRASTRUCTURE

4.11.1 Overview

One of the significant features of the real estate industry is that the projects are completed over a period of time and revenues are also normally received over time. IAS 11 permitted the use of the percentage of completion method though the risks and rewards of the property are not completely transferred – one of the essential requirements of IAS 18.

4.11.2 IFRS Standards that could impact the industry

Wikipedia defines real estate as "property consisting of land and the buildings on it, along with its natural resources such as crops, minerals, or water; immovable property of this nature; an interest vested in this; (also) an item of real property; (more generally) buildings or housing in general. Also: the business of real estate; the profession of buying, selling, or renting land, buildings or housing."

It is apparent by definition that IAS 16 and IAS 40 (*Property, Plant and Equipment* and *Investment Property* respectively) would be critical standards for the real estate industry. However, due to the nature of the business real estate entities can also hold land banks which could be accounted for as per IAS 2 *Inventories*.

4.11.2.1 IAS 16/IAS 2/IAS 40

Entities in the real estate space deal with land and buildings. These could be classified as PPE under IAS 16, Inventories under IAS 2 or Investment Property under IAS 40. It would seem that IAS 40 is a Standard that has been written only with the real estate sector in mind since they hold properties either for rental or for capital appreciation. Since IAS 2 uses the term "held for sale" in the ordinary course of business, it is clear that houses, apartments, and land and property under construction would fall under inventory and only those that are not held in the ordinary course of business would fall under Investment Property. It may be reasonable to conclude that IAS 16 would apply to a real estate entity only when the both IAS 2 and IAS 40 do not apply. When an entity in the course of its ordinary activities routinely sells items that it has held for rental to others, it transfers those assets to inventories at their carrying amount when they cease to be rented and become held for sale. Sale proceeds from such assets are recognised as revenue in accordance with IAS 18. When such assets are transferred to inventories, IFRS 5 does not apply.

Investment Property

This is likely to be the most significant item in the statement of financial position of entities in the real estate sector. IAS 40 *Investment Property* is a distinct standard addressing investment property, (e.g. land held for long-term capital appreciation and not for short-term sale in the ordinary course of business) and it allows the choice of using either the fair-value model or the cost model to account for such properties. Investment Property and PPE held for sale represents property that management intends to sell, but, unlike inventory, the sale of such property is not in the ordinary course of business.

Properties under construction (for sale): real estate companies sometimes sell properties e.g. houses and units apartments while they are under construction or development. The point is that IFRS principles treat sale of apartment and properties as a sale of a product (inventory) that is arguably also the underlying substance of such transactions, as against contracts for provision of construction services.

However, where there is an agreement to provide construction services, the real estate company is in the position of a contractor engaged in contracting activities. Hence, property being constructed on behalf of third parties is within the scope of IAS 11 *Construction Contracts* which deals with the accounting for construction contracts in the financial statements of contractors.

Land Securities Group – Investment Property

Investment properties are those properties, either owned by the Group or where the Group is a lessee under a finance lease, that are held either to earn rental income or for capital appreciation, or both. In addition, properties held under operating leases are accounted for as investment properties when the rest of the definition of an investment property is met. In such cases, the operating leases concerned are accounted for as if they were finance leases.

Investment properties are measured initially at cost, including related transaction costs. After initial recognition at cost, investment properties are carried at their fair values based on market value determined by professional independent valuers at each reporting date. The difference between the fair value of an investment property at the reporting date and its carrying amount prior to re-measurement is included in the income statement as a valuation surplus or deficit. Properties are treated as acquired at the point when the Group assumes the significant risks and returns of ownership and as disposed when these are transferred to the buyer. This generally occurs on unconditional exchange, except where completion is expected to occur significantly after exchange. Additions to investment properties consist of costs of a capital nature and, in the case of investment properties under development, capitalised interest. Certain internal staff and associated costs directly attributable to the management of major schemes during the construction phase are also capitalised.

When the Group begins to redevelop an existing investment property for continued future use as an investment property, the property continues to be held as an investment property. When the Group begins to redevelop an existing investment property with a view to sell, the property is transferred to trading properties and held as a current asset. The property is re-measured to fair value as at the date of the transfer with any gain or loss being taken to the income statement. The re-measured amount becomes the deemed cost at which the property is then carried in trading properties.

Borrowing costs associated with direct expenditure on properties under development or undergoing major refurbishment are capitalised. The interest capitalised is calculated using the Group's weighted average cost of borrowings after adjusting for borrowings associated with specific developments. Where borrowings are associated with specific developments, the amount capitalised is the gross interest incurred on those borrowings less any investment income arising on their temporary investment. Interest is capitalised as from the commencement of the development work until the date of practical completion. The capitalisation of finance costs is suspended if there are prolonged periods when development activity is interrupted. Interest is also capitalised on the purchase cost of land or property acquired specifically for redevelopment in the short-term but only where activities necessary to prepare the asset for redevelopment are in progress.

The valuation of the Group's property portfolio is inherently subjective due to, among other factors, the individual nature of each property, its location and the expected future rental revenues from that particular property. As a result, the valuations the Group places on its property portfolio are subject to a degree of uncertainty and are made on the basis of assumptions which may not prove to be accurate, particularly in periods of volatility or low transaction flow in the property market.

The investment property valuation contains a number of assumptions upon which Knight Frank and JLL have based their valuation of the Group's properties as at 31 March 2014. The assumptions on which the valuations have been based include, but are not limited to, matters such as the tenure and tenancy details for the properties, ground conditions at the properties, the structural condition of the properties, prevailing market yields and comparable market transactions. These assumptions are market standard and accord with the Royal Institution of Chartered Surveyors (RICS) Valuation – Professional Standards 2012. However, if any assumptions made by the property valuer prove to be inaccurate, this may mean that the value of the Group's properties differs from their valuation, which could have a material effect on the Group's financial condition.

Source: Land Securities Group Annual Report, page 105

Trading Properties

Trading properties are those properties held for sale, or those being developed with a view to sell, and are shown at the lower of cost and net realisable value. Proceeds received on the sale of trading properties are recognised within Revenue.

Revenue on long-term development contracts is recognised according to the stage reached in the contract by reference to the value of work completed using the percentage of completion method. An appropriate estimate of the profit attributable to work completed is recognised once the outcome of the contract can be estimated reliably. The gross amount due from customers for contract work is shown as a receivable. The gross amount due comprises costs incurred plus recognised profits less the sum of recognised losses and progress billings. Where the sum of recognised losses and progress billings exceeds costs incurred plus recognised profits, the amount is shown as a liability.

CRITICAL

Trading properties are carried at the lower of cost and net realisable value. The latter is assessed by the Group having regard to suitable valuations performed by its external valuer, Knight Frank.

The estimation of the net realisable value of the Group's trading properties, especially the development land and infrastructure programmes, is inherently subjective due to a number of factors, including their complexity, unusually large size, the substantial expenditure required and long timescales to completion. In addition, as a result of these timescales to completion, the plans associated with these programmes could be subject to significant variation. As a result, and similar to the valuation of investment properties, the net realisable values of the Group's trading properties are subject to a degree of uncertainty and are determined on the basis of assumptions which may not prove to be accurate.

If the assumptions upon which the external valuer has based the valuation prove to be inaccurate, this may have an impact on the net realisable value of the Group's trading properties, which would in turn have an effect on the Group's financial condition.

Source: Land Securities Group Annual Report, page 112

4.11.2.2 IAS 18 Revenue

There is general agreement that IAS 18 *Revenue* does not answer all questions on Revenue Recognition particularly for real estate entities with their different models. IAS 11 *Construction Contracts* provides some guidance but a question quickly arose as to which Standard has to be chosen – IAS 18 or IAS 11.

An IFRIC had to be issued to answer this question. IFRIC 15 provides guidance on how to determine whether an agreement for the construction of real estate is within the scope of IAS 11 *Construction Contracts* or IAS 18 *Revenue* and, accordingly, when revenue from the construction should be recognised:

- An agreement for the construction of real estate is a construction contract within the scope of IAS 11 only when the buyer is able to specify the major structural elements of the design of the real estate before construction begins and/or specify major structural changes once construction is in progress (whether it exercises that ability or not).
- If the buyer has that ability, IAS 11 applies.
- If the buyer does not have that ability, IAS 18 applies.

If IAS 11 applies, what is the accounting?

If IAS 11 applies, revenue is recognised on a percentage-of-completion basis provided that reliable estimates of construction progress and future costs can be made.

If IAS 18 applies, service or goods?

Even if IAS 18 applies, the agreement may be to provide construction services rather than goods. This would likely be the case, for instance, if the entity is not required to acquire and supply construction materials. If the entity is required to provide services together with construction materials in order to perform its contractual obligation to deliver real estate to the buyer, the agreement is accounted for as the sale of goods under IAS 18.

4.11.2.3 IFRS 15

IFRS 15, which replaces all other Standards on Revenue, is expected to have a significant impact on the real estate sector. As per approach mandated by IFRD 15,

Revenue may be recognised over time, in a manner that best reflects the company's performance, or at a point in time, when control of the good or service is transferred to the customer. For complex transactions with multiple components and/or variable amounts of consideration, or when the work is carried out under contract for an extended period of time, applying the standard may lead to revenue being accelerated or deferred in comparison with current requirements. The Standard has also introduced new estimates and judgemental thresholds have been introduced, which may affect the amount and/or timing of revenue recognised. Some of these are:

- estimating and recognising variable consideration;
- identifying separate goods and services in a contract; and
- estimating stand-alone selling prices.

The standard includes new criteria to determine when revenue should be recognised over time, addressing fact patterns such as construction contracts and contracts for services. Some contracts that are currently accounted for under the stage-of-completion method may now require revenue to be recognised on contract completion; but for other contracts, the stage-of-completion method may be applied for the first time under the new model. Making this assessment based on the criteria provided will require a detailed review of contract terms and – for contracts to sell development property – property law.

Unlike the limited guidance available in IAS18 and its related Standards, in IFRS 15:

- all guidance contained in a single standard;
- control-based model ("risks and rewards" concept is retained as an indicator of control transfer);
- consideration measured as the amount to which the company expects to be entitled, rather than fair value;
- new guidance on separating goods and services in a contract; and
- new guidance on recognising revenue over time.

Costs and Disclosures

New judgements will be required when accounting for contract costs, as the new standard replaces existing cost guidance in IAS 11 Construction Contracts with limited new guidance on the costs of obtaining and fulfilling a contract. This will directly affect profit recognition, especially when revenue is recognised over time. You will need to evaluate the impact of the new guidance on the costs to be capitalised and also consider the period over which they can be amortised.

The standard includes extensive new disclosure requirements. You may have to redesign, and in many cases significantly expand, the information captured about unfulfilled performance obligations in order to draft the notes to the financial statements dealing with revenue. The new disclosures could convey important additional information about business practices and prospects to investors and competitors. No exemptions have been provided for commercially sensitive information.

Revenue Recognition – Land Securities Group

The Group recognises revenue on an accruals basis, when the amount of revenue can be reliably measured and it is probable that future economic benefits will flow to the Group. Revenue comprises rental income, service charge income and other recoveries, proceeds from the sale of trading properties, finance lease interest and income arising on long-term development contracts. Rental income includes the income from managed operations such as car parks, food courts, serviced offices and flats. Service charge income includes income in relation to service charges together with any chargeable management fees.

Rental income, including fixed rental uplifts, from investment property leased out under an operating lease is recognised in the income statement on a straight-line basis over the term of the lease. Lease incentives being offered to occupiers to enter into a lease, such as an initial rent-free period or a cash contribution to fit-out or similar costs are an integral part of the net consideration for the use of the property and are therefore recognised on the same straight-line basis. Service charge income is recorded as income in the periods in which it is earned.

When property is let under a finance lease, the Group recognises a receivable at an amount equal to the net investment in the lease at inception of the lease.

Rentals received are accounted for as repayments of principal and finance income as appropriate. Finance income is allocated to each period during the lease term so as to produce a constant periodic rate of interest on the remaining net investment in the finance lease. Contingent rents, being lease payments that are not fixed at the inception of a lease, for example turnover rents, are recorded as income in the periods in which they are earned.

Proceeds received on the sale of trading properties are recognised within Revenue when the significant risks and rewards of ownership have been transferred tithe buyer.

Revenue on long-term development contracts is recognised according to the stage reached in the contract by reference to the value of work completed using the percentage of completion method. An appropriate estimate of the profit attributable to work completed is recognised once the outcome of the contract can be estimated reliably.

All revenue is classified within the "Revenue profit" column of the income statement, with the exception of proceeds on the sale of trading properties and income arising on long-term development contracts, which are presented in the "Capital and other items" column. Also included in the "Capital and other items" column is the difference between the relevant line item on a proportionate basis and the amount included in the Group income statement.

Source: Land Securities Group Annual Report 2014, page 94

4.11.2.4 IFRIC 12 Service Concession Arrangements

IFRIC 12 would apply to entities in the real estate and infrastructure space who enter into contracts that would involve a grantor and an operator.

The IFRIC specifies two types of service concession arrangement.

- The operator receives a **financial asset**, specifically an unconditional contractual right to receive a specified or determinable amount of cash or another financial asset from the government in return for constructing or upgrading a public sector asset, and then operating and maintaining the asset for a specified period of time. This category includes guarantees by the government to pay for any shortfall between amounts received from users of the public service and specified or determinable amounts.

- The Operator receives an **intangible asset** – a right to charge for use of a public sector asset that it constructs or upgrades and then must operate and maintain for a specified period of time. A right to charge users is not an unconditional right to receive cash because the amounts are contingent on the extent to which the public uses the service.

The IFRIC allows for the possibility that both types of arrangement may exist within a single contract: to the extent that the government has given an unconditional guarantee of payment for the construction of the public sector asset, the operator has a financial asset; to the extent that the operator has to rely on the public using the service in order to obtain payment, the operator has an intangible asset.

Accounting – Financial asset model

The operator recognises a **financial asset** to the extent that it has an unconditional contractual right to receive cash or another financial asset from or at the direction of the grantor for the construction services. The operator has an unconditional right to receive cash if the grantor contractually guarantees to pay the operator:

(a) specified or determinable amounts, or
(b) the shortfall, if any, between amounts received from users of the public service and specified or determinable amounts, even if payment is contingent on the operator ensuring that the infrastructure meets specified quality or efficiency requirements.

The operator measures the financial asset at fair value.

Accounting – Intangible asset model

The operator recognises an **intangible asset** to the extent that it receives a right (a licence) to charge users of the public service. A right to charge users of the public service is not an unconditional right to receive cash because the amounts are contingent on the extent that the public uses the service.

The operator measures the intangible asset at fair value.

Operating revenue

The operator of a service concession arrangement recognises and measures revenue in accordance with IASs 11 and 18 for the services it performs.

Presented below is how Aberdis reflected the impact of IFRIC 12 in their financial statements:

Impact of Application of IFRIC 12 on abertis

IFRIC 12 is an interpretation of the International Financial Reporting Standards (IFRS) for public-private concessions which regulates the accounting treatment to be adopted in relation to service concession contracts and establishes different accounting methods for infrastructure items which had previously been recorded as tangible fixed assets: the intangible model (the risk of recovery of the investment is taken on by the operator), the financial asset model (the grantor guarantees recovery of the investment by the concessionaire), and the mixed model (a combination of the previous two models), according to the agreements reached between the concessionaire and the grantor.

It is applicable from 1 January 2010, and the abertis Group's results for the first quarter, to be presented on 13 May, will therefore already reflect the new standard, with comparable figures for 2009. As part of its Investor Day, the company today presented the impacts resulting from the application of this new accounting regulation. It does not affect the whole of abertis and the main effects will be seen in the toll road sector. It is anticipated that the application of the regulations to abertis' closed accounts for the year 2009 will not have a significant effect: it will entail a decrease of 0.8% income, -3.3% in EBITDA and -4.5% in net profit.

IFRIC 12 basically entails a reclassification of concession assets for abertis, in most cases as intangible assets. It also establishes advance provisions for large cyclical items (road surfaces, maintenance and large interventions), which until now were either recognised as a cost at the time they were carried out, or were activated and depreciated at a later date. In the initial application of IFRIC 12, the provision deficit will be set off against equity so that these costs will in future no longer pass through the profit and loss account. The impact on abertis' equity is also fairly insignificant.

Source: http://www.abertis.com/actualites/impact-of-the-application-of-the-ifric-12-accounting-standard-on-abertis/var/lang/fr/idm/588/idc/3326/ano/2010/mes/4

Key Takeaways

- Ascertaining whether IAS 2 , IAS 40 or IAS 16 applies
- Revenue Recognition for complicated agreements
- Revenue Recognition as per IFRS 15
- Service Concession Arrangements – Financial Asset or Intangible Asset

4.12 OIL AND GAS

4.12.1 Overview

The petroleum industry is capital intensive. Setting up a petroleum plant involves very high costs. Such plants have to operate in remote locations which give rise to a number of business risks. The entire process of exploration, evaluation, extraction, refining, transportation and marketing can take a significant amount of time and costs.

4.12.2 IFRS Standards that could impact the industry

4.12.2.1 IFRS 6 Exploration and Evaluation of Mineral Resources

Exploration and evaluation expenditure/assets

IFRS 6 deals only with Exploration and Evaluation Expenditure. IFRS 6 is a temporary Standard as the IASB is working on a larger project on extractive activities. Prior to IFRS 6, mining entities used to follow different methods in treating exploration and evaluation expenditure – some used to expense it, some used to capitalise it while some used to do a bit of both depending on the type of expenditure.

IFRS 6 can be summarised as follows:

- It permits an entity to develop an accounting policy for exploration and evaluation assets without specifically considering the requirements of paragraphs 11 and 12 of IAS 8. Thus, an entity adopting IFRS 6 may continue to use the accounting policies applied immediately before adopting the IFRS. This includes continuing to use recognition and measurement practices that are part of those accounting policies.
- It requires entities recognising exploration and evaluation assets to perform an impairment test on those assets when facts and circumstances suggest that the carrying amount of the assets may exceed their recoverable amount.
- It varies the recognition of impairment from that in IAS 36 but measures the impairment in accordance with that Standard once the impairment is identified.

However, IFRS 6 states that an entity shall not apply the IFRS to expenditures incurred:

- before the exploration for and evaluation of mineral resources, such as expenditures incurred before the entity has obtained the legal rights to explore a specific area; and
- after the technical feasibility and commercial viability of extracting a mineral resource has been demonstrated.

Para 9 of IFRS 6 provides the following indicative list of expenditures that might be included in the initial measurement of exploration and evaluation assets:

   (a) acquisition of rights to explore;
   (b) topographical, geological, geochemical and geophysical studies;
   (c) exploratory drilling;
   (d) trenching;
   (e) sampling; and

(f)   activities in relation to evaluating the technical feasibility and commercial viability of extracting a mineral resource.

It is common practice for entities in the Oil and Gas Industry to use the "successful efforts" method of accounting for exploration and development (E&D) expenditure. Under this method, the costs associated with locating, purchasing, and developing reserves are capitalised on a field-by-field basis. Once the reserves are proven, the capitalised costs can be assigned to the discovery; if discovery is not attained, then the expenditures are charged as an expense.

However, "successful efforts" is by no means a universal method. In its place, a number of upstream companies employ the full cost method of accounting for E&D expenditure. In contrast to the field-by-field approach of successful efforts, full cost is based on the aggregation of fields around geographic cost centers, typically organised on a country or regional basis.

Under IFRS, the proper application of full cost remains unsettled. IFRS 6 *Exploration for and Evaluation of Mineral Assets* allows for the use of full cost only for exploration and evaluation. After this phase, companies must switch to the successful efforts method.

Presented below is an extract from the financial statements of British Petroleum. It is interesting to note that instead of a generic statement of significant estimate or judgement at the beginning of the Statement of Accounting Policies, BP has chosen to give statements of significant estimate or judgement in their disclosures of every significant accounting policy.

OIL AND NATURAL GAS EXPLORATION, APPRAISAL AND DEVELOPMENT EXPENDITURE

Oil and natural gas exploration, appraisal and development expenditure is accounted for using the principles of the successful efforts method of accounting.

LICENCE AND PROPERTY ACQUISITION COSTS

Exploration licence and leasehold property acquisition costs are capitalised within intangible assets and are reviewed at each reporting date to confirm that there is no indication that the carrying amount exceeds the recoverable amount. This review includes confirming that exploration drilling is still under way or firmly planned or that it has been determined, or work is under way to determine, that the discovery is economically viable based on a range of technical and commercial considerations and sufficient progress is being made on establishing development plans and timing. If no future activity is planned, the remaining balance of the licence and property acquisition costs is written off. Lower value licences are pooled and amortised on a straight-line basis over the estimated period of exploration. Upon recognition of proved reserves and internal approval for development, the relevant expenditure is transferred to property, plant and equipment.

EXPLORATION AND APPRAISAL EXPENDITURE

Geological and geophysical exploration costs are charged against income as incurred. Costs directly associated with an exploration well are initially capitalised as an intangible asset until the drilling of the well is complete and the results have been evaluated. These costs include employee remuneration, materials and fuel used, rig costs and payments made to contractors. If potentially commercial quantities of hydrocarbons are not found, the exploration well is written off as a dry hole. If hydrocarbons are found and, subject to further appraisal activity, are likely to be capable of commercial development, the costs continue to be carried as an asset.

Costs directly associated with appraisal activity, undertaken to determine the size, characteristics and commercial potential of a reservoir following the initial discovery of hydrocarbons, including the costs of appraisal wells where hydrocarbons were not found, are initially capitalised as an intangible asset. When proved reserves of oil and natural gas are determined and development is approved by management, the relevant expenditure is **transferred to property, plant and equipment**.

DEVELOPMENT EXPENDITURE

Expenditure on the construction, installation and completion of infrastructure facilities such as platforms, pipelines and the drilling of development wells, including service and unsuccessful development or delineation wells, is capitalised within property, plant and equipment and is depreciated from the commencement of production as described below in the accounting policy for property, plant and equipment.

SIGNIFICANT ESTIMATE OR JUDGEMENT

The determination of whether potentially economic oil and natural gas reserves have been discovered by an exploration well is usually made within one year after well completion, but can take longer, depending on the complexity of the geological structure. Exploration wells that discover potentially economic quantities of oil and natural gas and are in areas where major capital expenditure (e.g. offshore platform or a pipeline) would be required before production could begin, and where the economic viability of that major capital expenditure depends on the successful completion of further exploration work in the area, remain capitalised on the balance sheet as long as additional exploration appraisal work is under way or firmly planned.

It is not unusual to have exploration wells and exploratory-type stratigraphic test wells remaining suspended on the balance sheet for several years while additional appraisal drilling and seismic work on the potential oil and natural gas field is performed or while the optimum development plans and timing are established. All such carried costs are subject to regular technical, commercial and management review on at least an annual basis to confirm the continued intent to develop, or otherwise extract value from, the discovery. Where this is no longer the case, the costs are immediately expensed.

Source: BP Annual Report and Form 20F 2013, page 129

4.12.2.2 IAS 37 Provisions, Contingent Liabilities and Contingent Assets

Oil and Gas Industries operate in difficult and remote terrains. Building infrastructure in these areas is difficult. Maintaining them is even more difficult. If the infrastructure gives way (if there is a leak in a pipeline, for instance), the oil or gas leaks. This causes great damage to the environment and threatens human beings and animals. Claims for damages are bound to follow bringing into play IAS 37 *Provisions,*

Contingent Liabilities and Contingent Assets. These claims for damages last over a few years so estimating the best estimate of the current obligation from a past event can be challenging. Wikipedia lists at least 12 major oil spills that have occurred since 1910 and have caused substantial damage.

The financial statements of British Petroleum (BP) provide an excellent example of how to provide for provisions and disclose Contingent Liabilities. The 2010 Gulf of Mexico oil spill has had a substantial impact on the financial statements of the company. This is a very long read but it epitomises the essence of what IFRS Standards seek in terms of disclosures.

Provisions and Contingent Liabilities

PROVISIONS

BP has recorded provisions relating to the Gulf of Mexico oil spill in relation to environmental expenditure, spill response costs, litigation and claims, and Clean Water Act penalties that can be measured reliably at this time.

Environmental

The environmental provision includes $320 million for BP's commitment to fund the Gulf of Mexico Research Initiative, which is a 10-year research programme to study the impact of the incident on the marine and shoreline environment of the Gulf of Mexico. In addition, BP faces claims under the Oil Pollution Act of 1990 (OPA 90) for natural resource damages. These damages include, among other things, the reasonable costs of assessing the injury to natural resources. During 2011, BP entered a framework agreement with natural resource trustees for the United States and five Gulf-coast states, providing for up to $1 billion to be spent on early restoration projects to address natural resource injuries resulting from the oil spill, to be funded from the $20-billion trust fund. In 2012, work began on the initial set of early restoration projects identified under this framework. At 31 December 2013 the amount provided for natural resource damage assessment costs and early restoration projects was $1,224 million. Until the size, location and duration of the impact is assessed, it is not possible to estimate reliably either the amounts or timing of the remaining natural resource damages claims other than the assessment and early restoration costs noted above, therefore no additional amounts have been provided for these items and they are disclosed as a contingent liability.

Spill response

The spill response provision relates primarily to ongoing shoreline operational activity.

Litigation and claims

The litigation and claims provision includes amounts that can be estimated reliably for the future cost of settling claims by individuals and businesses for damage to real or personal property, lost profits or impairment of earning capacity and loss of subsistence use of natural resources ("Individual and Business Claims"), and claims by state and local government entities for removal costs, damage to real or personal property, loss of government revenue and increased public services costs ("State and Local Claims"), under OPA 90 and other legislation, except as described under Contingent liabilities below. Claims administration costs and legal costs have also been provided for. The timing of payment of litigation and claims provisions classified as non-current is dependent on on-going legal activity and is therefore uncertain.

BP has provided for its best estimate of the cost associated with the PSC settlement agreements with the exception of the cost of business economic loss claims. As part of its monitoring of payments made by the DHCSSP, BP identified multiple business economic loss claim determinations that appeared to result from an interpretation of the EPD Settlement Agreement by the claims administrator that BP believes was incorrect.

Between March 2013 and March 2014, there were various rulings from both the federal District Court in New Orleans (the District Court) and a panel of the US Court of Appeals for the Fifth Circuit (the business economic loss panel) on matters relating to the interpretation of the EPD Settlement Agreement, in particular on the issue of matching revenue and expenses as well as causation requirements of the EPD Settlement Agreement.

As reported in *BP Annual Report and Form 20-F 2012*, the estimated cost of the PSC settlement for Individual and Business Claims was $7.7 billion at 31 December 2012. This estimate increased during the year to $9.6 billion to reflect all claims processed by the DHCSSP for which eligibility notices had been issued and increases in claims administration costs. As a result of the District Court's preliminary injunction issued on 18 October 2013 that, amongst other things, required the claims administrator to temporarily suspend payments of business economic loss claims other than those claims supported by sufficiently matched accrual-basis accounting or any other business economic loss claim for which the claims administrator determines that the matching of revenue and expenses is not an issue, the provision for $0.4 billion of claims for which eligibility notices had been issued but had not yet been paid was derecognised as BP considered and continues to consider that no reliable estimate can be made for these claims. At 31 December 2013, the total costs of the PSC settlement that BP considers can be reliably estimated is therefore $9.2 billion.

On 5 December 2013, the District Court amended its earlier preliminary injunction and temporarily suspended the issuance of final determination notices and payments of business economic loss claims, until the business economic loss issues have been resolved. On 24 December 2013, the District Court ruled on the issues in relation to the matching of revenue and expenses and causation that were remanded to it by the business economic loss panel. Regarding matching, the District Court reversed its earlier decision and ruled that the claims administrator, in administering business economic loss claims, must match revenue with the variable expenses incurred by claimants in conducting their business, even where the revenues and expenses were recorded at different times. The District Court assigned to the claims administrator the development of more detailed matching requirements. On 12 February 2014, the claims administrator issued a draft policy addressing the matching of revenue and expenses for business economic loss claims. The parties have made written submissions on the draft policy and the claims administrator will issue a final policy to which BP and the PSC have the right to object and seek review by the District Court. Regarding causation, the District Court ruled that the EPD Settlement Agreement contained no causation requirement beyond the revenue and related tests set out in an exhibit to that agreement. BP appealed the District Court's ruling on causation to the business economic loss panel and moved for a permanent injunction that would prevent the claims administrator from making awards to claimants whose alleged injuries are not traceable to the spill. On 3 March 2014, the business economic loss panel affirmed the District Court's ruling on causation and denied BP's motion for a permanent injunction. BP is considering its appeal options, including a potential petition that all the active judges of the Fifth Circuit review the 3 March decision. Under the terms of the business economic loss panel's ruling, the injunction temporarily suspending issuance of final determination notices and payments of business economic loss claims will be lifted when the matter is transferred back to the District Court; the timing of this would be affected by the status of any such petition by BP.

In addition to the proceedings in relation to the interpretation of the EPD Settlement Agreement, following the District Court's final order and judgment approving the EPD Settlement in January 2013, groups of purported members of the Economic and Property Damages Settlement Class (the Appellants) appealed from the District Court's approval of that settlement to a different panel of the Fifth Circuit. On 10 January 2014, that other panel of the Fifth Circuit affirmed the District Court's approval of the EPD Settlement but left to the business economic loss panel of the Fifth Circuit the question of how to interpret the EPD Settlement Agreement, including the meaning of the causation requirements of that agreement (see above). BP and several Appellants have filed petitions requesting that all the active judges of the Fifth Circuit review the decision to uphold approval of the EPD Settlement.

Until the uncertainties described below are resolved, management is unable to estimate reliably the value and volume of future business economic loss claims and whether and to what extent received or processed but unpaid business economic loss claims will be paid. Firstly, the inherent uncertainty as to the interpretation of the EPD Settlement Agreement in respect of matching and causation issues will continue until the more detailed matching requirements are finalised by the claims administrator and are implemented by the DHCSSP; the issue of causation and the requirements for class membership under the EPD Settlement Agreement are resolved on appeal; and the impact of any new policies and procedures in response to these issues on the value and volume of business economic loss claims becomes clear. Furthermore, the Fifth Circuit has yet to decide whether to grant the petitions seeking review of its decision affirming approval of the EPD Settlement and, if granted, whether to alter its decision in that appeal. Secondly, uncertainty arises from the lack of sufficient claims data under the DHCSSP from which to extrapolate any reliable trends – the number of business economic loss claims received and the average amounts paid in respect of such claims prior to the District Court's injunction were higher than previously assumed by BP. This inability to extrapolate any reliable trends may or may not continue once the uncertainties concerning the interpretation of the EPD Settlement Agreement described above have been resolved. Thirdly, there is uncertainty as to the ultimate deadline for filing business economic loss claims, which is dependent on the date on which all relevant appeals are concluded. Management believes, therefore, that no reliable estimate can currently be made of any business economic loss claims not yet received, processed and paid by the DHCSSP. A provision for business economic loss claims will be established when a reliable estimate can be made of the liability.

The total cost of the PSC settlement is likely to be significantly higher than the amount recognised to date of $9.2 billion because the current estimate does not reflect business economic loss claims not yet received, processed and paid. The DHCSSP has issued eligibility notices, disputed by BP, in respect of business economic loss claims of $1,019 million which have not yet been paid. Furthermore, a significant number of business economic loss claims have been received but have not yet been processed, and further claims are likely to be received.

The provision recognised for litigation and claims includes an estimate for State and Local Claims. Although the provision recognised is BP's current reliable best estimate of the amount required to settle these obligations, significant uncertainty exists in relation to the outcome of any litigation proceedings and the amount of claims that will become payable by BP. See Contingent liabilities below for further details.

Clean Water Act penalties

A charge for potential Clean Water Act Section 311 penalties was first included in BP's second-quarter 2010 interim financial statements. At the time that charge was taken, the latest estimate from the intra-agency Flow Rate Technical Group created by the National Incident Commander in charge of the spill response was between 35,000 and 60,000 barrels per day. The mid-point of that range, 47,500 barrels per day, was used for the purposes of calculating the charge. For the purposes of calculating the amount of the oil flow that was discharged into the Gulf of Mexico, the amount of oil that had been or was projected to be captured in vessels on the surface was subtracted from the total estimated flow up until when the well was capped on 15 July 2010. The result of this calculation was an estimate that approximately 3.2 million barrels of oil had been discharged into the Gulf. This estimate of 3.2 million barrels was calculated using a total flow of 47,500 barrels per day multiplied by the 85 days from 22 April 2010 to 15 July 2010 less an estimate of the amount captured on the surface (approximately 850,000 barrels). This estimated discharge volume was then multiplied by $1,100 per barrel – the maximum amount the statute allows in the absence of gross negligence or wilful misconduct – for the purposes of estimating a potential penalty. This resulted in a provision of $3,510 million for potential penalties under Section 311. BP intends to argue for a penalty lower than $1,100 per barrel. The actual penalty a court may impose could be lower than $1,100 per barrel if it were determined that such a lower penalty was appropriate based on the factors a court is directed to consider in assessing a penalty. In particular, in determining the amount of a civil penalty, Section 311 directs a court to consider a number of enumerated factors, including "the seriousness of the violation or violations, the economic benefit to the violator, if any, resulting from the violation, the degree of culpability involved, any other penalty for the same incident, any history of prior violations, the nature, extent, and degree of success of any efforts of the violator to minimise or mitigate the effects of the discharge, the economic impact of the penalty on the violator, and any other matters as justice may require." Civil penalties above $1,100 per barrel up to a statutory maximum of $4,300 per barrel of oil discharged would only be imposed if alleged gross negligence or wilful misconduct were proven. The $1,100 per-barrel rate has been utilised for the purposes of calculating the provision after considering and weighing all possible outcomes and in light of: (i) the company's conclusion that it did not act with gross negligence or engage in wilful misconduct; and (ii) the uncertainty as to whether a court would assess a penalty below the $1,100 statutory maximum. On 2 August 2010, the United States Department of Energy and the Flow Rate Technical Group had issued an estimate that 4.9 million barrels of oil had flowed from the Macondo well, and 4.05 million barrels had been discharged into the

Gulf (the difference being the amount of oil captured by vessels on the surface as part of BP's well containment efforts). It was and remains BP's view, based on the analysis of available data by its experts, that the 2 August 2010 Government estimate is not reliable. BP believes that the 2 August 2010 discharge estimate is overstated by at least 20%. If the flow rate were 20% lower than the 2 August 2010 estimate, then the amount of oil that flowed from the Macondo well would be approximately 3.9 million barrels and the amount discharged into the Gulf would be approximately 3.1 million barrels (using a current estimate of barrels captured by vessels on the surface of 810,000 in line with the stipulation entered with the US government – see Legal proceedings), which is not materially different from the amount we used for our original estimate at the end of the second quarter 2010. For the purposes of calculating a provision for fines and penalties under Section 311 of the Clean Water Act, BP has continued to use an estimate of 3.2 million barrels of oil discharged to the Gulf of Mexico and a penalty of $1,100 per barrel, as its current best estimate, as defined in paragraphs 36-40 of IAS 37 "Provisions, Contingent Liabilities and Contingent Assets," of the amounts which may be used in calculating the penalty under Section 311 of the Clean Water Act and as a result, the provision at the end of the year was $3,510 million. The amount and timing of the amount to be paid ultimately is subject to significant uncertainty since it will depend on what is determined by the court in the federal multi-district litigation proceedings in New Orleans (MDL 2179) as to negligence, gross negligence or wilful misconduct, the volume of oil spilled and the application of statutory penalty factors. The trial court could issue its decision on the first two phases of the trial (which considered the issues of negligence or gross negligence in phase one, and source control efforts and the volume of oil spilled in phase two) at any time and has not yet scheduled a hearing on the subsequent phase regarding the application of statutory penalty factors. The court has wide discretion in its determination as to whether a defendant's conduct involved negligence or gross negligence as well as in its determinations on the volume of oil spilled and the application of statutory penalty factors.

PROVISION MOVEMENTS

The total amount recognised as an increase in provisions during the year was $2,239 million, including $1,921 million for items covered by the trust fund and $318 million for other items (2012 $6,868 million, including $1,985 million for items covered by the trust fund and $4,883 million for other items). In addition, $379 million (2012 $794 million) was derecognised relating to items that will be covered by the trust fund but which can no longer be reliably estimated. After deducting amounts utilised during the year totalling $3,777 million, including payments from the trust fund of $3,051 million and payments made directly by BP of $726 million (2012 $5,864 million, including payments from the trust fund of $4,624 million and payments made directly by BP of $1,240 million), and after reclassifications and adjustments for discounting, the remaining provision as at 31 December 2013 was $9,346 million (2012 $15,200 million).

The total amounts that will ultimately be paid by BP in relation to all obligations relating to the incident are subject to significant uncertainty and the ultimate exposure and cost to BP will be dependent on many factors. Furthermore, significant uncertainty exists in relation to the amount of claims that will become payable by BP, the amount of fines that will ultimately be levied on BP (including any determination of BP's culpability based on any findings of negligence, gross negligence or wilful misconduct), the outcome of litigation and arbitration proceedings, and any costs arising from any longer-term environmental consequences of the oil spill, which will also impact upon the ultimate cost for BP. The amount and timing of any amounts payable could also be impacted by any further settlements which may or may not occur. Although the provision recognised is the current best reliable estimate of expenditures required to settle certain present obligations at the end of the reporting period, there are future expenditures for which it is not possible to measure the obligation reliably.

CONTINGENT LIABILITIES

BP has provided for its best estimate of amounts expected to be paid from the trust fund that can be measured reliably. This includes certain amounts expected to be paid pursuant to the Oil Pollution Act of 1990 (OPA 90). It is not possible, at this time, to measure reliably other obligations arising from the incident that are under the terms of the trust fund, namely any obligation in relation to natural resource damages claims or associated legal costs (except for the estimated costs of the assessment phase and costs relating to early restoration agreements under the $1-billion framework agreement referred to above), claims asserted in civil litigation including any further litigation through excluded parties from the PSC settlement including as set out in Legal proceedings, the cost of business economic loss claims under the PSC settlement not yet received, processed and paid by the DHCSSP, any further obligation that may arise from state and local government submissions under OPA 90 and any obligation in relation to other potential private or governmental litigation, nor is it practicable to estimate their magnitude or possible timing of payment. Therefore, no amounts have been provided for these obligations as at 31 December 2013.

Natural resource damages resulting from the oil spill are currently being assessed. BP and the federal and state trustees are collecting extensive data in order to assess the extent of damage to wildlife, shoreline, near shore and deepwater habitats, and recreational uses, among other things. The study data will inform an assessment of injury to the Gulf Coast natural resources and the development of a restoration plan to address the identified injuries.

Detailed analysis and interpretation continue on the data that have been collected. Any early restoration projects undertaken pursuant to the $1-billion framework agreement could mitigate the total damages resulting from the incident. Accordingly, until the size, location and duration of the impact is assessed, it is not possible to estimate reliably either the amounts or timing of the remaining natural resource damages claims, therefore no such amounts have been provided as at 31 December 2013.

As described under Provisions above, BP has identified multiple business economic loss claim determinations under the PSC settlement that appeared to result from an interpretation of the EPD Settlement Agreement by the claims administrator that BP believes was incorrect. Uncertainty as to the interpretation of the EPD Settlement Agreement will continue until the effects of the implementation of new policies and procedures are known, the issue of causation and the requirements for class membership under the EPD Settlement Agreement are resolved on appeal and the courts have ruled on the appeals in relation to the final order and judgment approving the EPD Settlement. Therefore the potential cost of business economic loss claims not yet received, processed and paid is not provided for and is disclosed as a contingent liability. A significant number of business economic loss claims have been received but have not yet been processed and paid, and further claims are likely to be received.

As described above in Provisions, a provision has been made for State and Local claims that can be measured reliably. In January 2013, the States of Alabama, Mississippi and Florida submitted or asserted claims to BP under OPA 90 for alleged losses including economic losses and property damage as a result of the Gulf of Mexico oil spill. BP is evaluating these claims. The States of Louisiana and Texas have also asserted similar claims. The amounts claimed, certain of which include punitive damages or other multipliers, are very substantial. However BP considers these claims unsubstantiated and the methodologies used to calculate these claims to be seriously flawed, not supported by OPA 90, not supported by documentation, and to substantially overstate the claims. Similar claims have also been submitted by various local government entities and a foreign government under OPA 90, and more claims are expected to be submitted. The amounts alleged in the submissions for these State and Local Claims total approximately $35 billion. BP will defend vigorously against these claims if adjudicated at trial.

Proceedings relating to securities class actions (MDL 2185) pending in federal court in Texas, including a purported class action on behalf of purchasers of American Depository Shares under US federal securities law, are continuing. A jury trial is scheduled to begin in October 2014. No reliable estimate can be made of the amounts that may be payable in relation to these proceedings, if any, so no provision has been recognised at 31 December 2013.

In addition to the State and Local claims and securities class actions described above, BP is named as a defendant in approximately 2,950 other civil lawsuits brought by individuals, corporations and government entities in US federal and state courts, as well as certain foreign jurisdictions, resulting from the Deepwater Horizon accident, the Gulf of Mexico oil spill, and the spill response efforts. Further actions are likely to be brought. Among other claims, these lawsuits assert claims for personal injury or wrongful death in connection with the accident and the spill response, commercial and economic injury, damage to real and personal property, breach of contract and violations of statutes, including, but not limited, to alleged violations of US securities and environmental statutes. Until further fact and expert disclosures occur, court rulings clarify the issues in dispute, liability and damage trial activity nears or progresses, or other actions such as further possible settlements occur, it is not possible given these uncertainties to arrive at a range of outcomes or a reliable estimate of the liabilities that may accrue to BP in connection with or as a result of these lawsuits. Therefore no amounts have been provided for these items as at 31 December 2013.

For those items not covered by the trust fund it is not possible to measure reliably any obligation in relation to other litigation or potential fines and penalties except, subject to certain assumptions detailed above, for those relating to the Clean Water Act. There are a number of federal and state environmental and other provisions of law, other than the Clean Water Act, under which one or more governmental agencies could seek civil fines and penalties from BP. For example, a complaint filed by the United States sought to reserve the ability to seek penalties and other relief under a number of other laws. Given the unsubstantiated nature of certain claims that may be asserted, it is not possible at this time to determine whether and to what extent any such claims would be successful or what penalties or fines would be assessed. Therefore no amounts have been provided for these items.

Under the settlement agreements with Anadarko and MOEX, and with Cameron International, the designer and manufacturer of the Deepwater Horizon blowout preventer, with M-I L.L.C. (M-I), the mud contractor, and with Weatherford, the designer and manufacturer of the float collar used on the Macondo well, BP has agreed to indemnify Anadarko, MOEX, Cameron, M-I and Weatherford for certain claims arising from the accident. It is therefore possible that BP may face claims under these indemnities, but it is not currently possible to reliably measure any obligation in relation to such claims and therefore no amount has been provided as at 31 December 2013.

The magnitude and timing of all possible obligations in relation to the Gulf of Mexico oil spill continue to be subject to a very high degree of uncertainty. Any such possible obligations are therefore contingent liabilities and, at present, it is not practicable to estimate their magnitude or possible timing of payment. Furthermore, other material unanticipated obligations may arise in future in relation to the incident.

Source: BP Annual Report and Form 20F 2013, pages 140–44

De-Commissioning Costs

The accounting for Decommissioning is well covered by the scope of IAS 37 *Provisions, Contingent Liabilities and Contingent Assets* and management will need to apply care and judgment in applying this standard. The objective of IAS 37 "is to ensure that appropriate recognition criteria and measurement bases are applied to provisions, contingent liabilities and contingent assets and to ensure that sufficient information is disclosed in the notes to enable users to understand their nature, timing and amount". Decommissioning obligations have a financial impact as they necessitate cash costs in the future IAS 37 requires recognition of a provision when there is: a present obligation (legal or constructive) as a result of a past event; it is probable that an outflow will occur; and a reliable estimate can be made. The "present obligation as a result of a past event" criterion means that only infrastructure that is currently in place will result in a provision. The liability will therefore exclude decommissioning costs of facilities yet to be installed. For an event to be an obligating event, it is necessary that the entity has no realistic alternative to settling the obligation created by the event. This is the case only when: the settlement of the obligation can be enforced by law, or in the case of a constructive obligation where the event creates valid expectations in other parties that the entity will discharge the obligation.

With respect to the initial recognition of decommissioning liabilities, provisions should only be recognised if the obligation arises from past events existing independently of an entity's future actions; thus, if an entity can avoid an obligation by its future actions, no provision is required. The cost of dismantling and removing an asset associated with the construction of the asset should be apportioned in the original cost of the asset. Obligations to decommission an asset should be recognised during the exploration and evaluation and development or production phases, as appropriate, rather than at the time the asset begins commercial production. This is an important consideration for an asset that takes a substantial period of time to prepare for its intended use.

Decommissioning liabilities and the related capitalised costs are measured at the best estimate of the costs required to settle the decommissioning liability or to transfer to third party. Decommissioning liability provisions are discounted using pre-tax rate that reflects current market assessments of the time value of money and the risks specific to the liability.

The standard requires that, in the event the time value of money is significant, the amount of a provision should be the present value of the expected expenditures necessary to discharge the obligation. It will be important for entities to be consistent in the choice and application of a discount rate, not only from period to period but also to situations in which discounting is required, e.g., impairment tests, cash flows from reserves, etc. IAS 37 explicitly prescribes that:

- the amount of the provision is the present value of the expenditure expected to be required to settle the obligation;
- the discount rate applied is a pre-tax rate that reflects current market assessments of the time value of money and the risks specific to the liability; and
- the discount rate should not reflect risks for which future cash flow estimates have been adjusted.

The Decommissioning Asset is depleted (depreciated), in the same way as the other oil and gas assets, using the unit of production (UOP) basis. This means that the cost of decommissioning is expensed to profit and loss over the life of the field, rather than in one big hit after the field has stopped producing. The Decommissioning Provision is increased over time as it is unwound, which adjusts for the year's worth of discount risk. The key idea is that by the time the field dries up, asset is down to 0 and provision is up to the full cost of decommissioning, in the money of the day when this takes place.

Costs estimates are based upon a number of assumptions and as a result changes in these estimates are almost inevitable over the life of a field, which will result in a change in the decommissioning asset and decommissioning provision. The decommissioning provision must be reviewed at each reporting date and adjusted to reflect management's current best estimates. In addition, at each reporting date the decommissioning provision is to be recalculated for changes in the estimated timing or amount of future cash outflows.

Accounting for changes in provisions is outlined in IFRIC 1 *Changes in Existing Decommissioning, Restoration and Similar Liabilities* and is applicable to decommissioning liabilities that have been both included in PP&E as part of an asset measured under IAS 16 and measured as a liability under IAS 37. It deals with the effect of the following three changes:

1. a change in the estimated timing of outflow of resources necessary to discharge the decommission obligation,
2. a change in the current market based discount rate (changes in the time value of money and risks specific to the liability), and
3. an increase that reflects the passage of time (also referred to as the unwinding of the discount or accretion of the discount).

For changes caused by items 1 and 2, the change is added to or deducted from the capitalised decommission cost of the asset to which it relates and the adjusted amount is amortised prospectively over the estimated life of the asset. A downward adjustment to the decommissioning and restoration asset cannot exceed the current carrying amount of the asset. Any excess should be recognised in the income statement in the current period.

The unwinding of the discount (item 3) arising from the passage of time is recognised as a financing cost in the income statement. It is not a borrowing cost as defined in IAS 23 *Borrowing Costs* and cannot be capitalised.

Key Takeaways

- Accounting for exploration and evaluation expenditure keeping in mind the requirements of IFRS 6
- Providing for claims as per a correct interpretation of the term current obligation from past events
- Providing for decommissioning costs

4.13 MEDIA

4.13.1 Overview

The main sources of income for an entity operating in the media space are subscription revenue and advertising revenue. IAS 18 provides guidance on both these areas. The media industry deals with rights to publish and broadcast. Entities would need to ascertain if these rights meet the definition of an Intangible Asset under IAS 38.

4.13.2 IFRS Standards that could impact the industry

4.13.2.1 IAS 18 Revenue Recognition

The media and broadcasting industry encompasses both physical media and online media. As a normal business practice, entities operating in the industry ship goods to the retail stores. The basic concept of risk and rewards enunciated in IAS 18 would need to be ascertained prior to recognising revenue. There could be restrictions on the selling of the shipped goods or the contract with the retailer could specify a right of return. In case there is a restriction on the sale of the shipped goods, it would appear appropriate to wait for the restriction to be lifted prior to recognising revenue.

Rights of return

For publishing and music companies converting to IFRSs, a key issue likely is determining an appropriate accounting policy for the rights of return. The nature of different arrangements with customers such as book and music stores will determine whether it is appropriate to recognise revenue under a consignment sale model, i.e. only as the book or music store sells the goods to the end customer, or whether it is appropriate to recognise revenue in full at the date of shipment to the book or music stores less a provision for expected returns.

Online downloads and e-books

It is now a norm to purchase media goods through online downloads, whereby the customer pays a fee to download content, such as books (e-books) and music, over the internet onto portable devices.

For music, risks and rewards generally are transferred upon the payment of fees and download of the file by the customer, and revenue would be recognised at that point.

Publishers selling e-books will require careful analysis of contractual terms of the arrangement prior to recognising revenue in order to reflect the substance of the arrangement. Two models are possible:

- the *purchase model*, whereby content is transferred to the customer in exchange for an upfront price. In this case, revenue is recognised upon download; or
- the *licensing model*, whereby the customer is offered access to individual e-books or a series of titles during the licence period. Typically in that case revenue is recognised over the period of access.

Bundled arrangements

Some publishing companies often sell both print and online products for a single price, such as in the case of educational or professional products. While print products have a fixed edition status at the time of sale, the online product often includes regular updates to the information contained in the printed product for a certain period of time. A key practice issue is determining when to separate the various components in a bundled arrangement.

Under IFRSs, if it is determined that (1) the component has stand-alone value to the customer; and (2) its fair value can be measured reliably, then generally the component is accounted for separately. In our experience, a large number of these transactions will be separated into individual components under IFRSs, with only the attributable revenue recognised as each component is delivered.

Once the individual components have been identified, the next step is to allocate the consideration among these components. IFRSs allow the relative fair value method or the fair value of the undelivered components (residual method) as a basis for allocating revenues to the separable components.

The detailed requirements of IFRS 15 would need to be considered for bundled contracts.

Sales incentives

Publishing and music companies often provide sales incentives such as cash discounts, volume rebates, free/discounted goods or services and vouchers to customers directly or through third parties. When an incentive programme is based on the volume or price of the products sold, the cost of these programmes generally is deducted from revenue when the corresponding sales are recorded.

Presented below are extracts from the Annual Report of the Guardian Media Group.

REVENUE RECOGNITION

Revenue comprises the fair value of consideration received or receivable for the sale of goods and services in the ordinary course of the Group's activities. Revenue is shown net of VAT, trade discounts and anticipated returns after eliminating sales within the Group.

The Group recognises revenue when the amount of revenue can be reliably measured, it is probable that future economic benefits will flow to the entity and when specific criteria have been met for each of the Group's activities as described below. The amount of revenue is not considered to be reliably measurable until all contingencies relating to the sale have been resolved. The Group bases its estimates on historical results, taking into consideration the type of customer, the type of transaction and the specifics of each arrangement.

Circulation and advertising revenue is recognised on publication, broadcast or display.

Revenues from barter transactions are recognised when the advertisements are displayed or broadcast and are recorded at the fair value of goods or services received.

SALE AND FINANCE LEASEBACK TRANSACTIONS

Where sale and finance leaseback transactions are entered into as a means of raising finance, the asset is regarded as being retained rather than disposed of and re-acquired. No adjustment to the carrying value or to the expected useful economic life of the asset is therefore made. The difference between the sale price and the fair value is recognised as a liability and charged to the income statement over the period of the lease agreement.

Source: Guardian Media Group

Purchased rights

Generally, publishing, title and distribution rights are acquired either separately or through a business combination. The costs incurred to acquire these rights are capitalised as intangible assets, provided that they meet the definition thereof as well as the recognition criteria under IAS 38 *Intangible Assets*.

Internally developed rights

Publishing companies often incur significant expenditure on internally generated intangible assets such as developing publishing rights and publishing titles. IFRSs include specific requirements in respect of such costs, and companies will need to carefully review their internal capitalisation policies on converting to IFRSs.

The internal cost of developing an intangible asset is classified into the *research* phase and the *development* phase. Only directly attributable costs incurred during the development phase are capitalised from the date that the publishing company can demonstrate that certain criteria are met. In our experience, the key criteria for publishing companies are: (1) the ability to demonstrate the probability of generating future economic benefits; and (2) the ability to reliably measure the expenditure incurred. Capitalising costs incurred during the development phase is not optional.

IFRSs specifically prohibit capitalising expenditure on internally generated intangible assets such as internally generated brands, mastheads, publishing titles and customer lists. This is because such expenditure cannot be distinguished from the costs of developing the business as a whole. Publishing companies often develop and publish magazines and incur significant costs in their research and development. These costs are not capitalised under IFRSs, since in practice publishing companies find it difficult to determine future economic benefits that will accrue on its sale. Publishing companies on converting to IFRSs should carefully review their internal capitalisation policies.

Development of database content

Developing content for a database and then selling the related access rights often is the main business for publishers, especially those in the business of developing and publishing professional and scientific material. Developing this content is similar to internally developed rights, and costs that are directly attributable to the development of the database content typically are capitalised as an intangible asset.

4.13.2.2 Intangible assets – amortisation, impairment and reversals

Amortisation

IFRSs do not require a specific method of amortisation, and publishing and music companies can choose between the straight-line, diminishing balance, unit-of-production method, or another method that appropriately reflects the pattern of consumption of the asset's economic benefits.

Impairment of non-financial assets

Under IAS 36 *Impairment of Assets*, publishing and music companies are required to assess at the end of each reporting period whether there are any indicators, external or internal, that an asset is impaired. In our experience, some of the indicators that publishing and music companies should consider include:

- the unexpected release of rival publications or albums;
- changes in the requirements within the advertising environment affecting publications that rely heavily on advertising;
- the adaptation of publications or music records to reflect the wishes of target groups;
- substantial differences between the quantities originally planned and those actually sold; and
- expected losses on a project as a whole.

Key Takeaways

- Recognition of Revenue considering the different methods of sale adopted by media and broadcasting companies
- Recognising Intangible Assets at their appropriate value

4.14 MINING

4.14.1 Overview

One of the first things that strikes one about the mining industry is that everything takes a lot of time. A mining company that has information that there are prospects for minerals to be mined in a particular region take a lot of time to explore the possibility of mining there. They then need to evaluate the technical feasibility and commercial viability of mining there. Both the activities of exploration and evaluation can take substantial periods of time. Once technical feasibility and commercial viability are proved, the entity takes a lot of time to develop the mine. The mine is then operated for several years before it is decommissioned. The entire cycle described above can last more than 25 years.

4.14.2 Present IFRS Standards that could impact the industry.

4.14.2.1 Exploration and evaluation expenditure/assets

IFRS 6 deals only with Exploration and Evaluation Expenditure. IFRS 6 is a temporary Standard as the IASB is working on a larger project on extractive activities. Prior to IFRS 6, mining entities used to follow different methods in treating exploration and evaluation expenditure – some used to expense it, some used to capitalize it while some used to do a bit of both depending on the type of expenditure.

IFRS 6 can be summarised as follows:

- It permits an entity to develop an accounting policy for exploration and evaluation assets. Thus, an entity adopting IFRS 6 may continue to use the accounting policies applied immediately before adopting the IFRS. This includes continuing to use recognition and measurement practices that are part of those accounting policies.
- It requires entities recognising exploration and evaluation assets to perform an impairment test on those assets when facts and circumstances suggest that the carrying amount of the assets may exceed their recoverable amount.
- It varies the recognition of impairment from that in IAS 36 but measures the impairment in accordance with that Standard once the impairment is identified.

However, IFRS 6 states that an entity shall not apply the IFRS to expenditures incurred:

- before the exploration for and evaluation of mineral resources, such as expenditures incurred before the entity has obtained the legal rights to explore a specific area;
- after the technical feasibility and commercial viability of extracting a mineral resource are demonstrable.

IFRS 6 provides the following indicative list of expenditure that might be included in the initial measurement of exploration and evaluation assets:

- (a) acquisition of rights to explore;
- (b) topographical, geological, geochemical and geophysical studies;
- (c) exploratory drilling;

(d) trenching;

(e) sampling; and

(f) activities in relation to evaluating the technical feasibility and commercial viability of extracting a mineral resource.

Impairment of exploration and evaluation assets

IFRS 6 effectively modifies the application of IAS 36 *Impairment of Assets* to exploration and evaluation assets recognised by an entity under its accounting policy. Specifically:

- entities recognising exploration and evaluation assets are required to perform an impairment test on those assets when specific facts and circumstances outlined in the standard indicate an impairment test is required. The facts and circumstances outlined in IFRS 6 are non-exhaustive, and are applied instead of the "indicators of impairment" in IAS 36;
- entities are permitted to determine an accounting policy for allocating exploration and evaluation assets to cash-generating units or groups of CGUs. This accounting policy may result in a different allocation than might otherwise arise on applying the requirements of IAS 36; and
- if an impairment test is required, any impairment loss is measured, presented and disclosed in accordance with IAS 36.

4.14.2.2 Start-up costs

It is not uncommon in the mining industry for there to be a long commissioning period, sometimes over 12 months, during which production is gradually increased towards design capacity. In these situations, a key question which arises under IFRS is how the revenues and costs incurred during the commissioning period should be accounted for.

IAS 16 *Property, Plant and Equipment* requires that costs can only be capitalised if they are "directly attributable" to the asset, and it also states that revenue from saleable material produced during the testing phase should be deducted from the cost of constructing the asset. Taking this into account along with the indicative list of costs that can be shown as E & E Assets as per IFRS 6, it would appear that most start-up costs would be expensed till the directly attributable and economic benefits tests are met.

4.14.2.3 Decommissioning and restoration costs

IAS 37 *Provisions, Contingent Liabilities and Contingent Assets* provides guidance on how to account for decommissioning, restoration and similar liabilities, which can be significant for mining entities. In addition, IFRIC 1 *Changes in Existing Decommissioning, Restoration and Similar Liabilities* contains specific rules on how revisions to these liabilities should be accounted for. In applying the requirements of IAS 37 and IFRIC 1, there are a number of areas where careful consideration is required. One question that could crop up is when should the liability be recognised – it appears that the ideal time would be the development stage and not the start-up stage.

4.14.2.4 Depreciation basis

There are various methods that can be used for depreciating property, plant and equipment in the mining industry. Under IAS 16, the method used should reflect the pattern in which the asset's future economic benefits are expected to be consumed by the entity.

The future economic benefits for some mining assets are closely matched to the production throughput or output – for example, the benefits associated with a crusher are linked to ore throughput. For other assets (such as administration office buildings), the benefits do not directly relate to production.

The most common depreciation methods are as follows:

- The straight-line method, which results in an equal annual depreciation expense over the asset's useful life.
- The units-of-production method, in which the depreciation expense reflects the pattern of reserve/resource depletion or throughput.
- The diminishing balance method, which results in a decreasing depreciation expense over the useful life of the asset. Conceptually, one would expect a lot of mining assets to be depreciated on a units-of-production basis. Certainly this is the most appropriate method for depreciating mining properties, with the annual charge reflecting the amount produced each year. However, some entities depreciate all or most of their mining equipment on a straight-line basis which is much simpler to apply. This needs to be considered on a case-by-case basis, but where equipment is operated at full capacity throughout its economic life, for example, the straight-line method is unlikely to give a materially different result from a units-of-production basis.

4.14.2.5 Deferred stripping

When India was planning to adopt IFRS, the Chairman of India's largest coal mining company, Coal India Limited made the following statement:

> *"Once we adopt IFRS accounting standards, we will get back some Rs 12,000 crore from provision kept as 'overburden removal reserve' used in our traditional accounting system of our mines. This will boost our networth from 2012–13," said the Chairman of Coal India Limited.*

> *Source: www.business-standard.com/article/companies/cil-net-worth-to-jump-by-rs-12k-cr-from-2012-13-110101800187_1.html*

The statement reflects the impact that removing overburden costs can have on a mine.

Mining entities often need to remove overburden and other waste materials to access ore reserves. The costs they incur are referred to as "stripping costs." During the development of a mine (before production begins), the stripping costs are capitalised as part of the depreciable cost of constructing the mine. Those capitalised costs are then depreciated over the productive life of the mine.

IFRIC 20 *Stripping Costs in the Production Phase* of a mine would be applicable to all such costs during the production phase of a mine.

IFRIC 20 requires the following:

- The costs of stripping activity to be accounted for in accordance with the principles of IAS 2 *Inventories* to the extent that the benefit from the stripping activity is realised in the form of inventory produced.
- The costs of stripping activity which provides a benefit in the form of improved access to ore is recognised as a non-current "stripping activity asset" where the following criteria are met:
  - ○ it is probable that the future economic benefit (improved access to the ore body) associated with the stripping activity will flow to the entity;
  - ○ the entity can identify the component of the ore body for which access has been improved; and
  - ○ the costs relating to the stripping activity associated with that component can be measured reliably.
- When the costs of the stripping activity asset and the inventory produced are not separately identifiable, production stripping costs are allocated between the inventory produced and the stripping activity asset by using an allocation basis that is based on a relevant production measure.
- A stripping activity asset is accounted for as an addition to, or as an enhancement of, an existing asset and classified as tangible or intangible according to the nature of the existing asset of which it forms part.
- A stripping activity asset is initially measured at cost and subsequently carried at cost or its revalued amount less depreciation or amortisation and impairment losses.
- A stripping activity asset is depreciated or amortised on a systematic basis, over the expected useful life of the identified component of the ore body that becomes more accessible as a result of the stripping activity. The units of production method is used unless another method is more appropriate.

4.14.2.6 *Joint ventures*

In the mining industry, joint ventures are common. Entities operating in the mining industry would need to take into account the provisions of *IFRS 11 Joint Arrangements*.

As per IFRS 11, the classification of a joint arrangement as a joint operation or a joint venture depends upon the rights and obligations of the parties to the arrangement. An entity determines the type of joint arrangement in which it is involved by considering the structure and form of the arrangement, the terms agreed by the parties in the contractual arrangement and other facts and circumstances. Regardless of the purpose, structure or form of the arrangement, the classification of joint arrangements depends upon the parties' rights and obligations arising from the arrangement.

Mining entities would need to recognise, measure and disclose the impact of Joint Arrangements in accordance with IFRS 11 which would involve a close and detailed study of the contracts.

4.14.2.7 *Joint and by-products*

It is common in the mining industry for more than one product to be extracted from a particular ore. Base metals such as lead and zinc are often found together, and gold is commonly found with copper. Reasons vary for treating mine production as joint products or by-products, but the treatment is usually related to the importance of the products to the viability of the mine.

- Joint products are defined in IAS 2 as "two or more products produced simultaneously from a common raw material source, with each product having a significant relative sales value." One joint product cannot be produced without the other, and the products cannot be identified separately until a certain production stage, often called the "split-off point," is reached.

- By-products are "secondary products obtained during the course of production or manufacture, having relatively small importance when compared with the principal product or products." IAS 2 allows any rational and consistent basis of cost allocation when the conversion costs of a product are not separately identifiable. Varying practices are used to value joint and by-products. In relation to joint products, one possible approach is to allocate the "common costs" based on the relative sales value of the joint products. This method can be justified where the profitability of the joint products is roughly equal, but not where the products have significantly different profit margins. An acceptable alternative may be to allocate costs based on the relative volume of production in some circumstances.

If the amounts involved are immaterial, it is common for by-products to be recorded at net realisable value (i.e. market value less any selling and residual processing costs). This approach is acceptable under IAS 2, so long as it is a well-established practice for the relevant commodity. Some entities, however, account for by-products on a cost basis by applying those costs incurred after the split off point, and carry the inventory at the lower of cost and net realisable value. This method is also acceptable. Whichever method is chosen it should be applied consistently.

4.14.3 First time conversion example

Presented below is an extract from the financial statements of Rio-Tinto when they first transitioned to IFRS from their previous GAAP.

Rio-Tinto: Adoption of International Financial Reporting Standards

The Group's transition date for IFRS is 1 January 2004. The principal differences between UK GAAP and IFRS are described below. All financial numbers are stated after tax and outside shareholders' interests.

REVERSAL OF GOODWILL AMORTISATION

The systematic amortisation of goodwill under UK GAAP, by an annual charge to the profit and loss account, will cease under IFRS. It will be replaced by annual impairment reviews of the carrying value of goodwill. Impairment charges relating to goodwill are quite likely in future reporting periods due to the finite life of the associated ore body. The charges may vary significantly from period to period.

The impact on Net Earnings in 2004 was a $77 million reduction (to zero) of the charge for amortisation of goodwill. At 31 December 2004, this increases the goodwill balance under IFRS by $74 million because the goodwill amortised under UK GAAP in 2004 has been reversed.

POST-RETIREMENT BENEFITS

Under UK GAAP, the Group applied SSAP 24, "Accounting for Pension Costs" under which post retirement benefit surpluses and deficits were spread over the expected average remaining service lives of relevant current employees. The International Accounting Standards Board (IASB) issued an amendment to IAS 19 "Employee Benefits" in December 2004. In preparing the IFRS information in this release, the directors have assumed that this revised standard will be endorsed by the EU and adopted in the Group's 2005 financial statements. Under IAS 19 the basis of calculating the surplus or deficit under IFRS differs from SSAP 24. In addition, IAS 19 permits three alternative ways in which the surplus or deficit can be recognised. The Group has chosen to recognise actuarial gains and losses directly in shareholders' equity via the Statement of Recognised Income and Expense. The annual service cost and net financial income on the assets and liabilities of the Group's post retirement benefit plans are recognised through Net Earnings.

The impact on Net Earnings in 2004 was a $25 million reduction in the charge for post retirement benefits.

At 31 December 2004, the different bases for calculating the surplus or deficit and determining the amounts recognised on the balance sheet results in additional provisions of $764 million (net of deferred tax and outside interests) in the IFRS balance sheet compared to the UK GAAP balance sheet.

SHARE BASED PAYMENTS

Under UK GAAP, no cost was recognised in respect of the Group's share option schemes. IFRS requires the economic cost of share option plans to be recognised by reference to fair value on the grant date, and charged to the Income Statement over the expected vesting period. The IFRS charge in 2004 was $27 million and is included in Underlying Earnings.

DEFERRED TAX ON FAIR VALUE ADJUSTMENTS ARISING ON ACQUISITIONS

UK GAAP requires the recognition of deferred tax on all fair value adjustments to monetary items, and on fair value adjustments which reduce the carrying value of non-monetary items. IFRS requires deferred tax to be recognised on all fair value adjustments, other than those recorded as goodwill. IFRS Net Earnings will therefore benefit as the additional deferred tax provisions on upward revaluations of non-monetary items are released to the Income Statement in line with the amortisation of the related fair value adjustments.

For future acquisitions, these additional deferred tax provisions will be offset by increases to the value of goodwill or other acquired assets. For acquisitions prior to 1 January 2004, the increase in provisions has been reflected as a reduction in opening shareholders' equity.

The impact on IFRS Net Earnings for 2004 was an increase of $29 million. At 31 December 2004, the IFRS balance sheet includes additional provisions of $720 million relating to deferred tax on fair value adjustments for prior year acquisitions.

DEFERRED TAX ON UNREMITTED EARNINGS

Under UK GAAP, tax was only provided on unremitted earnings to the extent that dividends were accrued or if there was a binding agreement for the distribution of earnings at the reporting date. Under IFRS, full provision must be made for tax arising on unremitted earnings from subsidiaries, joint ventures and associated companies, except to the extent that the Group can control the timing of remittances and remittance is not probable in the foreseeable future.

The impact on IFRS net earnings was a reduction of $16 million. At 31 December 2004, the IFRS balance sheet includes additional provisions of $74 million relating to deferred tax balances on unremitted earnings.

DEFERRED TAX RELATED TO CLOSURE COSTS

Under IFRS, deferred tax is not provided on the depreciation of capitalised closure costs except to the extent that the capitalised amount was first recognised in accounting for an acquisition. This reduced IFRS Net Earnings for 2004 by $20 million and reduced IFRS shareholders' equity at 31 December 2004 by $105 million.

PROFITS ON DISPOSAL OF SUBSIDIARIES, JOINT VENTURES, ASSOCIATES AND UNDEVELOPED PROPERTIES

Differences occur in the measurement of the accounting gain on such transactions where there are differences in the book value of assets under the respective accounting rules. In 2004, the majority of the additional profit under IFRS arose because under UK GAAP goodwill that had been eliminated against reserves at the time of acquisition was reinstated and charged against earnings at the time of disposal. Such reinstatement does not apply under IFRS. In 2004 this increased IFRS Net Earnings by $262 million.

EXCHANGE DIFFERENCES ON NET DEBT

The Group finances its operations primarily in US dollars, which is the currency in which the majority of its revenues are denominated. A substantial part of the Group's US dollar debt is located in subsidiaries having functional currencies other than the US dollar. Under IFRS, exchange gains and losses relating to US dollar debt and certain intragroup financing balances are included in the Group's US dollar Income Statement, whereas under UK GAAP they were taken to reserves. In 2004 this increased IFRS net earnings by $80 million. Under both IFRS and UK GAAP the offsetting differences arising on the translation into US dollars of the local currency balance sheets are taken to reserves.

There is no difference between the IFRS Balance Sheet and the UK GAAP Balance Sheet due to these items.

At 1 January 2005, the main currency exposures arising from net debt and intragroup financing balances were liabilities of US$1.7 billion accounted for in Australian dollars and liabilities of US$0.5 billion accounted for in Canadian dollars. The exchange differences recorded in the Income Statement are a function not only of fluctuations in exchange rates but also fluctuations in the level of these balances during the period.

MARK TO MARKET OF DERIVATIVE CONTRACTS

It remains the Group's general policy not to hedge on-going exposures to fluctuations in exchange rates, prices or interest rates although the Group is party to some derivative contracts. For example, the Group holds derivative contracts taken out by Group companies prior to their acquisition and from time to time the Group has used forward foreign currency contracts to hedge the non US dollar component of capital projects.

Some derivative contracts that qualified for hedge accounting under UK GAAP do not qualify for hedge accounting under IFRS because the instrument is not located in the operation which carries the exposure. These contracts are marked to market under IFRS, thereby giving rise to charges or credits to the Income Statement in periods before the hedged transaction is recognised.

At 31 December 2004, the marked to market value of derivative contracts, that under UK GAAP would have been eligible for hedge accounting, increases shareholders' equity by $99 million.

EXCHANGE DIFFERENCES ON CAPITAL EXPENDITURE HEDGES

Some of the derivative contracts that were taken out to fix the non US dollar component of capital expenditure in previous periods do not qualify for hedge accounting under IFRS. The adjustment to the carrying value of property, plant & equipment that under UK GAAP had been stated net of realised exchange gains and losses on forward contracts hedging capital expenditure, increases shareholders' equity by $162 million.

DIVIDENDS

Under IFRS, dividends that do not represent a present obligation at the reporting date are not included in the balance sheet. Hence, the Companies' proposed dividends are not recognised in the Group accounts until the period in which they are declared by the directors.

This has no effect on Net Earnings or Underlying Earnings, but increases shareholders' equity at 31 December 2004 by $626 million.

FUNCTIONAL CURRENCIES

From 2005, the functional currencies of Rio Tinto's operations will be their local currencies with the exception of Escondida, Grasberg JV and Lihir for which the functional currency is the US dollar.

IAS 39 AND IAS 32

The Group has elected to adopt IAS 32 "Financial Instruments: Disclosure and Presentation" and IAS 39 "Financial Instruments: Recognition and Measurement" with effect from 1 January 2005 with no restatement of comparative information. The financial information for 30 June 2004 and 31 December 2004 does not therefore incorporate the effect of these Standards.

Subsidiaries, joint ventures and associates
The basis for determining the presentation of partially owned operations in the Group's financial statements differs in certain respects between IFRS and UK GAAP. The Group has decided to adopt equity accounting for all jointly controlled entities.

Kennecott Energy's Colowyo operation, which under UK GAAP was equity accounted, is consolidated under IFRS. Anglesey Aluminium, which was consolidated is now equity accounted.

Boyne Island Smelters, Queensland Alumina Limited, Eurallumina and NZAS which were proportionately consolidated under UK GAAP will be equity accounted under IFRS. This results in significant increases in accounts receivable and accounts payable in the Group balance sheet because amounts due to or from these operations by the rest of the Group are no longer eliminated on consolidation.

Rio Tinto Coal Australia's Bengalla, Mount Thorley, Blair Athol, Hail Creek, Kestrel and Warkworth mines, Kennecott Minerals' Greens Creek mine and the Grasberg Joint Venture which were equity accounted under UK GAAP will be proportionately consolidated under IFRS.

CASH FLOW STATEMENT AND NET DEBT

The pre-tax cash flow from operations of $4,452 million, including dividends from equity accounted joint ventures and associates, is practically the same under IFRS as it was under UK GAAP. Some operations previously equity accounted under UK GAAP are proportionately consolidated under IFRS and vice versa, with the effect that the increase in cash flow from subsidiary operations is largely offset by lower reported dividends from equity accounted joint ventures and associates. These reclassifications are explained fully above.

Similarly, net debt of $3,809 million is only $58 million higher under IFRS reflecting changes between equity accounting and proportionate consolidation for some operations. A sizeable proportion of Rio Tinto's borrowings are denominated in currencies other than US dollar and then swapped into US dollars. Under UK GAAP, these borrowings are accounted for as if they were in US dollars. Under IFRS, the exchange gains and losses on the swaps must be shown separately in the balance sheet as financial assets or financial liabilities as appropriate. A reconciliation of net debt to the various balance sheet categories is shown on page 19. There is no change to the Group's treasury policy, which is to manage net debt after taking account of such currency swaps.

Gearing increases from 22 per cent under UK GAAP to 23 per cent under IFRS because of the reduction in shareholders' equity shown above. IFRS interest cover is 20 times.

Source: http://www.proactiveinvestors.co.uk/companies/rns/050505rio9036l

Key Takeaways

- Exploration and Evaluation Expenditure would need to be carefully segregated and accounted taking into consideration the requirements of IFRS 6
- IFRIC 20 would need to be considered for stripping costs in the production phase of a mine
- Useful lives of Assets would need to be carefully estimated
- Decommissioning Costs would need to be provided for and monitored regularly

4.15 RETAIL

4.15.1 Overview

The retail industry can be said to be one of the most "popular" industries – everyone needs to consume goods and receive services from retail players to meet their requirements. As indicated in another Chapter, the retail industry "front-ends" most of the fast moving consumer goods (FMCG) industry.

Accountants in the retail industry could have issues with Inventories – valuations and methods, accounting for warranties, guarantees and returns and revenue recognition.

4.15.2 IFRS Standards that could impact the industry

4.15.2.1 IAS 18 Revenue Recognition

(a) Revenue

Revenue recognition issues in the retail industry could involve timing of the revenue recognition. The main questions that would need to be answered here are:

1. When does the margin/commission of the retailer accrue?
2. What is the process to be followed by the retailer to account for incentives/rebates given by the manufacturer?
3. How does the retailer account for Barter transactions?

(b) Rebates

Under IFRS, non-cash rebates (e.g., free gift with purchase or buy one get one free) are generally treated as a reduction in revenues. This may not be the case in other GAAP requirements.

(c) Layaway sales

Under IAS 18 layaway sales would generally be recognised when the goods are delivered. Under IFRS revenue could also be recognised when a significant deposit is received, provided that the goods are on hand, identified, and ready for delivery to the buyer. Because "significant" is not defined under IFRS, one will have to carefully apply judgment upon determining when to recognise revenue.

4.15.2.2 IFRIC 13 Customer loyalty programmes

The International Financial Reporting Interpretations Committee (IFRIC) has issued guidance on accounting for customer loyalty programmes. When loyalty awards are granted, IFRS requires that the consideration be separated into two components – the fair value of the goods and services provided, and the fair value of the awards given to the customer. The value of the award is then deferred as a liability until the obligation has been fulfilled.

IFRS has an answer to each issue indicated above. These IFRS requirements could significantly change the timing of when revenue is recognised.

Tesco

REVENUE

Revenue comprises the fair value of consideration received or receivable for the sale of goods and services in the ordinary course of the Group's activities.

SALE OF GOODS

Revenue is recognised when the significant risks and rewards of ownership of the goods have transferred to the buyer and the amount of revenue can be measured reliably.

Revenue is recorded net of returns, discounts/offers and value added taxes.

PROVISION OF SERVICES

Revenue from the provision of services is recognised when the service is provided and the revenue can be measured reliably, based on the terms of the contract.

Where the Group acts as an agent selling goods or services, only the commission income is included within revenue.

FINANCIAL SERVICES

Revenue consists of interest, fees and income from the provision of insurance.

Interest income on financial assets that are classified as loans and receivables is determined using the effective interest rate method.

Calculation of the effective interest rate takes into account fees receivable that are an integral part of the instrument's yield, premiums or discounts on acquisition or issue, early redemption fees and transaction costs.

Fees in respect of services (credit card interchange fees, late payment and ATM revenue) are recognised as the right to consideration accrues through the provision of the service to the customer. The arrangements are generally contractual and the cost of providing the service is incurred as the service is rendered.

The Group generates commission from the sale and service of motor and home insurance policies underwritten by Tesco Underwriting Limited, or in a minority of cases by a third party underwriter. This is based on commission rates which are independent of the profitability of underlying insurance policies. Similar commission income is also generated from the sale of white label insurance products underwritten by other third party providers.

CLUBCARD, LOYALTY AND OTHER INITIATIVES

The cost of Clubcard and loyalty initiatives is part of the fair value of the consideration received and is deferred and subsequently recognised over the period that the awards are redeemed. The deferral is treated as a deduction from revenue.

The fair value of the points awarded is determined with reference to the fair value to the customer and considers factors such as redemption via Clubcard deals versus money-off-in-store and redemption rate.

Source: Tesco Annual Report and Financial Statements 2014 Page 75

There has been enough literature written on the Revenue Recognition issues at Tesco. It is not my intention to add to the existing literature. More than a revenue recognition issue, the Tesco issue was an error in judgement – the problem was that the error of judgement was huge.

4.15.2.3 *IAS 16* **Property, Plant, and Equipment**

Retail operations typically incur significant expenditures for evaluating store locations, building and/or refurbishing stores.

IFRS requires that costs for feasibility assessments be expensed and that each item of property, plant, and equipment be identified and recorded at a component level, with individually significant components depreciated separately over their respective useful lives. Under IFRS, additional components may need to be captured, and you may require modifications to fixed assets systems.

IFRS also provides separate guidance for accounting for investment property (property held for purposes of generating rental income or capital appreciation).

IFRS permits companies to elect to carry property, plant, and equipment as well as investment property at fair value.

4.15.2.4 *IAS 37* **Provisions**

Under IFRS, a provision is recognised for both legal and constructive obligations when it arises from a past event, the outflow of resources is probable, and the amount can be estimated reliably. In this context, "probable" means "more likely than not" and represents a lower threshold than "likely." More items may, therefore, need to be provided for under IFRS, particularly for obligations to restore sites to certain conditions.

Under IFRS, provisions are measured based on management's best estimate of the amount required to settle the obligation.

IFRS also requires discounting on all provisions for which the effect of the time value of money is material. The discount rate should reflect current market assessments of the time value of money and the risks specific to the liability. Provisions should be re-measured when discount rates change.

4.15.2.5 *IAS 17* **Leases**

Retailers operate numerous stores. Consequently, retailers enter into multiple leases. Retailers would need to ascertain the nature of the lease – operating or finance – as per the mandate of IAS 17. In some instances, the lessor is the same for multiple properties of the retailer and thus offers lease incentives such as rent-free periods. Retailers would also need to take into consideration the requirements of IFRIC 4 *Determining Whether an Arrangement Contains a Lease*.

4.15.2.6 *Other Accounting Areas*

Web site development costs – Such costs can generally be capitalised under IFRS when it is probable that expected future economic benefits will arise. However, for Web sites for which the primary purpose is to advertise, promote, and facilitate the on-line sale of goods or services, the associated costs should be expensed.

Enterprises may encounter difficulties where they cannot differentiate whether the costs are associated with the on-lines sales function or other Web functions.

Deferred store opening costs/pre- operating costs – Under IFRS, such costs are expensed as incurred.

Multi-employer pension plans – Under IFRS, multi-employer pension plans are not automatically accounted for as defined contribution plans and, even when they are, further assets and liabilities may be required where the employers have a contractual agreement to share plan surpluses and fund plan shortfalls.

4.15.3 First time conversion case study

Presented below is the explanatory statement of differences when J. Sainsbury converted to IFRS for the first time.

First-time adoption of IFRS

IFRS 1 *First-time adoption of International Financial Reporting Standards* allows companies adopting IFRS for the first time to take certain exemptions from the full requirements of IFRS in the year of transition (i.e. the 52 weeks to 26 March 2005).

The Group has elected to take the following key exemptions:

(I) IFRS 3 BUSINESS COMBINATIONS

The Group has elected not to apply IFRS 3 *Business Combinations* retrospectively to acquisitions that took place before the date of transition. As a result, the carrying amount of goodwill in the UK GAAP balance sheet at 27 March 2004 is brought forward to the IFRS opening balance sheet without adjustment.

(II) IAS 19 EMPLOYEE BENEFITS – ACTUARIAL GAINS AND LOSSES

The Group has elected to recognise all cumulative actuarial gains and losses at the date of transition.

(III) IAS 21 – CUMULATIVE TRANSLATION DIFFERENCES

Under IFRS, cumulative translation differences arising on the consolidation of foreign entities are required to be recycled through the income statement when a foreign entity is sold as part of the gain or loss on sale. IFRS 1 allows the Group to not record cumulative translation differences arising before the date of transition. The Group has elected to take this exemption and has brought forward a nil balance in respect of these translation differences.

(IV) IAS 32 AND IAS 39 – FINANCIAL INSTRUMENTS

The Group has taken the option to defer the implementation of IAS 32 and IAS 39 to the financial year beginning 27 March 2005. Therefore, financial instruments continue to be accounted for and presented in accordance with UK GAAP for the 52 weeks to 26 March 2005.

(V) IAS 16 – VALUATION OF PROPERTIES

The Group has elected to treat the revalued amount of properties at 28 March 2004 as deemed cost as at that date and will not revalue properties for accounting purposes in the future.

(VI) IFRS 2 – SHARE-BASED PAYMENT

IFRS 1 provides an exemption which allows entities to only apply IFRS 2 *Share-based Payment* to share-based payment awards granted after 7 November 2002. The Group has not taken this exemption but has elected to apply IFRS 2 to share options granted before 7 November 2002. The fair value of those options has been published on our website.

Explanation of reconciling items between UK GAAP and IFRS – Group

(A) CAPITALISATION OF BUILDING LEASES

Under UK GAAP, the Group recognised finance leases under the recognition criteria set out in SSAP 21. Although the accounting treatment of finance leases remains largely the same under IFRS, the application of IAS 17 *Leases* results in the building element of a number of property leases being classified as finance leases.

The impact on the Group's financial statements is set out below:

- The Group's IFRS opening balance sheet at 28 March 2004 includes additional property, plant and equipment of £37 million and additional finance lease obligations of £53 million resulting in a reduction in net assets of £11 million after deferred tax of £5 million.
- The main impact on the income statement is that the operating lease payment charged to operating profit under UK GAAP is replaced with a depreciation charge on the finance lease asset and a financing charge on the obligation. The pre-tax impact on the income statement for the 52 weeks to 26 March 2005 is a reduction in administrative expenses of £2 million and an increase in finance costs of £3 million. This results in a net charge of £1 million (£1 million after deferred tax).
- The Group's IFRS balance sheet at 26 March 2005 includes additional property, plant and equipment of £36 million and additional finance lease obligations of £53 million resulting in a reduction in net assets of £12 million after deferred tax of £5 million.

(B) LEASE INCENTIVES

Under UK GAAP, rent-free periods were recognised over the period to the first market rent review. Under IAS 17, these are amortised over the term of the lease. The impact on the Group's financial statements is set out below:

- The Group's IFRS opening balance sheet at 28 March 2004 includes additional deferred income of £4 million, resulting in a reduction in net assets of £3 million after deferred tax.
- The pre-tax impact on the income statement for the 52 weeks to 26 March 2005 is an increase in administrative expenses of £2 million (£1 million after deferred tax).
- The Group's IFRS balance sheet at 26 March 2005 includes additional deferred income of £6 million, resulting in a reduction in net assets of £4 million after deferred tax.

(C) LEASES WITH PREDETERMINED FIXED RENTAL INCREASES

Comments by IFRIC have indicated that under IFRS it is necessary to account for leases with predetermined fixed rental increases on a straight-line basis over the life of the lease. Under UK GAAP, the Group accounted for these rental increases in the year they arose.

The impact on the Group's financial statements is set out below:

- The impact of this change at the date of transition, 28 March 2004, is an addition of deferred income of £17 million, resulting in a reduction in net assets of £12 million after deferred tax.
- The pre-tax impact on the income statement for the 52 weeks to 26 March 2005 is an increase in cost of sales of £4 million (£3 million after deferred tax).
- The Group's IFRS balance sheet at 26 March 2005 includes additional deferred income of £21 million, resulting in a reduction in net assets of £15 million after deferred tax.

(D) PENSIONS

The Group applied the provisions of SSAP 24 under UK GAAP and provided detailed disclosure under FRS 17 in accounting for pensions. Under IFRS, the Group's balance sheet reflects the assets and liabilities of the Group's defined benefit pension schemes. As allowed in the amendment to IAS 19, the Group has elected to recognise all cumulative actuarial gains and losses through the statement of recognised income and expense.

The impact on the Group's financial statements is set out below:

- The Group's opening balance sheet at 28 March 2004 reflects the liabilities of the defined benefit pension schemes, with a total gross deficit of £715 million. This liability represents a gross deficit of £665 million relating to the UK defined benefit pension schemes and £50 million relating to the US supermarkets business, Shaw's.

  The gross deficit relating to the UK defined benefit pension schemes of £665 million is shown together with £7 million of unfunded pension liabilities, previously recorded within provisions under UK GAAP. The associated deferred income tax asset of £202 million is shown within deferred income tax liability on the transition balance sheet.

  The net pension deficit relating to Shaw's of £30 million (£50 million gross deficit before deferred tax of £20 million – calculated at the US corporate tax rate of 40 per cent) has been transferred as part of the sale of Shaw's and has been included under "Non-current liabilities held for sale" in the IFRS balance sheet at 28 March 2004 (note (l)).

- The income statement adjustment for the 52 weeks to 26 March 2005 is a small increase in cost of sales of £2 million and a reduction in finance costs of £11 million, resulting in a net credit of £9 million (£6 million after deferred tax).

  The annual charge through the income statement is lower under IAS 19 than under SSAP 24 because the SSAP 24 charge included additional contributions to amortise the £161 million actuarial deficit identified in March 2003. The calculation of the IAS 19 income statement charge does not include these contributions.

  In addition, the net pension deficit of £30 million relating to Shaw's has been transferred as part of the sale of Shaw's with the effect of increasing the reported gain on sale. This is recorded as an increase in the "Profit attributable to discontinued operations" in the income statement for the 52 weeks to 26 March 2005.

- The Group's IFRS balance sheet at 26 March 2005 reflects the gross deficit of £527 million relating to the UK defined benefit pension schemes and £9 million of unfunded pension liabilities previously recorded within provisions under UK GAAP. The associated deferred income tax asset of £161 million is shown separately within deferred income tax liability.

The gross actuarial gain of £128 million and its associated deferred tax impact of £38 million (net actuarial gain of £90 million) has been recognised in the statement of recognised income and expense for the 52 weeks to 26 March 2005.

(E) OTHER EMPLOYEE BENEFITS

Under UK GAAP no provision was made for long service awards. Under IAS 19, the costs of long service awards are accrued over the period the service is provided by the employee.

The impact on the Group's financial statements is set out below:

- A provision for long service awards is included in the opening IFRS balance sheet at 28 March 2004 to the value of £7 million (£5 million after deferred tax).
- There is no income statement charge in respect of this provision for the 52 weeks to 26 March 2005 and the provision for long service awards remains at £7 million (£5 million after deferred tax) in the Group's IFRS balance sheet at 26 March 2005.

(F) SHARE-BASED PAYMENTS

IFRS 2 *Share-based Payment* requires that an expense for share-based payments, including SAYE schemes, be recognised in the financial statements based on their fair value at the date of grant. The expense is recognised over the vesting period of the share-based payment scheme.

The additional pre-tax charge arising from the adoption of IFRS 2 on the Group's income statement for the 52 weeks to 26 March 2005 is £8 million (cost of sales: £5 million; administrative expenses: £3 million), resulting in a net charge of £7 million after deferred tax. The adjustment is comparatively low because the executive share options granted since 2002 are unlikely to vest and as a result there is no charge relating to these awards.

(G) SOFTWARE CAPITALISATION

Under UK GAAP, software was included within tangible fixed assets. Under IFRS, software is reclassified from tangible fixed assets and recorded within intangible assets. The balance sheet reclassification amounts to £86 million at date of transition 28 March 2004 and £74 million at 26 March 2005. There is no income statement impact.

(H) GOODWILL

Previously goodwill on acquisitions was capitalised and amortised over its useful economic life. Under IFRS, amortisation is no longer charged, instead goodwill is tested for impairment annually and again where indicators are deemed to exist. Goodwill is carried at cost less accumulated impairment losses.

The impact on the Group's financial statements is set out below:

- The goodwill amortisation charge for the 52 weeks to 26 March 2005 under UK GAAP of £5 million (including £1 million of goodwill amortisation relating to Shaw's) reverses in the IFRS financial statements. No impairment charge relating to acquired goodwill has been recognised as at 26 March 2005.
- The impact on the Group's IFRS balance sheet at 26 March 2005 is to increase the goodwill balance by £4 million, resulting in an increase in net assets of £4 million.

(I) GOODWILL – SALE OF US SUPERMARKETS BUSINESS, SHAW'S

Under UK GAAP, goodwill previously set off against reserves was recycled on the sale of the entity to which it related. However, this "recycling" is not permitted under IFRS.

As a result, the goodwill recycled upon disposal of the US supermarkets business,

Shaw's is reversed, resulting in an increase of £86 million to the gain on sale. This is recorded as an increase in the "Profit attributable to discontinued operations" on the face of the income statement for the 52 weeks to 26 March 2005.

(J) IMPAIRMENT OF NON-FINANCIAL ASSETS

Under IFRS, the Group reviews the carrying amounts of its tangible and intangible assets to determine whether there is any indication that those assets are impaired.

If any such indication exists, the recoverable amount of the asset is estimated in order to determine the extent of the impairment loss (if any). Where the asset does not generate cash flows that are independent from other assets, the Group estimates the recoverable amount of the cash-generating unit ("CGU") to which the asset belongs. For tangible and intangible assets, excluding goodwill, the CGU is deemed to be each trading store. For goodwill, the CGU is deemed to be each retail chain of stores acquired.

The impact on the Group's financial statements is set out below:

- As at the opening balance sheet date, 28 March 2004, 27 stores were deemed to be impaired, resulting in an impairment loss of £51 million (£44 million after deferred tax) for property, plant and equipment. This total includes the 13 stores that the Group announced would be closed as part of the Business Review.
- A similar impairment review was performed for the 52 weeks to 26 March 2005 and no further impairment was deemed necessary. However, as a result of the above IFRS impairment adjustment at transition date, £11 million (£9 million after deferred tax) of UK GAAP depreciation charges and write-down costs relating to those impaired stores is reversed for the 52 weeks to 26 March 2005.
- The impact on the Group's IFRS balance sheet at 26 March 2005 is an impairment loss of £40 million (£35 million after deferred tax) for property, plant and equipment.

(K) DIVIDENDS

Under UK GAAP, dividends were recognised in the period to which they relate. IFRS requires that dividends be recognised as a liability when they are declared (i.e. approved by shareholders or, in the case of interim dividends, when paid). Accordingly, the accrued final dividends of £218 million and £95 million are reversed in the balance sheets at 28 March 2004 and 26 March 2005 respectively. The final dividend of £218 million is recognised directly as an appropriation of retained earnings in the balance sheet at 26 March 2005.

(L) DISCONTINUED OPERATIONS

Under IFRS, assets and liabilities of disposal groups are shown separately on the balance sheet. This has the effect of having a single line "Non-current assets held for sale" represent the total assets of disposal groups and a single line "Non-current liabilities held for sale" represent the total liabilities of disposal groups.

Similarly, the results of discontinued operations are shown in the income statement separately from continuing operations. This has the effect of having one line representing the trading profit of discontinued operations and any gain or loss on sale. This is a re-presentation and there is no impact on the total Group profit after tax as presented under UK GAAP.

The change in presentation on the Group's IFRS financial statements is set out below:

- At the date of transition 28 March 2004, the Group held a disposal group relating to the US supermarkets business, Shaw's. As a result, the assets and liabilities of Shaw's are excluded from the Group's assets and liabilities and are shown separately in the balance sheet.

(M) CASH AND CASH EQUIVALENTS

The definition of cash and cash equivalents under IFRS resulted in certain current assets being reclassified from investments to cash equivalents. The balance sheet reclassification amounts to £19 million at date of transition, 28 March 2004 and £24 million at 26 March 2005. There is no income statement impact.

(N) REVALUATION RESERVE

Under IFRS, deferred tax is accounted for on the basis of taxable temporary differences between the tax base and accounting base of assets and liabilities.

As a result, an additional deferred tax liability of £7 million arising from the revaluation reserve of £22 million has been recognised in the IFRS balance sheets at 28 March 2004 and 26 March 2005.

In addition, the Group has elected to treat the revalued amount of properties as deemed cost at date of transition 28 March 2004 and will not revalue properties for accounting purposes in the future. As a result, the revaluation reserve of £22 million under UK GAAP has been transferred directly to retained earnings in the Group's IFRS balance sheets at 28 March 2004 and 26 March 2005.

Source: J Sainsbury Annual Report 2005

4.16 TELECOM

4.16.1 Overview

The telecommunication industry is marked by high capital costs. The revenue model is distributed over millions of customers with tariff plans that change regularly. Telecom companies also charge customers for browsing the internet on their mobile phones and downloading data.

4.16.2 Present IFRS Standards that could impact the industry

4.16.2.1 IAS 18/IFRS 15

Telecoms face challenges when applying the revenue recognition requirements under IFRS. International Accounting Standard (IAS) 18 *Revenue* and related International Financial Reporting Interpretations Committee (IFRIC) interpretations are principle – based rather than sector-specific, which has resulted in a degree of inconsistency in the recognition of revenues by telecoms.

When faced with arrangements such as bundled products, free handsets, broadband connectivity and television and installation fees, telecoms reporting under IFRS must assess whether the risks and rewards of ownership have been transferred in order to determine when to recognise revenue. Accordingly, the individual facts and circumstances always will need careful consideration as they may vary between entities and also between different contracts within the same entity.

Separating arrangements into the underlying multiple deliverables, including customer loyalty programmes. Are you able to separate equipment sales from service arrangements? Can broadband installation or mobile activation fees be separated from the ongoing network provision? Such examples require a careful analysis of the entire revenue arrangement, rather than the constituent parts of the contract. Under IAS 18, two or more transactions are considered a single arrangement when they are "linked" in such a way that the commercial effect cannot be understood without reference to the series of transactions as a whole. This will usually revolve around the nature of the components of the transaction and the stand-alone value of those components.

In today's era of fierce competition and bundled pricing, "free" products, such as free handsets, modems or set-top boxes, are offered to customers by telecoms on subscribing to their wireless or fixed-line services.

In basic terms, if it is determined that (1) the component has stand-alone value to the customer and (2) its fair value can be measured reliably, then the component should be accounted for separately.

We would expect large numbers of these transactions to be separated into individual components under IFRS, with only the attributable revenue recognised as each component is delivered. The separation guidance equally applies to customer loyalty programmes, which are required to be accounted for as separate revenue-generating deliverables rather than as cost deferrals. The accounting for customer loyalty programmes will be a significant change for many telecoms.

4.16.2.2 Gross revenue reporting versus net revenue reporting

IFRS have specific guidance on determining whether an entity is acting as principal (indicative of reporting a transaction on a gross basis) or agent (indicative of reporting a transaction on a net basis) in a transaction. The issue is of particular importance to telecoms when it comes to mobile content downloads, premium rate services and call transmission such as international calls.

Mobile content downloads and premium rate services

Consideration received by telecoms from customers relating to mobile content downloads and premium rate services generally can be recorded on a gross basis only if the telecom has acquired the content rights and sells them to the users. In such cases, the telecom has the risks and rewards of the ownership rights. If the telecom merely passes the consideration received to the content owner after taking its share, then it may be appropriate that the consideration received by the telecom be recorded on a net basis reflective of its "commission."

However, telecoms need to exercise judgement when determining whether a transaction should be recorded on a gross or net basis. For example, in some cases the customer's credit risk for amounts receivable resides with the telecom but control over the content and price resides with the content provider.

Call transmission

Telecoms will need to consider various contractual rights and obligations before arriving at the decision that revenues from international calls are recorded on a net or gross basis, as facts and circumstances likely will be different in each case. Some of the questions to consider include the following:

- Does the telecom control decisions on the routing of traffic?
- Is the telecom involved in determining the scope of services provided?
- Do end customers have claim over the telecom for service interruption or poor quality of transmission?

Vodafone

REVENUE

Revenue is recognised to the extent the Group has delivered goods or rendered services under an agreement, the amount of revenue can be measured reliably and it is probable that the economic benefits associated with the transaction will flow to the Group. Revenue is measured at the fair value of the consideration receivable, exclusive of sales taxes and discounts.

The Group principally obtains revenue from providing the following telecommunication services: access charges, airtime usage, messaging, interconnect fees, data services and information provision, connection fees and equipment sales. Products and services may be sold separately or in bundled packages.

Revenue for access charges, airtime usage and messaging by contract customers is recognised as services are performed, with unbilled revenue resulting from services already provided accrued at the end of each period and unearned revenue from services to be provided in future periods deferred. Revenue from the sale of prepaid credit is deferred until such time as the customer uses the airtime, or the credit expires.

Revenue from interconnect fees is recognised at the time the services are performed.

Revenue from data services and information provision is recognised when the Group has performed the related service and, depending on the nature of the service, is recognised either at the gross amount billed to the customer or the amount receivable by the Group as commission for facilitating the service.

Customer connection revenue is recognised together with the related equipment revenue to the extent that the aggregate equipment and connection revenue does not exceed the fair value of the equipment delivered to the customer. Any customer connection revenue not recognised together with related equipment revenue is deferred and recognised over the period in which services are expected to be provided to the customer.

Revenue for device sales is recognised when the device is delivered to the end customer and the sale is considered complete. For device sales made to intermediaries, revenue is recognised if the significant risks associated with the device are transferred to the intermediary and the intermediary has no general right of return. If the significant risks are not transferred, revenue recognition is deferred until sale of the device to an end customer by the intermediary or the expiry of the right of return.

In revenue arrangements including more than one deliverable, the arrangements are divided into separate units of accounting. Deliverables are considered separate units of accounting if the following two conditions are met: (1) the deliverable has value to the customer on a stand-alone basis and (2) there is evidence of the fair value of the item. The arrangement consideration is allocated to each separate unit of accounting based on its relative fair value.

COMMISSIONS

Intermediaries are given cash incentives by the Group to connect new customers and upgrade existing customers.

For intermediaries who do not purchase products and services from the Group, such cash incentives are accounted for as an expense. Such cash incentives to other intermediaries are also accounted for as an expense if:

- the Group receives an identifiable benefit in exchange for the cash incentive that is separable from sales transactions to that intermediary; and
- the Group can reliably estimate the fair value of that benefit.

Cash incentives that do not meet these criteria are recognised as a reduction of the related revenue.

Source: Vodafone Annual Report 2014, page 111

4.16.2.3 Intangible assets

Spectrum or wireless licences, software (both acquired and internally developed) and goodwill are significant to the statement of financial position of telecoms and to the decision maker in any acquisition.

Spectrum licences are either acquired through government auctions or as part of an acquisition of another telecom, i.e., a business combination. The measurement of cost when purchased as part of a government auction includes the purchase price and any directly attributable costs such as borrowing costs, legal and professional fees. Alternatively, when such licences are acquired as part of a business combination, they are measured at fair value.

An internally generated intangible asset, such as billing software, is measured based on the direct costs incurred in preparing the asset for its intended use. Internal costs relating to the research phase of research and development (R&D) are generally expensed. However, development costs are capitalised if certain criteria are met. This requirement for an entity to define the criteria for research separately from development may affect telecoms who define R&D by reference to the criteria of other GAAPs.

4.16.2.4 Amortisation of intangible assets

Intangible assets are classified into those with a finite life, which are subject to amortisation, and those with an indefinite life including goodwill, which are not amortised but are subject to annual impairment testing.

The method of amortisation for an intangible asset with a finite useful life should reflect the pattern of consumption of the economic benefits. This should be consistent with management's assumptions in their budgeting, with amortisation beginning at the earliest point at which economic benefits are received from the intangible asset. Under IFRS, difficulties in determining useful life do not imply that an intangible asset has an indefinite useful life. This may cause issues for example, with spectrum licences in which it is likely that technology will eventually render a licence obsolete.

4.16.2.5 Property, plant and equipment

Telecoms are faced with the challenging task of reviewing capitalisation policies, detailed asset tracking and component depreciation.

4.16.2.6 Costs eligible for capitalisation

All costs such as material costs, labour and related benefits, installation costs, cost relating to network testing activities, site preparatory costs, among others, that are directly attributable to bringing an asset to the present condition and location necessary for intended use are eligible for capitalisation. However, all non-directly attributable costs such as allocations of general overhead including training costs may not be capitalised under IFRS. Telecoms, on conversion to IFRS, therefore will need to carefully review their asset capitalisation policies.

4.16.2.7 Component and depreciation methods

A telecom is required to allocate the initial amount relating to an item of property, plant and equipment into its significant parts or "components" and depreciate each part separately. This may involve significant judgement on part of the telecom.

When an item of property, plant and equipment comprises significant individual components for which different depreciation methods or rates are appropriate, each component is depreciated separately. A separate component may be either a physical component or a non-physical component that represents a major inspection or over-haul. An item of property, plant and equipment should be separated into components when those parts are significant in relation to the total cost of the item. Component accounting is compulsory when it would be applicable. However, this does not mean that an entity should split its assets into an infinite number of components if the effect on the financial statements would be immaterial.

IFRS do not specify one particular method of depreciation as preferable. Telecoms have the option to use the straight-line method, the diminishing or reducing balance method or the units-of-production method, as long as it reflects the pattern in which the economic benefits associated with the asset are consumed.

4.16.2.8 Asset retirement obligations or "decommissioning liabilities" under IFRS – contractual and constructive obligations

Under IAS 37 *Provisions, Contingent Liabilities and Contingent Assets*, telecoms recognise obligations, both contractual and constructive, as part of the carrying amount of an asset. However, there are often differences in practice relating to recognition where rectification obligations may exist but they are not enforced. For example, obligations in respect of cables laid in international waters on the seabed or on coastal "landing stations" may be unclear and inconsistently accounted for between telecoms. Some telecoms may consider that removing the original cables may cause more environmental damage than leaving them in place. In our experience, judgment is required in the area of recognition and measurement of such provisions.

4.16.2.9 Impairment of non-financial assets

A one-step approach requiring impairment losses to be recorded in the event the carrying amount of an asset exceeds its recoverable value. Consideration of the time value of money (i.e., discounting) is required.

4.16.2.10 Long-lived assets other than goodwill

Under IAS 36 *Impairment of Assets*, entities assess at the end of each reporting period whether there are any indicators, external or internal, that an asset is impaired. An impairment loss is recognised and measured for an individual asset, other than goodwill, at an amount by which its carrying amount exceeds its "recoverable amount." If the recoverable amount cannot be determined for the individual asset, because the asset does not generate independent cash inflows separate from those of other assets, then the impairment loss is recognised and measured based on the cash-generating unit ("CGU") to which the asset belongs.

4.16.2.11 Cash-generating units

A CGU is defined as the smallest group of assets that generates cash inflows from continuing use that are largely independent of the cash inflows from other assets or group of assets of the telecom.

Identifying CGUs can become more complex in the telecoms sector because of multiple products across different networks, especially if a telecom has operations in various countries. Further, certain telecoms may have their operating segments based on "type of customers" (e.g., residential or commercial), or "type of network" (e.g., fixed-line or wireless).

Telecoms are also faced with the challenge of allocating revenues from bundled products and services to the various networks in the current environment. This may be difficult when a customer is typically offered fixed-line calls, wireless, broadband and TV bundled as one service, while individual products are declining or rising in volume (e.g., fixed-line calls versus broadband line rentals).

4.16.2.12 Indicators of impairment

Some examples of indicators of impairment are outlined below:

- **Market value has declined significantly or the entity has operating or cash losses.** For example, the migration of customers from fixed-line to wireless services may result in operating cash losses in the fixed-line business and result in a trigger for impairment.
- **Technological obsolescence.** For example, the technology shift from copper-based network to fibre-based network may be an indicator of impairment for the copper-based network.
- **Competition.** For example, the saturation of the mobile market intensifies competition for customers, which may reduce revenues and operating profits, thereby indicating potential impairment.
- **Market capitalisation.** For example, the carrying amount of the telecom's net assets exceeds its market capitalisation.
- **Significant regulatory changes.** For example, regulation of roaming charges in the European Union.
- **Physical damage to the asset.**
- **Significant adverse effect on the entity that will change the way the asset is used or expected to be used.** For example, the impact of sharing networks with other telecoms or exchanging network capacity, which may lead to stranded network assets that may be impaired.
- **Goodwill.** Under IFRS, telecoms are required to test goodwill (and intangible assets with indefinite lives) for the purposes of impairment at least annually irrespective of whether indicators of impairment exist and more frequently at interim periods if impairment indicators are present. Goodwill by itself does not generate cash inflows independently of other assets or group of assets and therefore is not tested for the impairment separately. Instead, it should be allocated to the acquirer's CGUs that are expected to benefit from the synergies of the business combination from which goodwill arose, irrespective of whether other assets or liabilities of the acquiree are assigned to those units. Goodwill is allocated to a CGU which represents: (1) the lowest level within the entity at which the goodwill is monitored for internal management purposes and (2) cannot be larger than an operating segment as defined in IFRS 8 *Operating Segments*. An impairment loss is recognised and measured at an amount by which the CGU's carrying amount, including goodwill, exceeds its recoverable amount.

- **Impairment reversals.** Impairment losses related to goodwill cannot be reversed. However, other impairment losses are reversed, subject to certain restrictions, if the recoverable amount has increased. However, as networks become more sophisticated, such a reversal of value in the assets used in legacy technology areas is perhaps unlikely in the telecoms sector.

4.16.2.13 Leases

Considering the operating costs required by telecoms and the changing face of the sector, lease accounting is gaining attention. IAS 17 *Leases* instead looks to the substance of the transaction to determine which party has the risks and rewards of ownership of a leased asset. This may affect those telecoms who adjust accounting models to come close to the bright-line benchmarks that keep assets off-balance sheet as operating leases, when the substance of the arrangement is that the telecom obtains substantially all of the risks and rewards incidental to ownership of the asset.

Land and building leases

Under IFRS, IAS 17 requires telecoms to assess the lease classification of land and building separately in the case of a combined lease of property, unless the value of the land is considered to be immaterial. As telecoms often have material property portfolios of specialised buildings owing to telephone exchange or mobile network structures, if such items include property lease arrangements, then this may be a significant issue under IFRS.

While not the sole deciding factor for operating versus finance lease classification, the minimum lease payments need to be allocated into the two components of land and buildings in proportion to the relative fair value of the *leasehold interest* as opposed to the relative fair values of the assets themselves. If the allocation cannot be done reliably, then the entire lease is classified as a finance lease, unless it is clear that both elements qualify as operating leases.

4.16.2.14 Financial instruments

Significant changes in accounting for financial instruments.

Telecoms generally have financial instrument accounting issues owing to the treasury structures used to assist material network infrastructure build.

As it currently stands, IAS 39 *Financial Instruments: Recognition and Measurement* requires financial assets to be classified into one of four categories (financial assets at fair value through profit and loss, loans and receivables, held-to-maturity or available-for-sale) and financial liabilities are categorised as either financial liabilities at fair value through profit and loss or other liabilities.

Financial assets and financial liabilities are initially measured at fair value. After initial recognition, loans and receivables and held-to-maturity investments are measured at amortised cost. All derivative instruments are measured at fair value with gains and losses recorded in profit and loss except when they qualify as hedging instruments in a cash flow hedge.

A financial asset is derecognised only when the contractual rights to cash flows from that particular asset expire or when substantially all risk and rewards of ownership of the asset are transferred. A financial liability is derecognised when it is extinguished or when the terms are modified substantially.

4.16.2.15 *Provisions and contingencies*

IFRS generally will result in earlier recognition of provisions.

Various types of provisions that affect telecoms include, but are not limited to warranties, environmental liabilities, decommissioning liabilities, disputes and legal claims which are covered under IAS 37 *Provisions, Contingent Liabilities and Contingent Assets*. The standard requires the recognition of a present obligation as a provision based on the probability of occurrence of outflow of resources, in which "probable" is defined as "more likely than not." This may result in the recognition of additional amounts or earlier recognition of such amounts in the financial statements, as compared to the existing standards currently applied by telecoms.

Management is required to recognise a provision for its best estimate of the expenditure to be incurred at the end of the reporting period. The time value of money is considered, if material. For single obligations (e.g., lawsuits) a provision may be measured based on the most likely outcome. For a large population of possible amounts (e.g., product warranties), a provision is measured at its expected value which is a probability-weighted approach. In the event there is a continuous range of possible outcomes and no one amount is considered to be equally likely, then management is required to consider the mid-point of the range as an estimate of the amount of provision.

4.16.2.16 *Tower companies*

The key issues in question are whether communication towers should be classified as investment property or as property plant and equipment (PPE). An understanding of both the physical structure as well as the ownership and usage of these towers is crucial in order to correctly account for them under IFRS. The IFRS Interpretations Committee (IFRIC) had earlier expressed support for broadening the scope of IAS 40 by focussing on the way the asset is used rather than on the physical characteristics of the structure.

Key Takeaways

- Revenue Recognition especially in the light of IFRS 15
- Providing for claims from customers

4.17 SERVICES

4.17.1 Overview

The services industry includes technology and consulting firms that provide services to clients across the globe. Such firms invariably have multiple office locations across the globe. Outsourcing and off-shoring are some of the terms used to describe their business model.

4.17.2 IFRS Standards that could impact the industry

It is often said that the Service Industry comprises two Ss – Service and Salary. IAS 18/IFRS 15 *Revenue* and IAS 19 *Employee Benefits* would be important standards for this industry.

4.17.2.1 IAS 18/IFRS 15

Entities in the Service Industry have different methods of invoicing customers for the services rendered.

Time and Material Contracts (T & M)

A T & M contract is an arrangement under which a contractor is paid on the basis of: (1) actual cost of direct labour, usually at specified hourly rates, (2) actual cost of materials and equipment usage, and (3) agreed upon fixed add-on to cover the contractor's overheads and profit.

Long term fixed price contracts

A fixed-price contract is a contract where the amount of payment does not depend on the amount of resources or time expended, as opposed to a cost-plus contract which is intended to cover the costs plus some amount of profit.

Outsourcing contracts

Outsourcing contracts can be complex affairs and would be take a lot of time to complete. Outsourcing contracts are normally detailed through Service Level Agreements (SLAs) which would detail the terms of the contract as well as the deliverables and the payment schedule.

Entities in the service industry would need to study the Standards on Revenue in detail. IAS 18 provided limited guidance on Revenue Recognition but its replacement IFRS 15 provides detailed requirements on Revenue from Contracts with customers. The five-step approach advocated by IFRS 15 is summarised below.

- Identify the contract(s) with a customer.
- Identify the performance obligations in the contract.
- Determine the transaction price.
- Allocate the transaction price to the performance obligations in the contract.
- Recognise revenue when (or as) the entity satisfies a performance obligation.

Service organisations that enter into long-term fixed price contracts as well as outsourcing contracts would need to study existing contracts in detail to ascertain their performance obligations and when they are rendered and allocate a portion of the transaction price to the performance obligations. Revenue on the portion so allocated is recognised only when the performance obligation is satisfied. A strict application of the provisions of IFRS 15 would imply that service organisations will defer a portion of their Revenue which was probably previously being recognised upfront.

Contracts that service-based organisations enter into are normally high-cost contracts. A strict application of IFRS 15 could impact the topline of some entities as they will have to reflect some amounts as Unbilled Revenue. In case this impact is material, entities may want to talk to their customers and renegotiate the service level agreements and payment schedule mentioned in the contracts to ensure that IFRS 15 does not deprive them of cash flows.

Cap Gemini

RECOGNITION OF REVENUES AND COST OF SERVICES RENDERED

The method for recognising revenues and costs depends on the nature of the services rendered:

(a) Time and materials contracts

Revenues and cost of services are recognised as services rendered.

(b) Long-term fixed-price contracts

Revenues, including systems development and integration contracts, are recognised using the "percentage-of-completion" method. Costs are recognised as they are incurred.

(c) Outsourcing contracts

Revenues from outsourcing agreements are recognised over the term of the contract as the services are rendered. When the services are made up of different components which are not separately identifiable, the related revenues are recognised on a straight-line basis over the term of the contract.

The related costs are recognised as they are incurred. However, a portion of costs incurred in the initial phase of outsourcing contracts (transition and/or transformation costs) may be deferred when they are specific to a given contract, relate to future activity on the contract and/ or will generate future economic benefits, and are recoverable. These costs are allocated to work-in-progress and any reimbursement by the client is recorded as a deduction from the costs incurred. When the projected cost of the contract exceeds contract revenues, a loss to completion is recognised in the amount of the difference.

Revenues receivable from these contracts are recognised in the Consolidated Statement of Financial Position under "Accounts and notes receivable" when invoiced to customers and "Accrued income" when they are not yet invoiced. Advances from customers and billed in advance are included in current liabilities.

Source: http://www.capgemini.com/resource-file-access/resource/pdf/consolidated_financial_statements_2013.pdf

4.17.2.2 IAS 19 Employee Benefits

Employees form the crux of a service organisation. Due to the need to keep employees engaged and happy, entities need to tailor their benefit schemes to attract talent. In addition to high wages, bonuses and other short-term benefits, these organisations also have defined contribution and defined benefit plans for employees. All these benefits would come under the scope of IAS 19 *Employee Benefits*.

IAS 19 outlines the accounting requirements for employee benefits, including short-term benefits (e.g. wages and salaries, annual leave), post-employment benefits such as retirement benefits, other long-term benefits (e.g. long service leave) and termination benefits. The standard establishes the principle that the cost of providing employee benefits should be recognised in the period in which the benefit is earned by the employee, rather than when it is paid or payable, and outlines how each category of employee benefits are measured, providing detailed guidance in particular about post-employment benefits.

Due to the criticality given to Employee Benefits in service entities, many organisations in this sector have their own retirement plans managed through trusts. IAS 26 *Accounting and Reporting by Retirement Benefit Plans* would be applicable here. IAS 26 *Accounting and Reporting by Retirement Benefit Plans* outlines the requirements for the preparation of financial statements of retirement benefit plans. It outlines the financial statements required and discusses the measurement of various line items, particularly the actuarial present value of promised retirement benefits for defined benefit plans.

4.17.2.3 IFRS 2 Share-based Payment

In addition to the employee benefits described above, large service organisations provide stock options, share appreciation rights and other such share-based payments to employees with a view to motivate them to stay with the company for some time and to get rewarded for that.

The issuance of shares or rights to shares requires an increase in a component of equity. IFRS 2 requires the offsetting debit entry to be expensed when the payment for goods or services does not represent an asset. The expense should be recognised as the goods or services are consumed. For example, the issuance of shares or rights to shares to purchase inventory would be presented as an increase in inventory and would be expensed only once the inventory is sold or impaired.

The issuance of fully vested shares, or rights to shares, is presumed to relate to past service, requiring the full amount of the grant-date fair value to be expensed immediately. The issuance of shares to employees with, say, a three-year vesting period is considered to relate to services over the vesting period. Therefore, the fair value of the share-based payment, determined at the grant date, should be expensed over the vesting period.

As a general principle, the total expense related to equity-settled share-based payments will equal the multiple of the total instruments that vest and the grant-date fair value of those instruments. In short, there is truing up to reflect what happens during the vesting period. However, if the equity-settled share-based payment has a market related performance condition, the expense would still be recognised even if all other vesting conditions were met.

In addition to the recognition and measurement requirements, IFRS 2 details a number of disclosures that need to be made by entities that issue share-based payments. IFRS 2 mandates the following disclosures.

(a) A description of each type of share-based payment arrangement that existed at any time during the period, including the general terms and conditions of each arrangement, such as vesting requirements, the maximum term of options granted, and the method of settlement (e.g. whether in cash or equity).

b) The number and weighted average exercise prices of share options for each of the following groups of options:
   (i)   outstanding at the beginning of the period;
   (ii)   granted during the period;
   (iii) forfeited during the period;
   (iv) exercised during the period;
   (v)   expired during the period;
   (vi) outstanding at the end of the period; and
   (vii) exercisable at the end of the period.

(c) For share options exercised during the period, the weighted average share price at the date of exercise. If options were exercised on a regular basis throughout the period, the entity may instead disclose the weighted average share price during the period.

(d) For share options outstanding at the end of the period, the range of exercise prices and weighted average remaining contractual life. If the range of exercise prices is wide, the outstanding options shall be divided into ranges that are meaningful for assessing the number and timing of additional shares that may be issued and the cash that may be received upon exercise of those options.

If the entity has measured the fair value of goods or services received as consideration for equity instruments of the entity indirectly, by reference to the fair value of the equity instruments granted, to give effect to the principle in paragraph 46, the entity shall disclose at least the following.

(a) For share options granted during the period, the weighted average fair value of those options at the measurement date and information on how that fair value was measured, including:
   (i)   the option pricing model used and the inputs to that model, including the weighted average share price, exercise price, expected volatility, option life, expected dividends, the risk-free interest rate and any other inputs to the model, including the method used and the assumptions made to incorporate the effects of expected early exercise;
   (ii)   how expected volatility was determined, including an explanation of the extent to which expected volatility was based on historical volatility; and
   (iii) whether and how any other features of the option grant were incorporated into the measurement of fair value, such as a market condition.

(b) For other equity instruments granted during the period (ie other than share options), the number and weighted average fair value of those equity instruments at the measurement date, and information on how that fair value was measured, including:

   (i) if fair value was not measured on the basis of an observable market price, how it was determined;

   (ii) whether and how expected dividends were incorporated into the measurement of fair value; and

   (iii) whether and how any other features of the equity instruments granted were incorporated into the measurement of fair value.

(c) For share-based payment arrangements that were modified during the period:

   (i) an explanation of those modifications;

   (ii) the incremental fair value granted (as a result of those modifications); and

   (iii) information on how the incremental fair value granted was measured, consistently with the requirements set out in (a) and (b) above, where applicable.

If the entity has measured directly the fair value of goods or services received during the period, the entity shall disclose how that fair value was determined, e.g. whether fair value was measured at a market price for those goods or services.

The following would also need to be disclosed:

(a) The total expense recognised for the period arising from share-based payment transactions in which the goods or services received did not qualify for recognition as assets and hence were recognised immediately as an expense, including separate disclosure of that portion of the total expense that arises from transactions accounted for as equity-settled share-based payment transactions.

(b) For liabilities arising from share-based payment transactions:

   (i) the total carrying amount at the end of the period; and

   (ii) the total intrinsic value at the end of the period of liabilities for which the counterparty's right to cash or other assets had vested by the end of the period (e.g. vested share appreciation rights).

As indicated in the Preface, there is a school of thought that so much of what disclosures provide is merely ready fodder for competition to benchmark their compensation schemes or, in some instances, to poach employees since there is so much information available on Employee Benefits.

Cap Gemini: Incentive Instruments and Employee Share Ownership

(a) Instruments granted to employees

Stock options

Stock options have been granted to certain Group employees entitling them to purchase Cap Gemini shares over a period of five years, at a strike price set when the options are granted. Stock options were measured at fair value, corresponding to the value of the benefit granted to the employee at the grant date. The fair value of stock options is calculated using the "Black & Scholes" model, which incorporates assumptions concerning the option strike price and term, the share price at the grant date, implicit share price volatility and the risk-free interest rate. The expense recognised took into account staff attrition rates for eligible employee categories which are reviewed each year.

This amount was recognised in "Other operating income and expense" in the Income Statement on a straight-line basis over the vesting period, with a corresponding adjustment to equity.

Performance and presence conditions

Performance shares are granted to a certain number of Group employees, subject to performance (internal and external) and presence conditions. Share grants become definitive after a vesting period of two or four years, depending on the geographic location of the subsidiaries employing the beneficiaries.

The shares are measured at fair value, corresponding to the value of the benefit granted to the employee at the grant date. The fair value of shares subject to external performance condition is calculated using the "Monte Carlo" model, which incorporates assumptions concerning the share price at the grant date, implicit share price volatility, the risk-free interest rate, the expected dividend yield and market performance conditions applied. The fair value of shares subject to internal performance and/or presence conditions is calculated using a model in compliance with IFRS 2, which incorporates assumptions concerning the share price at the grant date, share transfer restrictions, the risk-free interest rate and the expected dividend yield.

The expense recognised also takes into account staff attrition rates for eligible employee categories, which are reviewed each year, and internal performance conditions (non-market conditions). This amount is recognised in "Other operating income and expense" in the Income Statement on a straight-line basis over the vesting period, with a corresponding adjustment to equity.

(b) Instruments proposed to employees

Redeemable share subscription or purchase warrants (BSAAR)

Redeemable share subscription or purchase warrants were proposed to employees and corporate officers of the Group. They confer entitlement to subscribe for Cap Gemini shares at a strike price determined at their date of acquisition by the employees and corporate officers of the Group. The exercise period commences the date of listing of the BSAAR warrants on the Euronext Paris market and terminates on the seventh anniversary of the issue date.

The issue price of these BSAAR warrants is equal to their market value and no benefit granted to beneficiaries is recognised in the consolidated financial statements of the Company.

Employee savings plan

Leveraged employee share ownership plans offering the possibility to subscribe for shares at a discounted preferential rate have been set up by the Group. When determining the IFRS 2 expense measuring the benefit granted to employees, the Group adjusts the amount of the discount granted by the Group to employees on the subscription price based on the following two items:

- the cost of the non-transferability of shares granted to employees during a period of five years. This cost is measured taking account of the five-year lock-in period. It corresponds to the cost of a two-stage strategy under which the market participant enters into a forward sale effective at the end of the five-year lock-in period and simultaneously borrows the amount necessary to buy a share available for immediate transfer. This borrowing is financed with the proceeds from the forward sale of the share and the dividends received during the lock-in period. This cost is calculated based on the following assumptions:

  the subscription price is set by the Chairman and Chief Executive Officer pursuant to the powers delegated by the Board of Directors. This subscription price is equal to the average Cap Gemini share price, adjusted for volume, during the twenty trading days preceding the decision of the Chairman and Chief Executive Officer, to which a discount is applied,

  the grant date is the date at which employees are fully informed of the specific characteristics and terms and conditions of the offer and particularly the subscription price,

  the loan rate granted to employees and used to determine the cost of the non-transferability of shares, is the rate at which a bank would grant a consumer loan repayable on maturity without allocation, to a private individual with an average risk profile, for a term corresponding to the term of the plan;

- the opportunity gain reflecting the possibility granted to employees to benefit from market terms and conditions identical to those of the Group.

  In certain countries where the introduction of leveraging through an Employee Savings Mutual Fund (Fonds Commun de Placement Entreprise) or directly in the name of the employee is not possible, the employee share ownership plan (ESOP) includes a Stock Appreciation Rights (SAR) mechanism. The benefit offered by the Group corresponds to the amount of the discount on the share subscription price.

Source: http://www.capgemini.com/resource-file-access/resource/pdf/consolidated_financial_statements_2013.pdf

Key Takeaways

- Revenue Recognition could be impacted due to the requirements of IFRS 15. Contracts may need to be renegotiated.
- Detailed Disclosures would need to be provided as per IAS 19 and IFRS 2

4.18 SHIPPING

4.18.1 Overview

History is evidence to the fact that transportation by sea is the most popular means of transport for cargo for centuries. This is obvious due to the lower costs associated with transporting by sea (the trade-off is the longer time it takes). Shipping companies maintain and run different types of ships – some of these could be bulk carriers, container ships, tankers, cruise ships and ocean liners. Transport of passengers through ships is normally for non-commercial purposes.

4.18.2 Present IFRS Standards that could impact the industry

4.18.2.1 IAS 16 Property, Plant and Equipment

A ship takes a long time to build. A ship is normally built in what is known as a yard. In accordance with IAS 16, all costs necessary to bring the ship to a seaworthy state would be capitalised – these could include charges incurred at the yard in addition to the contract price.

Non-specific or operating costs are expensed as incurred, including costs associated with crew training.

Component Accounting

One of the fundamental concepts of IAS 16 is that when an item of property, plant and equipment individual components for which different depreciation methods or rates are appropriate, each component is depreciated separately. A separate component may be either a physical component or a non-physical component that represents a major inspection or overhaul. PPE is separated into parts (components) when those parts are significant in relation to the total cost of the item. Component accounting is compulsory, but this does not mean that a company should necessarily split its assets into an infinite number of components if the effect on the financial statements would be immaterial.

Presented below is how a normal shipping company could identify different components (the data is illustrative only).

Ship's name: MV Santaclaus

Component	Allocated Cost	Residual Value	Useful Life (years)	Depreciation
Keel	xxx	xxx	xxx	xxx
Bridge	xxx	xxx	xxx	xxx
Anchor Windlass With Chains	xxx	xxx	xxx	xxx
Bulkheads	xxx	xxx	xxx	xxx
Propulsion System	xxx	xxx	xxx	xxx
Decks	xxx	xxx	xxx	xxx
Boiler	xxx	xxx	xxx	xxx
Hydraulic Crane	xxx	xxx	xxx	xxx

Turbine Generator	xxx	xxx	xxx	xxx
Bow Thruster	xxx	xxx	xxx	xxx
Refrigeration System	xxx	xxx	xxx	xxx

Dry-docking

Dry-docking is a term used for repairs or when a ship is taken to the service yard. During dry-docking, the whole ship is brought to a dry land so that the submerged portions of the hull can be cleaned or inspected. Usually dry-docking is done every 12 months to 24 months, as there could be machinery and systems that cannot be stopped while the ship is in use; these are also serviced, repaired or replaced at the same time. The normal steps followed are – the hull is cleaned of marine plants, painting with anti-corrosive and anti-fouling paints, hull inspection and repairs, shipside gratings cleaned and repaired, cleaning and surveying of tanks, rudder and carrier ring.

Locking devices clearances are also examined. All overboard and sea suction valves are overhauled. Tail shaft bearing wear down is checked. Tail shaft is removed and inspected. Anchor chain is examined, cleaned and re-marked.

Dry-docking expenses would need to be capitalised under IAS 16.

Residual value

At the time when a ship is to be sold, the future value of the ship will have to be ascertained – this is also known as the residual value. The residual value has a substantial effect on the Internal Rate of Return of a proposed ship investment. Consequently, the final agreement between buyer and seller is often significantly influenced by the residual value.

During the recent credit crisis, a lot of debate was generated around the fact that the residual value of ships was incorrectly estimated.

Given the obvious importance of the residual value estimate, estimating this value requires a great deal of thought and judgement. Help is available though in the form of agencies such as Shipping Intelligence.

4.18.2.2 IAS 36 **Impairment of Assets**

IAS 36 provides a number of example indicators of possible impairment, such as:

- a significant adverse change in the market and economic environment in which a company operates or to which an asset is dedicated; and
- evidence being available from internal reporting that indicates economic performance of an asset is worse than expected.

Practical triggers therefore include:

- general downturn in global economy;
- depressed freight rates;
- vessels being laid up;
- higher than normal scrapping rates;
- substantial physical damage to the vessel;
- technological obsolescence (e.g. driven by regulatory change); and
- operating losses.

Impairment model

Where an impairment test is performed, the carrying amount of an asset or group of assets is compared to its recoverable amount, which is the higher of:

- fair value less costs to sell (generally based on the market price); or
- the value expected to be generated from the continuing use of the asset – its value in use.

If the carrying value is greater than the recoverable amount then the asset is written down.

Identifying fair value

The best evidence of fair value is a binding sale agreement in an arm's length transaction. In the absence of liquid markets, entities use the best information available to estimate the amount that could be obtained through the disposal of the asset at the reporting date. The use of one or more independent brokers may be appropriate and the recently introduced on-line valuation tools can also provide supporting evidence.

Assessing value in use

The value in use of an asset (or group of assets) is defined as the present value of the future cash flows expected to be derived from the asset or CGU. The key factors in assessing a value in use are therefore the composition of cash flows and the discount rate applied.

For instance, in the dry bulk segment a large ship during 2008 could be rented at a daily rate in excess of $200,000, and less than $5,000 per day during the winter of 2009. As daily rental rates plummeted, so did asset values. A large five-year old ship in 2007 could be sold for around $150 million was worth less than $40 million at the peak of the credit crisis.

Onerous Contracts

It is possible that some vessels under construction may test positive for impairment if the agreed costs to build a vessel become higher than its estimated value in use or fair value. As observed above, during the credit crisis, the sale value of ships dropped dramatically. A shipping company will have to make an estimation if the costs to fulfill the contract exceed the benefits – in which case it would meet the definition of an onerous contract as per IAS 37.

If this is the case and the contract with the shipyard cannot be cancelled without a penalty, then it is necessary to consider whether the contract is onerous under IAS 37 *Provisions, Contingent Liabilities and Contingent Assets*. In assessing whether a contract is onerous, a shipping company compares the expected benefits from the vessel with the lower of the cost to fulfil the contract and any compensation or penalty to cancel the contract. If the expected costs to fulfil or cancel the contract are higher than the expected benefits from the vessel, then the contract is onerous. Before a separate provision for an onerous contract is established, the shipping company recognises an impairment loss on the vessel under construction.

Operating vs. finance leases

As per IAS 17- Leases, the assessment of whether a lease is a finance or operating lease depends on whether substantially all of the risks and rewards incidental to ownership of the leased asset have been transferred from the lessor to the lessee.

Under a finance lease, the lessor recognises a finance lease receivable and the lessee a finance lease liability for future lease payments. Under an operating lease both parties treat the lease as an executory contract with rentals being recognised in the income statement over the term of the lease on a straight-line basis. Under a finance lease of a vessel the lessee recognises an asset on its balance sheet, and under an operating lease, the asset remains on the balance sheet of the lessor. Shipping companies would need to be careful in calculating the present value of future lease rentals by using an appropriate discount rate.

Joint arrangements

Under IFRS 11, joint arrangements are essentially defined in the same way as under IAS 31 *Interests in Joint Ventures*; however, the classification of joint arrangements, which affects the accounting, has changed to:

- joint operations, whereby the parties with joint control have rights to the assets and obligations for the liabilities, relating to the arrangement; and
- joint ventures, whereby the parties with joint control have rights to the net assets of the arrangement.

The key to determining the type of the arrangements, and therefore the subsequent accounting, is the rights and obligations of the parties arising from the arrangements in the normal course of business. If a joint arrangement is determined to be a joint operation, then the joint operator accounts for its own assets, liabilities and transactions, including its share of those incurred jointly. If a joint arrangement is determined to be a joint venture, then the joint venture accounts for its investment using the equity method; the free choice between using the equity method or proportionate consolidation has been eliminated.

As a risk management measure, it is common for shipping companies to enter into pooling arrangements with others in the same line of business. Such pooling arrangements are structured in different ways – these structures need to be closely studied to ascertain if the arrangement would be either a joint operation or a joint venture as per IFRS 11 or would need to be consolidated as per IFRS 10.

4.18.3 Accounting Policies

The accounting policies of A.P.Moller-Maersk A/S provide further inputs to the issues narrated above.

CONSOLIDATION

The consolidated financial statements comprise the parent company A.P. Møller-Mærsk A/S, its subsidiaries and proportionate shares in joint arrangements classified as joint operations. Subsidiaries are entities controlled by A.P. Møller – Mærsk A/S. Control is based on the power to direct the relevant activities of an entity and the exposure, or right, to variable returns arising from it. In that connection relevant activities are those that significantly affect the investee's returns. Control is usually achieved by directly or indirectly owning or commanding more than 50% of the voting rights or by other rights, such as agreements on management control.

Joint arrangements are entities in which the Group, according to contractual agreements with one or more other parties, has joint control. The arrangements are classified as joint ventures, if the contracting parties' rights are limited to net assets in the separate legal entities, and as joint operations, if the parties have direct and unlimited rights to the assets and obligations for the liabilities of the arrangement.

Entities in which the Group exercises a significant but non-controlling influence are considered to be associated companies. A significant influence is usually achieved by directly or indirectly owning or controlling 20–50% of the voting rights. Agreements and other circumstances are considered when assessing the degree of influence. Consolidation is performed by summarising the financial statements of the parent company and its subsidiaries, inclusive of the proportionate share of accounts related to joint operations, part-owned vessels and pool arrangements, which have been prepared in accordance with the Group's accounting policies. Intra-group income and expenses, shareholdings, dividends, intra-group balances and gains on intra-group transactions are eliminated. Unrealised gains on transactions with associated companies and joint arrangements are eliminated in proportion to the Group's ownership share. Unrealised losses are eliminated in the same way, unless they indicate impairment.

Non-controlling interests' share of profit or loss for the year and of equity in subsidiaries which are not wholly owned is included as part of the Group's profit and equity respectively, but shown as separate items.

BUSINESS COMBINATIONS

Upon acquisition of new entities, the acquired assets, liabilities and contingent liabilities are measured at fair value at the date control was achieved using the acquisition method. Identifiable intangible assets are recognised if they arise from a contractual right or can otherwise be separately identified. The difference between the fair value of the acquisition cost and the fair value of acquired identifiable net assets is recognised as goodwill under intangible assets. Any subsequent changes to contingent acquisition costs are recognised as other income or other costs in the income statement. Transaction costs are recognised as operating costs as they are incurred. In business combinations achieved in stages, value adjustments of previously recognised investments are recognised in the income statement.

When surrendering control, the value of any retained investment is adjusted at fair value and the value adjustment is recognised in the income statement as gain on sale of non-current assets, etc., net. The effect of the purchase and sale of non-controlling interests without changes in control is included directly in equity.

FOREIGN CURRENCY TRANSLATION

The Group uses DKK as its presentation currency. In the translation to the presentation currency for entities with a functional currency different from DKK, the statement of comprehensive income is translated into DKK at average exchange rates and the balance sheet is translated at the exchange rates as at the balance sheet date. Exchange differences arising from such translations are recognised directly in other comprehensive income. The functional currency varies from business area to business area. For the Group's principal shipping and drilling activities and oil and gas activities, the functional currency is USD. This means that, among other things, the carrying amounts of property, plant and equipment and intangible assets and, hence, depreciation and amortisation are maintained in USD from the date of acquisition. For other activities, including container terminal activities and land-based container activities, the functional currency is generally the local currency in the country in which such activities are performed.

Transactions in other currencies than the functional currency are translated at the exchange rate prevailing at the date of the transaction.

Monetary items in foreign currencies not settled at the balance sheet date are translated at the exchange rate as at the balance sheet date.

Foreign exchange gains and losses are included in the income statement as financial income or expenses.

DERIVATIVE FINANCIAL INSTRUMENTS

Derivative financial instruments are recognised on the trading date and measured at fair value using generally acknowledged valuation techniques based on relevant observable swap curves and exchange rates. The effective portion of changes in the value of derivative financial instruments designated to hedge future transactions is recognised directly in other comprehensive income until the hedged transactions are realised. At that time, the cumulated gains/losses are transferred to the items under which the hedged transactions are recognised. The effective portion of changes in the value of derivative financial instruments used to hedge the value of recognised financial assets and liabilities is recognised in the income statement together with changes in the fair value of the hedged assets or liabilities which can be attributed to the hedging relationship. The ineffective portion of hedge transactions, including time value for oil price hedges, and changes in the fair values of derivative financial instruments, which do not qualify for hedge accounting are recognised in the income statement as financial income or expenses for financial instruments, and as other income/costs for oil price hedges and forward freight agreements.

SEGMENT INFORMATION

The allocation of business activities into segments reflects the Group's character as a conglomerate and is in line with the internal management reporting. Some activities are related, but are managed as independent units. The segments are as follows:

- Maersk Line Global container services
- Maersk Oil and gas production and exploration activities
- APM Terminals Container terminal activities, inland transportation, container depots and repair of containers, etc.
- Maersk Drilling Offshore drilling activities and operation of land-rigs through 50% ownership of Egyptian Drilling Company
- Maersk Supply Service Supply vessel activities with anchor handling and platform supply vessels, etc.
- Maersk Tankers Tanker shipping of crude oil, oil products and gas
- Damco Logistic and forwarding activities
- Svitzer Towing and salvage activities, etc.

In addition, the Group comprises other businesses, which does not constitute a reportable segment. This includes, *inter alia*, investments in the associated companies Danske Bank, Höegh Autoliners and DFDS. Revenue from Other businesses consists mainly of income from sale of containers, air freight, and services sold to the energy industry.

The reportable segments do not comprise costs in group functions. Also, oil hedging activities in Maersk Oil Trading and the results of Maersk Oil Trading's trading activity in the form of purchasing bunker and lubricating oil on behalf of entities in the Group are not allocated to business segments.

Revenue between segments is limited except for Terminal activities and Damco, which deliver a large part of their services to the Group's container shipping activities. Sales of products and services between segments are based on market terms.

Segment profit or loss (NOPAT), assets and liabilities comprise items directly related to or which can be allocated to segments. With no effect on the Group, long-term agreements between segments on reserved capacity in container terminals are treated as operating leases, where under IFRS they are classified as finance leases (cf. IFRIC 4). Financial assets and liabilities and financial income and expenses are not attributed to business segments.

INCOME STATEMENT

Revenue from sale of goods is recognised upon the transfer of risk to the buyer.

Revenue from shipping activities is recognised as the service is rendered, by which incomplete voyages are recognised at the share related to the financial year.

Oil and gas sales are recognised as revenue upon discharge from the production site. In agreements where tax is settled in oil, this tax is recognised both as revenue and tax. Revenue from terminal operations, logistics, forwarding activities and towing activities is recognised upon completion of the service. In container terminals operated under certain restrictive terms of pricing and service, etc., the value of tangible assets constructed on behalf of the concession grantor is also included. For drilling activities, which are typically carried out under long-term agreements with fixed day rates, revenue is recognised for the production time related to the financial year.

Lease income from operational leases is recognised over the lease term.

Source: Maersk, Group Annual Report 2013

4.19 SMALL AND MEDIUM ENTERPRISES

4.19.1 Overview

Small and medium enterprises (SME) form the economic backbone of many nations. Generally, an entity is classified as an SME on the basis of the number of persons it employs. Other data points that could be included to define a SME could be turnover or net worth. Wikipedia states that the European definition of SME as follows- The category of micro, small and medium-sized enterprises (SMEs) is made up of enterprises which employ fewer than 250 persons and which have an annual turnover not exceeding 50 million euro, and/or an annual balance sheet total not exceeding 43 million euro.

The *IFRS for SMEs* is a self-contained Standard of 230 pages, designed to meet the needs and capabilities of small and medium-sized entities (SMEs), which are estimated to account for over 95 per cent of all companies around the world. Compared with full IFRSs (and many national GAAPs), the *IFRS for SMEs* is less complex in a number of ways. The Standard is available for any jurisdiction to adopt, whether or not it has adopted full IFRSs. Each jurisdiction must determine which entities should use the Standard. The IASB's only restriction is that listed companies and financial institutions should not use it.

However, the IASB has not gone by benchmark criteria such as employee strength, turnover or balance sheet value to define an SME. The IFRS for SME's states that an entity that publishes general purpose financial statements for external users and does not have public accountability can use the IFRS for SMEs. An entity has 'public accountability' if it files or is in the process of filing its financial statements with a securities commission or other regulatory organisation for the purpose of issuing any class of instrument in a public market or if it holds assets in a fiduciary capacity for a broad group of outsiders. Banks, insurance companies, securities brokers and dealers, and pension funds are examples of entities that hold assets in a fiduciary capacity for a broad group of outsiders. Small listed entities are not included in the scope of standard. If a subsidiary of an IFRS entity uses the recognition and measurement principles according to full IFRS, it must provide the disclosures required by full IFRS.

In a departure from its others Standards, the IASB has also not advised an effective date to implement the IFRS for SMEs. It has left this decision to local regulators.

4.19.2 Major differences between IFRS and IFRS for SMEs

The purpose of issuing a separate IFRS for SMEs was to simplify some of the rigorous provisions of full-blown IFRS for SMEs who may not be able to afford the cost, employ dedicated resources or allocate sufficient time for a full-blown IFRS. The table below summarizes how this simplification has been attempted.

IFRS	*IFRS FOR SMEs*
Standards numbered as they are published	Organised by topic
Almost 3000 pages	Under 300 pages
Around 3000 disclosure items	About 300 disclosure items
Updated constantly	Updated once every two or three years

4.19.3 Other differences

Topic	Full IFRS	IFRS FOR SMEs
Financial statements	A statement of changes in equity is required, presenting a reconciliation of equity items between the beginning and end of the period.	Same requirement. However, if the only changes to the equity during the period are a result of profit or loss, payment of dividends, correction of prior-period errors or changes in accounting policy, a combined statement of income and retained earnings can be presented instead of both a statement of comprehensive income and a statement of changes in equity.
Business combinations	Transaction costs are excluded under IFRS 3 (revised). Contingent consideration is recognised regardless of the probability of payment.	Transaction costs are included in the acquisition costs. Contingent considerations are included as part of the acquisition cost if it is probable that the amount will be paid and its fair value can be measured reliably. Investments in associates and joint ventures
Investment in associates	Investments in associates are accounted for using the equity method. The cost and fair value model are not permitted except in separate financial statements. To account for a jointly controlled entity, either the proportionate consolidation method or the equity method are allowed. The cost and fair value model are not permitted.	An entity may account for its investments in associates or jointly controlled entities using one of the following: • The cost model (cost less any accumulated impairment losses); • The equity method; • The fair value through profit or loss model.
Research and Development costs	Research costs are expensed as incurred; development costs are capitalised and amortised, but only when specific criteria are met. Borrowing costs are capitalised if certain criteria are met.	All research and development costs and all borrowing costs are recognised as an expense.
Financial instruments – derivatives and hedging	IAS 39 *Financial instruments: Recognition and measurement*, distinguishes four measurement categories of financial instruments – that is, financial assets or liabilities at fair value through profit or loss, held-to-maturity investments, loans and receivables and available-for-sale financial assets.	There are two sections dealing with financial instruments: a section for simple payables and receivables, and other basic financial instruments; and a section for other, more complex financial instruments. Most of the basic financial instruments are measured at amortised cost; the complex instruments are generally measured at fair value through profit or loss. The hedging models under IFRS and IFRS for SMEs are based on the principles in full IFRS. However, there are a number of detailed application differences, some of which are more restrictive under IFRS for SMEs (for example, a limited number of risks and hedging instruments are permitted). However, no quantitative effectiveness test required under IFRS for SMEs.

Non-financial assets and goodwill	For tangible and intangible assets, there is an accounting policy choice between the cost model and the revaluation model. Goodwill and other intangibles with indefinite lives are reviewed for impairment and not amortised.	The cost model is the only permitted model. All intangible assets, including goodwill, are assumed to have finite lives and are amortised.
Intangible Assets	Under IAS 38 *Intangible assets*, the useful life of an intangible asset is either finite or indefinite. The latter are not amortised and an annual impairment test is required.	There is no distinction between assets with finite or infinite lives. The amortisation approach therefore applies to all intangible assets. These intangibles are tested for impairment only when there is an indication.
Investment Property	IAS 40 *Investment property*, offers a choice of fair value and the cost method.	Investment property is carried at fair value if this fair value can be measured without undue cost or effort.
Non-current assets held for sale	IFRS 5 *Non-current assets held for sale and discontinued operations*, requires non-current assets to be classified as held for sale where the carrying amount is recovered principally through a sale transaction rather than though continuing use.	Assets held for sale are not covered, the decision to sell an asset is considered an impairment indicator.
Employee Benefits – defined benefit plans	1. Under IAS 19 *Employee benefits*, actuarial gains or losses can be recognised immediately or amortised into profit or loss over the expected remaining working lives of participating employees. 2. The use of an accrued benefit valuation method (the projected unit credit method) is required for calculating defined benefit obligations.	1. Requires immediate recognition and splits the expense into different components. 2. The circumstance-driven approach is applicable, which means that the use of an accrued benefit valuation method (the projected unit credit method) is required if the information that is needed to make such a calculation is already available, or if it can be obtained without undue cost or effort. If not, simplifications are permitted in which future salary progression, future service or possible mortality during an employee's period of service are not considered.
Taxes	1. A deferred tax asset is only recognised to the extent that it is probable that there will be sufficient future taxable profit to enable recovery of the deferred tax asset. 2. No deferred tax is recognised upon the initial recognition of an asset and liability in a transaction that is not a business combination and affects neither accounting profit nor taxable profit at the time of the transaction.	1. A valuation allowance is recognised so that the net carrying amount of the deferred tax asset equals the highest amount that is more likely than not to be recovered. The net carrying amount of deferred tax asset is likely to be the same between full IFRS and IFRS for SMEs. 2. No such exemption.

3. There is no specific guidance on uncertain tax positions. In practice, management will record the liability measured as either a single best estimate or a weighted average probability of the possible outcomes, if the likelihood is greater than 50%.

3. Management recognises the effect of the possible outcomes of a review by the tax authorities. It should be measured using the probability-weighted average amount of all the possible outcomes. There is no probable recognition threshold.

4.19.4 Comprehensive Review

The IASB is conducting a comprehensive review of the *IFRS for SMEs* to consider whether there is a need for any amendments to the Standard.

Key Takeaways

- SMEs in which local jurisdictions wherein regulators have not prescribed IFRS for SMEs would need to follow the normal IFRS which could be a costly and time-consuming process
- Disclosure requirements for IFRS for SMEs have to be studied thoroughly
- SMEs should keep track of the changes to the IFRS for SMEs

4.20 SOFTWARE AND INFORMATION TECHNOLOGY

4.20.1 Overview

The software industry is human-resource intensive. A good portion of their expenses are employee benefits. On the revenue side, they invoice their clients either for the products they sell or the services they render or a combination of both. The services are invoiced either on a time and material basis or on a pre-determined rate. Some software installations are complex and the time from sale of product to installation could take a few years – the challenge in such cases would be to match revenues with costs.

4.20.2 Present IFRS Standards that could impact the industry

4.20.2.1 *IAS 18/IFRS 15* **Revenue/Revenue from Contracts with Customers**

IAS 18

Since the implementation of IFRS 15 has been deferred by a year, the Standard on Revenue that would be applicable would be IAS 18 Revenue. IAS 18 permits entities to recognise revenue when substantial risks and rewards of the goods sold have been transferred and on services on the basis of the percentage of completion of the services. Software companies usually have a combination of both goods as well as services – for instance, an off-the-shelf ERP package can be considered to be goods while the implementation of the package would involve services. In many instances, the goods are delivered in one accounting year and the services performed in a subsequent accounting year. IAS 18 provides some guidance by stating that the recognition criteria in this Standard are usually applied separately to each transaction. However, in certain circumstances, it is necessary to apply the recognition criteria to the separately identifiable components of a single transaction in order to reflect the substance of the transaction. For example, when the selling price of a product includes an identifiable amount for subsequent servicing, that amount is deferred and recognised as revenue over the period during which the service is performed. Software companies offer their customers servicing of the product sold or maintenance services post-implementation. The services are either bundled into the price of the product or are negotiated separately. While US GAAP had strict rules for segregating such transactions as per Statement No 606, and the erstwhile SOP 97-2, IAS 18 left it to the principle that the segregation would be needed only if it reflected the substance of the transaction.

IFRS 15

IFRS 15 attempts to rectify this apparent weakness in IAS 18 with its five-step approach.

1. Identify the contract(s) with a customer
2. Identify the performance obligations in the contract
3. Determine the transaction price
4. Allocate the transaction price to the performance obligations in the contract
5. Recognise revenue when (or as) the entity satisfies a performance obligation

Assuming that the entity expects that it is probable that the customer will pay the contract consideration, Step 1 requires that the entity consider whether two or more legal contracts should be aggregated together to account for the substance of the arrangement in a similar way to existing IFRS. Step 1 also includes detailed guidance on how contract modifications should be accounted for – a common feature in many construction-type contracts. Step 2 is focused on identifying the deliverables promised in the contract or, to use IFRS 15 terminology, the performance obligations. Performance obligations can be implicit or explicit and may be documented in writing or agreed orally. IFRS 15 requires that performance obligations are accounted for separately when the goods or services promised are distinct. A good or service is distinct if the customer is capable of using the deliverable by itself, or in conjunction with other goods and services generally available in the market. A deliverable that has no use to the customer without further purchases of goods and services from the same supplier is not distinct. Goods or services that are not distinct should be aggregated together until a distinct deliverable emerges. Even if a good or service is capable of being distinct, the requirements of IFRS 15 might require aggregation of those goods or services if they are not distinct in the context of the contract. For example a construction company building a house aggregates the bricks, timber and tiles because, although those goods are capable of being distinct, in the context of a contract to build a house they do not transfer the promised good or service to the customer on their own. The requirement to identify all of the performance obligations in a contract could impact industries that currently treat these promises as marketing costs, for example in the retail and automotive industries.

Usually the amount of consideration is easy to determine, but the two areas where challenges may arise in Step 3 are in respect of the time value of money and contingent consideration. IFRS 15 grants a practical expedient that discounting is not required when receipt of cash and performance occur within 12 months of each other, or when the date of performance is at the customer's discretion such as in the case of a customer loyalty programme. However, outside of this 12-month window, entities will now need to consider whether they should charge themselves interest on consideration received in advance in addition to discounting consideration received in arrears. The treatment of contingent consideration (for example where the amount of consideration can vary because of an entity's performance or customer return rights) will be broadly similar to IAS 18, but further guidance will increase consistency between entities. Contingent amounts will be recognised as revenue under IFRS 15 if it is highly probable that the amount recognised will not result in a significant reversal of revenue in subsequent periods. Investment management companies are likely to be particularly affected by the revised contingent consideration guidance.

Step 4 introduces a significant change to many entities' existing practice under IAS 18. Consideration must be allocated on a "relative stand-alone selling price" basis to each of the performance obligations in the contract. The stand-alone selling price of a good or service is the price that a customer would pay for that good or service if it was acquired on its own. In other words, any discount in a bundled arrangement is allocated pro rata to each deliverable based on that deliverable's relative stand-alone selling price. The free choice to apply a residual method under IAS 18, whereby the entire discount in a bundled arrangement is allocated to the delivered goods, is not acceptable under IFRS 15. This will have a significant impact on mobile telecommunication companies because this new guidance will force more consideration to be allocated to the handset and recognised up-front. Subsequent revenue recognised over the contract period will consequently be lower than the monthly bills issued. Entities with customer loyalty programmes will also be affected by this because most entities currently apply the residual method to the loyalty points under IFRIC 13 Customer loyalty programmes.

Finally, in Step 5, revenue is recognised when control of goods or services is transferred to the customer. For sales of goods, a list of indicators provides guidance as to when control transfers. For sales of services, control transfers over time and so revenue is recognised over time. When revenue is recognised over time, the new standard requires companies to critically consider what the most appropriate measure of progress is to depict faithfully the transfer of the promised goods or services. Consequently entities will need to assess whether using "input methods" (such as costs incurred compared to total expected costs) is the most appropriate measure of progress.

Existing IFRS has no guidance in determining what is a good and what is a service. Under IFRS 15 the arrangement is a service with revenue recognised over time if any of the following three criteria is met:

1. The customer receives and consumes the benefits of the entity's performance as the entity performs (for instance a cleaning or security service).
2. The entity's performance creates or enhances an asset that the customer clearly controls as the asset is created or enhanced (for example construction of a building on the customer's land).
3. The entity's performance does not create an asset with an alternative use to the entity (because of the asset is specific to the customer or because of a contractual restriction) and the entity has a right to payment for any performance completed to date (for example audit services and some types of contract manufacturing and construction contracts).

Specific guidance has also been included in the new standard in respect of licences with some licences being seen as similar to the sale of goods while others being services. Indicators are included in the new standard to help entities differentiate between the two different types of licence. Entities in the software industry should pay particular attention to this distinction, because it may require changes to existing practice for some entities.

In addition to dealing with revenue, IFRS 15 includes guidance as to when costs incurred as part of a revenue contract must be capitalised and carried forward against future contract performance. More of these contract costs will be capitalised under IFRS 15 than existing IFRS, and industries with significant up-front costs such as outsourcing should carefully consider the revised guidance. In addition, entities in the software industry may also experience a change in current practice as a result of mandatory capitalisation of some contract costs.

Software contracts can be of various types: customers can be given licences to use the software, software can be sold off the shelf in packages or they can be custom-made for the customer. In each of these instances, entities would need to look at the five-step approach to determine two critical aspects of Revenue Recognition – the timing and the amount. The contract with the customer would drive this.

The software major SAP provides a detailed example of how Revenue is recognised in a software company. An extract from their Accounting Policies is reproduced below. It is interesting to note that for accounting of multiple element arrangements are following the principles enunciated in US GAAP 985-605 and not IAS 18. Since the provisions of IFRS 15 are similar to US GAAP, there would be no impact on Revenue Recognition when IFRS 15 is implemented or early-adopted by SAP.

We derive our revenue from fees charged to our customers for (a) licenses to our on-premise software products, (b) the use of our hosted cloud subscription software offerings and (c) support, consulting, development, training, and other services. The majority of our software arrangements include support services, and many also include professional services and other elements.

For any of our product or service offerings, we determine at the outset of an arrangement that the amount of revenue cannot be measured reliably, we conclude that the inflow of economic benefits associated with the transaction is not probable, and we defer revenue recognition until the arrangement fee becomes due and payable by the customer. If, at the outset of an arrangement, we determine that collectability is not probable, we conclude that the inflow of economic benefits associated with the transaction is not probable, and we defer revenue recognition until the earlier of when collectability becomes probable or payment is received. If collectability becomes not probable before all revenue from an arrangement is recognised, we recognise revenue only to the extent of the fees that are successfully collected unless collectability becomes probable again. If a customer is specifically identified as a bad debtor, we stop recognising revenue from the customer except to the extent of the fees that have already been collected.

We account for out-of-pocket expenses invoiced by SAP and reimbursed by customers as support, cloud subscription and support, consulting, or other service revenue, depending on the nature of the service for which the out-of-pocket expenses were incurred.

Software revenue represents fees earned from the sale or license of software to customers for use on the customer's premises, in other words, where the customer has the right to take possession of the software for installation on the customer's premises (on-premise software). Revenue from the sale of perpetual licenses of our standard software products is recognised in line with the requirements for selling goods stated in IAS 18 *Revenue* when evidence of an arrangement exists, delivery has occurred, the risks and rewards of ownership have been transferred to the customer, the amount of revenue and associated costs can be measured reliably, and collection of the related receivable is probable. The fee of the sale is recognised net of returns and allowances, trade discounts, and volume rebates.

We usually sell or license on-premise software on a perpetual basis. Occasionally, we license on-premise software for a specified period of time. Revenue from short-term time-based licenses, which usually include support services during the license period, is recognised ratably over the license term. Revenue from multi-year time-based licenses that include support services, whether separately priced or not, is recognised ratably over the license term unless a substantive support service renewal rate exists; if this is the case, the amount allocated to the delivered software is recognised as software revenue based on the residual method once the basic criteria described above have been met.

In general, our software license agreements do not include acceptance-testing provisions. If an arrangement allows for customer acceptance-testing of the software, we defer revenue until the earlier of customer acceptance or when the acceptance right lapses.

We usually recognise revenue from on-premise software arrangements involving resellers on evidence of sell-through by the reseller to the end-customer, because the inflow of the economic benefits associated with the arrangements to us is not probable before sell-through has occurred.

Sometimes we enter into customer-specific on-premise software development agreements. We recognise software revenue in connection with these arrangements using the percentage-of-completion method based on contract costs incurred to date as a percentage of total estimated contract costs required to complete the development work. If we do not have a sufficient basis to reasonably measure the progress of completion or to estimate the total contract revenue and costs, revenue is recognised only to the extent of the contract costs incurred for which we believe recoverability to be probable. When it becomes probable that total contract costs exceed total contract revenue in an arrangement, the expected losses are recognised immediately as an expense based on the costs attributable to the contract.

On-premise software subscription contracts combine software and support service elements, as under these contracts the customer is provided with current software products, rights to receive unspecified future software products, and rights to product support during the on-premise software subscription term. Customers pay a periodic fee for a defined subscription term, and we recognise such fees ratably over the term of the arrangement beginning with the delivery of the first product. Revenue from on-premise software subscription contracts is allocated to the software revenue and support revenue line items in our Consolidated Income Statements.

On-premise software rental contracts also combine software and support service elements. Under such contracts the customer is provided with current software products and product support, but not with the right to receive unspecified future software products. Customers pay a periodic fee over the rental term. We recognise fees from software rental contracts ratably over the term of the arrangement. Revenue from rental contracts is allocated to the software revenue and support revenue line items in our Consolidated Income Statements.

Support revenue represents fees earned from providing customers with unspecified future software updates, upgrades, and enhancements, and technical product support services for on-premise software products. We recognise support revenue based on our performance under the support arrangements. Under our major support services our performance obligation is to stand ready to provide technical product support and to provide unspecified updates and enhancements on a when-and-if-available basis. For these support services we recognise revenue ratably over the term of the support arrangement. We do not sell separately technical product support or unspecified software upgrades, updates, and enhancements. Accordingly, we do not distinguish within software and software-related service revenue or within cost of software and software-related services the amounts attributable to technical support services and unspecified software upgrades, updates, and enhancements.

Revenue from cloud subscriptions and support represents fees earned from providing customers with:

- The right to use software in a cloud-based-infrastructure (hosting) provided by SAP, where the customer does not have the right to terminate the hosting contract and take possession of the software to run it on the customer's own IT infrastructure or by a third party hosting provider without significant penalty, or
- Additional premium support beyond the standard support which is included in SAP's basic cloud subscription fees, or
- Hosting services and related application management services for software hosted by SAP, where the customer has the right to terminate the hosting contract and take possession of the software without significant penalty.

Cloud subscription and support revenue is recognised as the services are performed. Where a fixed fee is agreed for the right to continuously access and use a cloud offering for a certain term, the fee is recognised ratably over the term covered by the fixed fee. Fees that are based on actual transaction volumes are recognised as the transactions occur.

Revenue from consulting primarily represents fees earned from providing customers with consulting services which primarily relate to the installation and configuration of our software products and cloud offerings. Usually, our consulting contracts do not involve significant production, modification, or customisation of software and the related revenue is recognised as the services are provided using the percentage-of-completion method of accounting as outlined above.

Revenue from other services represents fees earned from providing customers with training services, application management services for software not hosted by SAP, messaging services, SAP marketing events, and referral services.

- Training services provide educational services to customers and partners regarding the use of our software products. We recognise training revenue and application management services as the services are rendered.
- Messaging services primarily comprise the transmission of electronic text messages from one mobile phone provider to another. We recognise revenue from message services based upon the number of messages successfully processed and delivered. Revenue from fixed-price messaging arrangements is recognised ratably over the contractual term of the arrangement.
- Revenue from marketing events hosted by SAP, for which SAP sells tickets to its customers, is recognised when the marketing event is completed.
- Referral services comprise referring customers to partners. We recognise revenue from referral services upon providing the referral. The majority of our arrangements contain multiple elements. We account for software, support, cloud subscription, consulting and other service deliverables as separate units of account and allocate revenue based on fair value. Fair value is determined by establishing either company-specific objective evidence, or an estimated stand-alone selling price. The revenue amounts allocated to the individual elements are recognised when the revenue recognition criteria described above have been met for the respective element. We generally determine the fair value of each element based on its company-specific objective evidence of fair

value, which is the price charged when that element is sold separately or, for elements not yet sold separately, the price established by our management if it is probable that the price will not change before the element is sold separately.

We derive the company-specific objective evidence of fair value for our support services from the rates charged to renew the support services annually after an initial period. Such renewal rates generally represent a fixed percentage of the discounted software license fee charged to the customer. The majority of our customers renew their annual support service contracts at these rates.

Where company-specific objective evidence of fair value or third-party evidence of selling price cannot be established for deliverables, we determine the fair value of the respective element by estimating its stand-alone selling price. This is generally the case for our cloud subscription offerings.

Estimated stand-alone selling price (ESP) for our cloud subscription offerings is determined based on the rates agreed with the individual customers to apply if and when the subscription arrangement renews. We determine ESP by considering multiple factors which include, but are not limited to, the following: i) substantive renewal rates contained within an arrangement for cloud subscription deliverables; ii) gross margin objectives and internal costs for services; and iii) pricing practices, market conditions, and competitive landscape.

We apply the residual method of revenue recognition when company-specific objective evidence of fair value or estimated stand-alone selling price exists for all of the undelivered elements in the arrangement, but does not exist for one or more delivered elements. This is generally the case in multiple element arrangements involving on-premise software and services related to on-premise software where company-specific objective evidence of fair value or estimated standalone selling price exists for all the services in the arrangement (for example, support services, consulting services, cloud subscription services), but does not exist for the on-premise software. Under the residual method, revenue is allocated to all undelivered elements in the amount of their respective fair values and the remaining amount of the arrangement fee is allocated to the delivered element. With this policy we have considered the guidance provided by FASB ASC Subtopic 985-605, Software Revenue Recognition (FASB ASC 985-605), where applicable, as authorised by IAS 8 Accounting Policies, Changes in Accounting Estimates and Errors (IAS 8).

In multiple element arrangements where company-specific objective evidence of fair value or an estimated stand-alone selling price exists for all elements, revenue is allocated to the elements based on their relative fair values (relative fair value method).

Our consideration of whether on-premise software, cloud subscriptions, consulting or other services are to be accounted for separately or as one combined element of the arrangement depends on:

- whether the arrangement involves significant production, modification, or customisation of the software or cloud subscription, and
- whether the services are not available from third-party vendors and are therefore deemed essential to the software.

If neither of the above is the case, revenue for the on-premise software or cloud subscription element, and the other elements, are recognised separately. In contrast, if one or both of the above applies, the respective elements of the arrangement are combined and accounted for as a single unit of account, and the portion of the arrangement fee allocated to this single unit of account is recognised using the percentage-of-completion method, as outlined above, or over the cloud subscription term, if applicable, depending on which service term is longer.

We consider FASB ASC 985-605 in our accounting for options that entitle the customer to purchase, in the future, additional on-premise software. We allocate revenue to future incremental discounts whenever customers are granted the right to license additional on-premise software at a higher discount than the one given within the initial software license arrangement, or to purchase or renew services at rates below the fair values established for these services.

Our contributions to resellers that allow our resellers to execute qualified and approved marketing activities are recognised as an offset to revenue, unless we obtain a separate identifiable benefit for the contribution, and the fair value of the benefit is reasonably estimable.

COST OF SOFTWARE AND SOFTWARE-RELATED SERVICES

Cost of software and software-related services includes the cost incurred in producing the goods and providing the services that generate software and software-related service revenue. Consequently, this line item includes primarily employee expenses relating to these services, amortisation of acquired intangibles, fees for third-party licenses, and shipping and ramp-up cost.

COST OF PROFESSIONAL SERVICES AND OTHER SERVICES

Cost of professional services and other services includes the cost incurred in providing the services that generate professional service and other service revenue including messaging revenues. The item also includes sales and marketing expenses related to our professional services and other services that result from sales and marketing efforts that cannot be clearly separated from providing the services.

Source: SAP Annual Report 2013, pages 175–79

IFRS 2 Share-based Payments

With their relentless focus on employees, it is quite probable to hazard a guess that technology companies were one of the first to introduce stock option schemes as a method to reward employees provided they proved their loyalty to the company. Like IAS 19, IFRS 2 focuses on employee benefits – though the scope of IFRS 2 is much larger as it encompasses all share-based payments and not those only meant for employees. Companies that are moving over to IFRS may have different accounting policies to account for share-based payments provided to employees. The requirements of IFRS 2 could be different as they intend to spread the cost of these benefits over the vesting period.

In addition to the measurement requirements of IFRS 2, the disclosure requirements are intense. It is felt in some quarters that the disclosure requirements provide competitors with sensitive data. This appears all the more pertinent to technology companies where the variable compensation and share-based payments constitute a significant portion of the total compensation.

Share-based Payments

Share-based payments cover cash-settled and equity-settled awards issued to our employees. The fair values of both equity-settled and cash-settled awards are initially measured at grant date using an option-pricing model.

The fair value of equity-settled awards is not subsequently remeasured. The grant date fair value of equity-settled awards is recognised as personnel expense in profit or loss over the period in which the employees become unconditionally entitled to the rights, with a corresponding increase in share premium. The amount recognised as an expense is adjusted to reflect the actual number of equity-settled awards that ultimately vest. We grant our employees discounts on certain share-based payments. Since those discounts are not dependent on future services to be provided by our employees, the discount is recognised as an expense when the rights are granted.

For the share-based payments that are settled by paying cash rather than by issuing equity instruments, a provision is recorded for the rights granted reflecting the vested portion of the fair value of the rights at the end of each reporting period. Personnel expense is recognised over the period the beneficiaries are expected to perform the related service (vesting period), with a corresponding increase in provisions. Cash-settled awards are remeasured to fair value at the end of each reporting date until the award is settled. Any changes in the fair value of the provision are recognised as personnel expense in profit or loss. The amount of unrecognised compensation expense is dependent on the future price of our ordinary shares which we cannot reasonably predict.

Where we hedge our exposure to cash-settled awards, changes in the fair value of the respective hedging instruments are also recognised as personnel expense in profit or loss. The fair values for hedged programmes are based on market data reflecting current market expectations.

Source: SAP Annual Report 2013, page 181

4.20.3 Research and Development Expenditure

Under IAS 38, internally generated intangible assets from the development phase are recognised if certain conditions are met. These conditions include the technical feasibility, intention to complete, the ability to use or sell the asset under development, and the demonstration of how the asset will generate probable future economic benefits. The cost of a recognised internally generated intangible asset comprises all directly attributable cost necessary to make the asset capable of being used as intended by management. In contrast, all expenditures arising from the research phase are expensed as incurred. We go back to SAP financial statements to see how this is applied in practice.

We believe that determining whether internally generated intangible assets from development are to be recognised as intangible assets requires significant judgment, particularly in the following areas:

- Determining whether activities should be considered research activities or development activities.
- Determining whether the conditions for recognising an intangible asset are met requires assumptions about future market conditions, customer demand and other developments.
- The term "technical feasibility" is not defined in IFRS, and therefore determining whether the completion of an asset is technically feasible requires judgment and a company-specific approach.
- Determining the future ability to use or sell the intangible asset arising from the development and the determination of the probability of future benefits from sale or use.
- Determining whether a cost is directly or indirectly attributable to an intangible asset and whether a cost is necessary for completing a development.

We have determined that the conditions for recognising internally generated intangible assets from our software development activities are not met until shortly before the developed products are available for sale. This assessment is monitored by us on a regular basis.

Source: SAP Annual Report 2013, page 189

4.20.3.1 IFRS 3 Business Combinations

Business Combinations are a norm in the technology industry. Many companies have internal teams to identify potential targets. As per IFRS 3, the purchase method of accounting has to be followed in which acquisition date fair values are assigned to all assets acquired and liabilities assumed. If it is not possible to determine accurate fair values on the acquisition date, IFRS 3 provides a period of one year from the acquisition date as measurement period to ascertain the accurate fair values and true up the values. Previously unrecognised Intangible Assets can be recognised in a Business Combination. Goodwill and other Intangible Assets are tested for Impairment every year and IFRS 3 has detailed methods to account for Contingent Consideration. As per IFRS 3, the net impact of a Bargain Purchase is reflected in the Profit and Loss Account.

The impact of IFRS 3 on technology companies is expected to increase in the future with the recent trend of technology companies displaying a penchant to acquire start-ups that have created an impact. Technologies change and start-up emerge and are acquired at the blink of an eye.

4.20.3.2 *Intangible Assets and their Impairment*

Entities in the technology industry create, acquire and possess Intangible Assets such as specific software, intellectual property rights, patents and trademarks and specific customer rights. In some instances, valuing Intangible Assets acquired could possess a challenge due to the lack of adequate information as the Assets could be so unique. An erroneous value at the time of initial recognition could pose complications later on since the initial base has been over estimated.

In the software and technology industries, technologies change at the blink of an eyelid. Entities in the industry would need to be particularly vigilant of impairment triggers. Accounting for an impairment loss is ultimately a matter of calculation but the critical aspect would be recognising the correct moment in time when the impairment was triggered.

Key Takeaways

- IFRS 15 could alter timing and amount of revenue recognition. Software entities should relook at contracts with customers. Since there is a postponement of the implementation of IFRS 15, entities could use this period to assess the impact of IFRS 15 and if necessary, amend their contracts with customers accordingly.

- In jurisdictions where there are no accounting standards for share-based payments, the impact of IFRS 2 would need to be considered.

- IFRS 3 *Business Combinations* would play a significant part in the industry due to the number of combination of businesses that occur.

- A combination of the Intangible Assets Standard and the Impairment Standard would play a significant role in the financials of players in this industry.

5 FORTHCOMING IFRS STANDARDS THAT COULD IMPACT INDUSTRY

When can we say that the IASB is done and dusted with issuing IFRS Standards? The answer to that question is probably "Never" because the IASB is constantly working on improving existing standards or issuing new ones thereby making the Standards an ongoing Work-in-Progress.

In 2015, the IASB targets a Revised IFRS on Leases. It is also redeliberating on IFRS 4 *Insurance Contracts* though the FASB has temporarily decided to go it alone on Insurance Contracts. An Exposure Draft on the Conceptual Framework is expected soon and there are discussion papers out on accounting for Dynamic Risk Management – a Portfolio approach to Macro Hedging and Rate regulated activities. There are upcoming Discussion Papers on Disclosures too.

We will focus on the two major Standards that would impact Industry: Leases and Insurance Contracts. There are other minor amendments to existing Standards, which are touched upon.

5.1   IFRS 16 *LEASES*

5.1.1   Industries Impacted: Airline industry, Retail industry and All Industries that have Leases as an integral part of their business

The revised Standard on Leasing turns the concepts of "Operating Lease" and "Finance Lease" that everyone is familiar with on its head and proposes a radically different approach.

5.1.2   Significant Changes

The new Standard mandates that for lessees, all leases must be on balance sheet if the Lease Term is greater than 12 months. Entities are supposed to reassess each lease under the new requirements. If the lease term is 12 months or less (including optional renewal periods), the lessee can elect to simply expense the lease payments and not apply the proposed new requirements. There is a new lease definition based on the right to use an "underlying asset."

5.1.3   Identification and Classification of a Lease

An entity would determine whether a contract contains a lease by assessing whether both of the following conditions are met:
- Fulfilment of the contract depends on the use of the identified asset.
- The contract conveys the right to control the use of the identified asset for a period of time in exchange for consideration.

- A contract conveys the right to control the use of an asset if the customer has the ability to direct the use and receive the benefits from use of the identified asset.
- Separable components of the lease shall be accounted for separately.

5.1.4   Impact on Lessees

The proposed Leasing Standard would impact all industries that depend on leasing as a major financing mechanism. The airline and retail industries stand out as examples. Due to the radical change that the Standard proposes, it is expected that the amount of Leased Assets on the Balance Sheet would change (there would be an increase) in the case of Lessees. Similarly, there would be an increase in the Liability. The Profit or Loss Account would see the impact of the interest expense as well as the amortisation.

5.1.5   Tax Terrors

It is expected that once the new Standard on Leases is implemented, there could be some tax terrors for entities in certain geographies. It is possible that the tax authorities would take a stand that an asset, which does not belong to the taxpayer, is being amortised. Lease Rental is tax deductible in most tax geographies but it is possible that there could be issues when the debit to the Profit or Loss Account appears not as a lease rental but as an amortisation.

5.1.6   Impact on Lessors

Lessors would find that the Leased Asset vanishes from their Balance Sheet. This would impact their balance-sheet strength, which would in turn impact their borrowing capacity. Though the Leased Asset would be moved to Lease Receivable in the Balance Sheet, there would still be an impact on capacity to borrow due to the current/ non-current classification.

5.2   IFRS 4 *INSURANCE CONTRACTS*

5.2.1   Industries Impacted: The Insurance Industry

When IFRS 4 *Insurance Contracts* was issued, it was clearly identified as an Interim Standard. The interim standard introduces some amendments to current practice such as: a liability cannot be set for possible future claims , changes in accounting are permitted (shadow accounting, fair value measurements and deferring acquisition costs) and a liability adequacy test (LAT) has to be performed to assess the sufficiency of regulatory reserves. For long, the IASB has been working on a complete Standard on Insurance an Exposure Draft of which is ready now.

The revised exposure draft proposes a market consistent measurement of insurance contracts under a four-block approach, which considers the insurance liability as the sum of the following elements:

- Contractual service margin: a component of the measurement of the insurance contract representing the risk-adjusted expected profit from the contract (it cannot be negative).

- Fulfilment cash flows: a current, updated estimate of the amounts the entity expects to collect from premiums and pay out for claims, benefits and expenses, adjusted for risk and the time value of money.

The fulfilment cash flows are divided into the following three blocks:

1. Future cash flows: expected cash flows from premiums, claims and benefits.
2. Discounting: an adjustment that converts future cash flows into current amounts.
3. Risk adjustment: an assessment of the uncertainty about the amount of future cash flows.

The measurement will be made at portfolio level.

The revenues and expenses of insurance contracts will be disclosed in the income statement except, optionally, the time value of money that might be partially recognised in OCI. OCI refers to Other Comprehensive Income. It represents the gains and losses of the entity that are not recognised in profit and loss account. The OCI is presented in the Equity section of the balance sheet. The unwinding of the original locked-in discount rate would be recognised in the income statement and the update of the liability to the current market interest rates would be recognised in OCI.

On the asset side, IFRS 9 *Financial Instruments* would come into play. Assuming a fair value measurement of assets and liabilities, insurance would be the first sector to be full mark-to-market.

The contractual service margin feature and the introduction of OCI accounting would reduce the income statement volatility but on the other hand assumptions (other than discounting) changes will increase it.

Insurers should anticipate the implementation of this new standard and consider whether they have the required data to measure their insurance contracts under the new standard, whether they have the relevant resources to manage this transition and whether their systems will be compatible.

5.3   SMES

5.3.1   Industries Impacted: Small and Medium enterprises in all industries.

The IASB is also planning a comprehensive review of IFRS for SMEs. However, since this is expected to take some time to come out, it has not been discussed in this edition.

5.4   FRAMEWORK

5.4.1   Industries Impacted: All Industries

All IFRS Standards live off the Framework to International Financial Reporting Standards. With over a decade of practical experience with the Framework, the IASB has embarked on a project to revise the Framework so that it enables the new IFRS Standards also to live off it. The thoughts of the IASB on the Framework are as follows:

These include: (a) definitions of assets and liabilities; (b) recognition and derecognition of assets and liabilities; (c) measurement; (d) equity; (e) profit or loss and other comprehensive income (OCI); and (f) presentation and disclosure.

5.4.1.1 Definition of Assets

An asset of an entity is a present economic resource controlled by the entity as a result of past events

5.4.1.2 Definition of Liabilities

A liability of an entity is a present obligation of the entity to transfer an economic resource as a result of past events.

5.4.1.3 Recognition

Although the existing Conceptual Framework includes criteria for the recognition of assets and liabilities, those criteria need to be updated. The Discussion Paper suggests that an entity should recognise all its assets and liabilities:

(a) recognising an asset or a liability would provide users of financial statements with information that is not relevant, or is not sufficiently relevant to justify the cost; or

(b) no measure of an asset or a liability would result in a sufficiently faithful representation of both that asset or liability and the resulting income or expense.

5.4.1.4 Derecognition

The existing Conceptual Framework does not address derecognition, although the IASB has addressed the derecognition of various assets or liabilities in some of its recent IFRSs. The Discussion Paper suggests that an entity should derecognise an asset or a liability (or part of an asset or a liability) when it no longer meets the recognition criteria. If, following a transaction, an entity retains part of a previously recognised asset or liability, the Discussion Paper suggests that the IASB may need to consider how best to reflect the transaction and the resulting changes to the underlying economic resource or obligation. For example, the IASB may decide to require enhanced disclosure, separate presentation or continued recognition of the asset or liability.

5.4.1.5 Measurement

The existing Conceptual Framework provides little guidance on measurement and when a particular measurement basis should be used. The Discussion Paper describes guidance on measurement that could be included in a revised Conceptual Framework. The Discussion Paper suggests that the IASB should limit the number of measurement bases used in financial statements to enhance their understandability and comparability. However, the Discussion Paper also suggests that a single measurement basis for all assets and liabilities may not provide the most relevant information.

Different classes of equity financial statements do not typically provide enough information about the claims of different classes of equity investors, such as the effect of senior equity claims on subordinate equity claims. The Discussion Paper suggests that entities should use an enhanced statement of changes in equity to provide more information about different classes of equity. An enhanced statement of changes in equity would provide more information about the different classes of equity claims and show how wealth is transferred between those classes. It might also enable the IASB to simplify the IFRSs that distinguish liabilities from equity instruments. Distinction between equity and liabilities Existing IFRSs do not apply the definition of a liability consistently when distinguishing liabilities from equity instruments. The resulting requirements can be complex, difficult to understand and apply. The Discussion Paper does not propose to change the existing definition of equity. To distinguish between equity instruments and liabilities, the IASB would use the existing definition of equity, and the definition of a liability, which focuses on whether the entity has an obligation to deliver economic resources.

The Discussion Paper suggests that the Conceptual Framework: (a) should require a profit or loss total or subtotal that also results, or could result, in some items of income or expense being recycled; and (b) should limit the use of OCI to items of income or expense resulting from changes in current measures of assets and liabilities (remeasurements). However, not all such remeasurements would be eligible for recognition in OCI.

The Discussion Paper discusses two approaches that describe which items could be included in OCI: (a) a "narrow" approach; and (b) a "broad" approach. Both of these approaches would require items of income and expense to be recognised in profit or loss, unless they are eligible for inclusion in OCI.

The existing Conceptual Framework does not have a section on disclosure. The IASB will aim to develop concepts that it will be able to use when developing future disclosure requirements in IFRSs. The Discussion Paper suggests that: (a) the objective of presenting information in the primary financial statements is to provide summarised information about recognised assets, liabilities, equity, income, expenses, changes in equity and cash flows, that has been classified and aggregated in a manner that is useful; and (b) the objective of disclosing information in the notes to the financial statements is to supplement the primary financial statements by providing additional useful information about the items recognised and unrecognised assets and liabilities.

5.5   OTHER MAJOR PROJECTS

Apart from the above, the IASB is conducting a couple of other major projects.

5.5.1   Disclosure Initiative

As we have observed elsewhere in this book, one of the major criticisms against IFRS Standards is the detailed disclosure requirement. The Board is aware of this and is working towards fixing this. We could expect amendments to clarify the distinction between a change in an accounting policy and a change in an accounting estimate, in relation to the application of IAS 8, to help preparers, auditors and regulators to use judgement when applying the concept of materiality and to improve existing guidance in IFRS that helps entities determine the basic structure and content of a complete set of financial statements.

5.5.2   Others

A couple of other initiatives are a portfolio revaluation approach to macro hedging and some changes to the IFRS 14 on rate regulated activities.

6 *COLLATERAL IMPACT OF A TRANSITION TO IFRS*

A conversion to IFRS is a paradigm change that impacts not only the Finance and Accounting functions of an entity but also the information technology systems, legal contracts and employee policies. It has the potential to have a spin-off and collateral impact on the working of an organisation in various ways. A few such areas are discussed below.

6.1   SIGNIFICANT ASSUMPTIONS AND JUDGEMENT

The notes to the financial statements prepared by the management start off with a statement, which goes somewhat like this:

> The preparation of financial statements in conformity with IFRS requires management to make estimates and assumptions that affect the reported amounts of assets and liabilities and disclosure of contingent assets and liabilities at the date of the financial statements and the reported amounts of revenue and expenses during the reporting period. A discussion on the Group's critical accounting judgements and key sources of estimation uncertainty is detailed below. Actual results could differ from those estimates. The estimates and underlying assumptions are reviewed on an ongoing basis. Revisions to accounting estimates are recognised in the period in which the estimate is revised if the revision affects only that period or in the period of the revision and future periods if the revision affects both current and future periods.

A novice reading this could be forgiven if he assumes that the financial statements are estimated financial statements. It is a fact though that such a disclaimer is needed because in the real world the estimates could change very fast. In 2014, petroleum companies who have been estimating the price of Brent Crude at around $100 had to revise their estimates to $60 within one quarter. Even $60 proved erroneous as the price soon slid to $50.

With its focus on Fair Value, the importance of the above statement in IFRS financial statements can never be over-emphasised. Any error in these estimates will have a significant impact on the reported numbers.

6.2   THE GOING CONCERN CONCEPT

Apart from other concepts, the concept of Going Concern is an integral part of the Framework to International Financial Reporting Standards. Though as a concept it is simple, applying this concept in practice can pose numerous challenges. What is the trigger-point for raising a red flag that an entity may not be a going concern? Based on present auditing literature and practical experience, two trigger-points seem to stand out- availability of credit and budgets and forecasts. In a few countries, it has been observed that auditors question the Going Concern concept in case banks do not renew large loans to an entity that is dependent on the loan.

6.2.1   Availability of credit

One major effect of the credit crisis and economic downturn is the lack of available credit to entities of all sizes. Turmoil in the banking sector has led to a general tightening of credit, which may have a pervasive effect on an entity's ability to continue as a going concern. In addition, as an entity's financial health changes, contractual terms in loans and other obligations, including debt covenants and guarantees, and an entity's compliance with such terms, are likely to be under greater scrutiny from lenders, and also from management and auditors. There are a number of factors that may, in the circumstances of the entity, need to be considered, including:

- Whether banks may withdraw credit from entities that had previously had easy access to credit whenever necessary;
- Whether reductions in asset values or trading losses have led to breaches in lending covenants;
- Whether failure to comply with the respective covenants has resulted, or will result, in immediate demands from the lenders, or changes in the terms on which finance is available;
- Whether on-demand clauses in term loans affect the classification of such liabilities on an entity's balance sheet and whether the lenders may in fact invoke such clauses, rather than continuing a practice of granting waivers;
- Whether it is reasonable to assume that lenders will roll over existing credit facilities on similar terms, if at all;
- Whether banks are likely to be unwilling to commit to future renewal of credit facilities.

6.2.2   Forecasts and budgets

An important component of the going concern assessment relates to an entity's ongoing forecasts and budgeting. Factors that may be relevant in evaluating forecasts prepared by management include:

- whether senior management and those charged with governance have been appropriately involved and have given appropriate attention to forecasts;
- whether the assumptions used in the forecasts are consistent with assumptions that have been used in asset valuations and models for impairment;
- whether the forecasts have been prepared on a monthly basis and, if so, how the forecasts reflect expected payment patterns (e.g., quarterly cash outflows such as tax installments, and variable cash inflows such as expected proceeds from the sale of assets);
- whether the forecasts indicate months of insufficient cash and, if so, management's plans to deal with any shortfalls;
- whether forecasts reflect an inappropriate management bias, in particular as broadly compared to others in a particular industry;

- how management's budget for the current period compares with results achieved to date;
- whether the forecasts consider potential losses of revenue, including whether an inability of an entity to obtain letters of credit affects its international trade;
- whether increases in the cost of borrowing have been factored into management's analysis, including potential increases in margin sought by banks and the effect of alternative sources of financing;
- whether the forecasts account for trends typically noted in recessionary periods, such as reduced revenues, increased bad debts (because of trading conditions or the withdrawal of credit insurance), and extended credit terms to customers;
- whether management has performed an appropriate sensitivity analysis, such as considering the effect of the loss of key customers or key suppliers due to bankruptcies;
- how the forecast deals with asset realisations, including whether these realisations are practicable and realistic in amount; and
- whether the forecasts imply any future concerns over the entity's ability to meet debt covenant requirements.

6.3 INFORMATION TECHNOLOGY

One is frequently asked the question "Which is the best ERP Accounting Package for IFRS?" Well, the honest answer should be "none". While all the reputed ERP Accounting packages are robust, flexible and scalable, it is a fact that most of these packages cannot ascertain the exact fair value of an Asset or test it for impairment. Many of such adjustments have to be made outside the ERP system and true-up entries should be passed later.

Introduction of IFRS would have an impact not only on the final financial position of the entity but also at the individual invoice level. For instance, with the adoption of IFRS-15, an entity may decide that the performance obligations in a contract are spread to later years and may allocate a portion of the consideration towards that. The entry for this would have to be done by the Sales Accountant who would need to be trained as he is used to passing a single entry and not hiving off individual components. Similarly, the need for componentisation of Property, Plant and Equipment in IAS 16 would add a lot of work to the Accountant in charge of Property, Plant and Equipment. The Fixed Assets Register would need to be updated and tracked for changes in the useful lives of the Assets. Enterprises would do well to:

1. Identify the areas where moving over to IFRS could impact ERP and IT systems.
2. Formulate Accounting Policies in line with IFRS in these specific areas.
3. Train all the Accounting staff on the implications of shifting over to IFRS.

6.4 COSTS

Whenever an entity is asked to undergo a major change, one of the points for debate that surfaces is the cost vs. the benefits. For instance, when Section 404 of the Sarbanes Oxley Act (SOX) was introduced in the USA, there was a criticism that the costs to revisit all internal controls over financial reporting and other compliance requirements of SOX far exceeded the benefits.

A transition to IFRS costs money. Major costs that would be incurred in a transition to IFRS would include:

1. Impact Assessment Study;
2. First time conversion to IFRS;
3. Information Technology Costs;
4. Training Costs.

Due to the intricacies involved in an IFRS conversion, entities normally employ consultants to assist them in the first time adoption of IFRS. There could also be a sense of security in outsourcing these to a consultant since they would have had a lot of experience in doing the conversion to IFRS. However, there are no free consultants in IFRS and hence the cost of a Consultant would be a direct cost on the enterprise. As we have seen above, an entity will have to bear the costs of additional or revamped information technology systems once the transition to IFRS is done. However, it has to be stated that most of these costs are one-time costs that are not expected to recur. While the cost-benefit ratio may be skewed in the year of transition to IFRS, these costs should be looked on more as investments for the future.

The Impact Assessment is meant to give the top management a summary view of what the impact of a transition to IFRS would do to the financials of an entity. The actual conversion exercise would involve preparing the IFRS Opening Balance Sheet on the date of transition to IFRS as per the procedures laid out in IFRS 1 *First Time Conversion to International Financial Reporting Standards*. Training Costs are the costs involved to bring all the accountants up to speed on what IFRS accounting involves. Due to the extensive disclosure requirements of IFRS, a considerable amount of time would need to be spent on providing detailed disclosures as per the requirements of each and every IFRS Standard. Entities for whom IAS 34 *Interim Financial Reporting* applies would need to do this transition quickly as the next interim financial statements would need to be as per IFRS Standards.

6.5   ACCOUNTING MANUAL

Entities that have an Accounting Manual under their previous GAAP would need to make a new one as per IFRS. There could be new heads of account (such as Unbilled Revenue in view of IFRS 15) or there could be additions to line items in the Fixed Assets due to componentisation. The revised Accounting Manual would have to be comprehensive enough to cover all the intricacies of IFRS.

6.6   TAXES

A transition to IFRS would have an impact on Taxes. Unless otherwise specified, IFRS thrives on the concept of Fair Value. The tax department may not bless the concept of Fair Value. The impact of this could be that entities could end up paying higher taxes due to the transition to IFRS and the Deferred Taxes on the Balance Sheet would also change. There could be recognition issues. For instance under IAS 18 and IFRS 15, there is an imputed interest for credit sales. This is shown as a financing component, which raises the question of how the tax department would view it – as Sales or Interest? If it were recognised as Interest, would there have to be a withholding tax done? Applying IFRS 9 would mean that there would be notional gains or losses hitting the Profit or Loss Account – would the tax department bless these notional amounts? Entities that are operating in different geographies would have established transfer-pricing agreements amongst themselves. Implementation of IFRS will impact the financials. These entities may have to revisit their transfer pricing agreements to see if the transactions with the associated enterprise are still at an arm's length. In case the answer is no, agreements would need to be revised which would result in a change in the tax outflow of the entity.

6.7 PRESENTATION OF FINANCIAL STATEMENTS

IAS 1 *Presentation of Financial Statements* specifies the overall requirements for financial statements, including how they should be structured, the minimum requirements for their content and overriding concepts such as going concern, the accrual basis of accounting and the current/non-current distinction. The standard requires a complete set of financial statements to comprise a statement of financial position, a statement of profit or loss and other comprehensive income, a statement of changes in equity and a statement of cash flows.

Entities who are moving over to IFRS may have different ways of presenting their financial statements and will have to change their accounting and reporting systems as per the new presentation requirements of IFRS. In some geographies (India being a good example) regulators may specify the format in which financial statements have to be presented. In such circumstances, the entity should assume that the format specified by the regulator complies with the provisions of IAS 1.

6.8 IMPACT OF IFRS ON FINANCIAL RATIOS

IFRS introduces many new concepts such as Fair Value, Componentisation, Testing Goodwill and other Intangible Assets for Impairment every year etc. There is a general feeling that a transition to IFRS could impact the financial ratios of an entity. Any impact on the financial ratios of an entity could impact its market price and, if the ratios are very adverse, the entity could be perceived as not doing too well.

Balios Dimitrios, Lecturer on Accounting, National and Kapodistrian University of Athens Department of Economics; Eriotis Nikolaos, Associate Professor of Accounting, National and Kapodistrian University of Athens, Department of Economics, Athens; Paraskevopoulos Konstantinos, Master in Banking and Finance, Open University of Cyprus; and Vasiliou Dimitrios, Professor of Bank Management, Hellenic Open University, Patra did some seminal research on this. In their paper, "The impact of IFRS on ratios of listed and new listed companies of Athens Exchange", (thejournalofbusiness.org/index.php/site/article/download/14/14), they conclude that:

According to the results of these tests, it appears that the ratios of the two groups of companies of the two samples behaved in a similar way during the transition from GAS to IFRS. There is no significant effect from the adoption and implementation of IFRS in Greece on the calculation of the financial ratios. Specifically, to determine more accurately the relationship between the financial ratios of the two accounting standards we applied statistical analysis in all fifteen examined ratios per sample. The results in their majority do not differ significantly. Exceptions for the first sample are the Leverage ratios: Debt Ratio and the Activity ratios: Asset Turnover, Fixed Assets Turnover, Net Profit Margin and Gross Profit Margin. Furthermore, based on regression analysis we demonstrated a strong linear relationship between the ratios of the two different accounting standards in the majority of the two samples, apart from EBITDA margin ratio in the first sample. As far as the comparison of the two samples of listed and new listed companies, it can be argued that there is not a significant difference in the results found, as well as the application of statistical tests to all ratios that were calculated, did not display any significant difference in its percentage of diversification. Comparable outcomes were reached by the application of multiple regression analysis, which displayed that the temporal point of the introduction of a company in AE did not have any significant effect on the diversification of ratios from the transition to IFRS, except for EBIT to invested capital. We conclude that the particular characteristics of each group of companies were not able to significantly affect the differences in the financial statements of companies after the implementation of IFRS.

The results of the above research cannot be questioned. However, it is a fact that the impact of IFRS would be felt when an entity moves over to IFRS for the first time, adopts IFRS 1 and parks the differences arising therefrom in Retained Earnings or another component of equity. After this, since the entity would prepare even it interim financial reports as per IFRS, it is possible that no significant impact is felt at the end of the financial year.

6.9   CHALLENGES IN IMPLEMENTING IFRS

After IFRS became a reality in the European Union, Eva K. Jermakowicz and Sylwia Gornik-Tomaszewski published a paper "Implementing IFRS from the perspective of EU publicly traded companies" in the *Journal of International Accounting, Auditing and Taxation* 15 (2006) 170–196. In this paper, they conducted a survey which *inter-alia*, detailed the main challenges that entities faced while moving over to IFRS which is reproduced below:

- Complex nature of IFRS, which is made for big companies
- Lack of IFRS implementation guidance
- Lack of uniform interpretation of IFRS
- Final rules not being ready for the 2005 deadline
- Impact on profit and loss account
- Continuing debate of IAS 39
- Constant change of IFRS, transformation of IASB decisions in EU Regulations

- Running of parallel accounting systems
- Preparation of comparative financial statements for the past years
- Lack of IFRS knowledge among employees and auditors
- Training of accounting staff and management
- To change the mindset of finance personnel
- Change of the IT Structure

While many of these have been addressed, there are some challenges that would appear to never go away. Change of the IT structure, constant change of IFRS and training costs could be some examples.

6.9.1   Where are the valuers?

One of the major challenges in IFRS could be finding valuers. Companies normally have a panel of qualified valuers to value their Property, Plant and Equipment. In the case of a Financial Instrument, which is quoted on the market, valuation should not pose an issue, as the Quoted Market Price is the best indicator of Fair Value as per IFRS 13. The challenge would like in valuing Intangible Assets and financial instruments which are not quoted in an active market. For instance, in case an entity acquires a Brand that is not related to its main line of business, who is the qualified and independent valuer who would value the Brand? Though the value of the Brand will be tested for Impairment in case any of the impairment indicators indicated by IAS 38 are triggered, the initial recognition cannot be way off the mark. To take another example, who would be the most appropriate person to value an inter-corporate deposit that is over-due for a year? There are press reports that the company that has received the inter-corporate deposits is going through a severe cash crisis and could be acquired.

Valuation involves making significant assumptions and exercising judgement. As required by IFRS 13, if these are disclosed in detail in the Notes on Accounts, there should be no controversies. Like all accountants, it would assist a lot if the valuer opts to err on the side of caution.

AFTERWORD

This book has attempted to provide an overview of how IFRS Standards could impact different industries. Due to the sheer quantum of industries that abound and the ever-changing nature of the business landscape, the book cannot and does not make the claim that it illustrates all the areas of impact that IFRS standards could have on all industries. As mentioned in the Preface, the impact illustrations narrated in this book have been based on a combination of my experience in a few industries and some research. Wiley and the author encourage readers to send in their comments on any impact that has been missed out in this edition of the book.

We can strive together to make future editions of this book better and more comprehensive.

@mohanlavi
mohan@mohanlavi.com

APPENDIX: IMPACT SUMMARY

A SNAPSHOT OF IFRS STANDARDS THAT WOULD IMPACT DIFFERENT INDUSTRIES

Industry	Indicative Critical Standards that would impact the industry	Brief Analysis
All Industries	IFRS 1, IAS 36, IAS 40, IFRS 3, IFRS 5, IFRS 8, IFRS 13, IAS 39/IFRS 9 IFRS 10 and Disclosures.	The reason as to why **IFRS 1** would impact all industries is a no-brainer as the Standard is a mandatory ready reckoner for anyone transitioning to IFRS.
		IAS 36 is included in this list because every industry goes through its dips and during those dips indicators of impairment could arise. **IAS 40** is a new concept brought in by IFRS for properties that are held for rental or capital appreciation, which most industries have. No industry can escape a Business Combination, which is why **IFRS 3** is in this list while **IFRS 5** is a small but powerful standard on non-current assets that are held for sale. **IFRS 8** changes the way segments are recognised. In the midst of wide-ranging criticism of the concept of Fair Value, **IFRS 13** has been issued which attempts to bring some sanity into fair valuation. Financial Instruments are to be found on the Balance-Sheet of every major company bringing the complexities of **IAS 39/IFRS 9** into play. **IFRS 10** redefines the concept of control and would impact any entities in all industries that acquire stakes in others. IFRS thrives on **disclosures**, which will impact every industry irrespective of size.
Airlines	IAS 18, IAS 16, IAS 36, IFRIC 13	Ascertaining useful lives of various components of an aircraft as per **IAS 16** would need to be done. Accounting for Frequent Flier schemes as per **IFRIC 13** would be necessary. Ticketing revenue would need to be done with the limited guidance in **IAS 18**. Cut-throat competition in the industry could impair assets as per **IAS 36**.
Agriculture	IAS 41, IFRS 13	Does the Asset meet the definition of a biological asset as per **IAS 41**? In the relatively limited world of biological assets, can accurate Fair Values be ascertained as per **IFRS 13**?

Automotive	IAS 16, IAS 38	Does all expenditure in setting up an automotive plant meet the definition of an Asset as per the Framework to IFRS and can they be classified as PPE under **IAS 16**? Assets transferred/received under Master Supply Agreement with suppliers would also need to pass this test. Does the production of a blockbuster car model give rise to an Intangible Asset as per **IAS 38**?
Banking	IAS 39/IFRS 9	It's all about Financial Instruments. The impact of changes in fair value as per **IAS 39** and the expected loss model enunciated by **IFRS 9** would need careful scrutiny.
Family Controlled Enterprises	IAS 24	The mantra of IFRS is "When in doubt, just disclose it" including all related party transactions as per **IAS 24**
Government Owned Enterprises	IPSAS	IPSAS Accounting Standards would need to be referred to.
FMCG	IAS 18/IFRS 15, IAS 37	By definition, these goods are fast moving. Recognising revenue/providing for returns as per **IAS 18** would need to be done. Being fast-moving and consumer-facing, numerous claims could arise bringing the provisions of **IAS 37** into the picture.
Insurance	IFRS 4, IAS 39	Though issued as a temporary standard **IFRS 4**, (and a complete standard looks far away) provides detailed guidance on some aspects of Insurance Contracts. There is a very thin line of difference between an Insurance Contract and a financial instrument these days. **IAS 39** could apply to many contracts.
Pharma	IAS 38, IAS 18, IAS 37	In the software industry, they call it outsourcing. In the pharma industry, they call it in-licensing and out licensing. Accounting for revenue on these contracts as per **IAS 18**, whether an Intangible Asset arises as per **IAS 38** and providing for claims as per **IAS 37** can prove tricky. Segregation of research and development costs is the key.
Real Estate & Infrastructure	IAS 18/IFRS 15, IAS 11, IFRIC 12	A unique industry that has two Standards on Revenue: **IAS 18/IFRS 15** and **IAS 11**. Some contracts would be classified as Service Concession Agreements under **IFRIC 12**.
Oil and Gas	IFRS 6, IAS 37	Exploration and Evaluation Expenditure would need to take into account the limited guidance provided in **IFRS 6**. Provisions for claims and decommissioning costs as per **IAS 37** would be needed.
Media & Broadcasting	IAS 18/IFRS -15	Revenue recognition for direct sales, online downloads, updates would need to take into consideration the principles in **IAS18/IFRS 15**.

Mining	IFRS 6, IAS 37	Exploration and Evaluation Expenditure would need to take into account the limited guidance provided in **IFRS 6**. Provisions for claims and decommissioning costs as per **IAS 37** would be needed.
Retail	IAS 18, IFRIC 13	Recognition of Revenue as per **IAS 18** for different types of Sales would need to be studied. Customer Loyalty programmes would make **IFRIC 13** applicable.
Telecom	IAS 18/IFRS 15/ IAS 37	How is Revenue to be recognised as per **IAS 18/ IFRS 15** when telecom companies announce different tariff plans every alternate day with some freebies bundled in? Dissatisfied customers could claim claims from the company which would need to be provided for as per **IAS 37**.
Shipping	IAS 16	Componentisation as per **IAS 16** and capitalising unique expenses such as dry-docking costs need attention as would determining the useful lives and residual value of ships.
Small and Medium Enterprises	IFRS for SMEs	A separate Standard has been issued that is supposed to make life for SMEs easier. The operative phrase is "supposed to".
Software	IAS 18/IFRS 15/IFRS 2	Bundled contracts with multiple deliverables are a part of the industry. The limited guidance in **IAS 18** and the exhaustive guidance in **IFRS 15** should be used. The industry believes in giving a part of its employee remuneration in shares for which there is a separate standard **IFRS 2**.
Private Equity	IFRS 10, IAS 39	Does the private equity firm control the investee? If yes, **IFRS 10**. Is the investment only an investment? If yes, **IAS 39**.
Service Industries	IAS 18/IFRS 15, IAS 19, IFRS 2	Recognition of Revenue on Time and Material and long term contracts as per **IAS18/IFRS 15**. Employee Benefits as per **IAS 19** and Share-based payments as per **IFRS 2** would need to be followed along with the detailed disclosures provided in the respective Standards.

INDEX